SO YOU WANT TO SING EARLY MUSIC

So You Want to Sing

Guides for Performers and Professionals

A Project of the National Association of Teachers of Singing

So You Want to Sing: Guides for Performers and Professionals is a series of works devoted to providing a complete survey of what it means to sing within a particular genre. Each contribution functions as a touchstone work not only for professional singers but also for students and teachers of singing. Titles in the series offer a common set of topics so readers can navigate easily through the various genres addressed in each volume. This series is produced under the direction of the National Association of Teachers of Singing, the leading professional organization devoted to the science and art of singing.

So You Want to Sing Music Theater: A Guide for Professionals, by Karen S. Hall, 2013

So You Want to Sing Rock 'n' Roll: A Guide for Professionals, by Matthew Edwards, 2014

So You Want to Sing Jazz: A Guide for Professionals, by Jan Shapiro, 2015

So You Want to Sing Country: A Guide for Performers, by Kelly K. Garner, 2016

So You Want to Sing Gospel: A Guide for Performers, by Trineice Robinson-Martin, 2016

So You Want to Sing Sacred Music: A Guide for Performers, edited by Matthew Hoch, 2017

So You Want to Sing Folk Music: A Guide for Performers, by Valerie Mindel, 2017

So You Want to Sing Barbershop: A Guide for Performers, by Diane M. Clarke and Billy J. Biffle, 2017

So You Want to Sing A Cappella: A Guide for Performers, by Deke Sharon, 2017

So You Want to Sing Light Opera: A Guide for Performers, by Linda Lister, 2018

So You Want to Sing CCM (Contemporary Commercial Music): A Guide for Performers, edited by Matthew Hoch, 2018

So You Want to Sing for a Lifetime: A Guide for Performers, by Brenda Smith, 2018

So You Want to Sing the Blues: A Guide for Performers, by Eli Yamin, 2018

So You Want to Sing Chamber Music: A Guide for Performers, by Susan Hochmiller, 2019

So You Want to Sing Early Music: A Guide for Performers, by Martha Elliott, 2019

SO YOU WANT TO SING EARLY MUSIC

A Guide for Performers

Martha Elliott

Allen Henderson
Executive Editor, NATS

Matthew Hoch
Series Editor

A Project of the National Association of
Teachers of Singing

ROWMAN & LITTLEFIELD
Lanham • Boulder • New York • London

Published by Rowman & Littlefield
A wholly owned subsidiary of
The Rowman & Littlefield Publishing Group, Inc.
4501 Forbes Boulevard, Suite 200, Lanham, Maryland 20706
www.rowman.com

6 Tinworth Street, London SE11 5AL

British Library Cataloguing in Publication Information Available

Library of Congress Cataloging-in-Publication Data

Names: Elliott, Martha, author.
Title: So you want to sing early music : a guide for performers / Martha
  Elliott.
Description: Lanham : Rowman & Littlefield, [2018] | Series: So you want to
  sing | Includes bibliographical references and index.
Identifiers: LCCN 2018040484 (print) | LCCN 2018042139 (ebook) | ISBN
  9781538105900 (electronic) | ISBN 9781538105894 (pbk. : alk. paper)
Subjects: LCSH: Singing—Instruction and study. | Vocal music—17th
  century—Instruction and study. | Vocal music—18th century—Instruction
  and study.
Classification: LCC MT820 (ebook) | LCC MT820 .E5 2018 (print) | DDC
  783/.043—dc23
LC record available at https://lccn.loc.gov/2018040484

♾️™ The paper used in this publication meets the minimum requirements
of American National Standard for Information Sciences—Permanence of
Paper for Printed Library Materials, ANSI/NISO Z39.48-1992.

Printed in the United States of America

For Michael and Emily

CONTENTS

SERIES EDITOR'S FOREWORD

So You Want to Sing Early Music: A Guide for Performers is the fifteenth book in the NATS/Rowman & Littlefield "So You Want to Sing" series and the twelfth book to fall under my editorship. We are grateful to Martha Elliott for her authorship of this important title. She brings to these pages a wealth of knowledge that she has gathered over the course of her long career as a scholar of early music. In addition to her impressive career as a performer, Elliott also maintains a private voice studio at Princeton University, so this entire book is also written from a pedagogue's perspective. She is well-known to the international voice teaching community through her 2006 book *Singing in Style: A Guide to Vocal Performance Practices*, published by Yale University Press.

The primary target audience of the "So You Want to Sing" series is singers and voice teachers who are trained in traditional "classical" programs where Western art song and operatic literature is emphasized. For this reason, a title devoted to early music—and, in particular, the solo singing style of the Renaissance and baroque periods—is a necessary book, as the canon of vocal literature studied at universities and conservatories tends to focus overwhelmingly on subsequent eras. In addition, the historically informed performance (HIP) practice that has emerged in recent decades has had an enormous impact on what audiences expect to hear when listening to early music. A book detailing these styles, and the technique required to sing this literature well, is a welcome and much-needed addition to our series.

In addition to a thorough discussion of vocal technique, Elliott also devotes chapters to style, ornamentation, score study, and singing as a chamber musician. Three appendices also offer supplemental essays on other important early music topics. Gabriel Crouch contributes "So You Want to Be a Consort Singer?"; Jamie Reuland writes "Approximating the Past"; and four authors—Mary Benton, Patricia Hlafter, Judith Klotz, and Amy Warren—offer advice when "Singing with Players." Like other books in the series, there are several "common chapters" that are included across multiple titles. These chapters include one devoted to voice science by Scott McCoy and another on vocal health by Wendy LeBorgne. These chapters help to bind the series together, ensuring consistency of fact when it comes to the most essential matters of voice production. Anthony Roth Costanzo, internationally renowned countertenor and friend of the author, contributes the guest foreword.

The collected volumes of the "So You Want to Sing" series offer a valuable opportunity for performers and teachers of singing to explore new styles and important pedagogies. I am confident that voice specialists, both amateur and professional, will benefit from Martha Elliott's important resource on singing early music. It has been a privilege to work with her on this project. This book is an invaluable resource for performers who are interested in adding early music to their repertoire.

Matthew Hoch
Series Editor

FOREWORD

Anthony Roth Costanzo

As a countertenor, my bread and butter is early music. When I was an undergraduate at Princeton University, I was lucky to have Martha Elliott as a resource, an expert, and an inspiration close at hand. What a joy to discover the considerable knowledge and skill she has accrued from a career of performing and teaching, distilled with such clarity and elegance in this book. Even at this point in my career, having sung baroque opera everywhere from the Metropolitan Opera to Versailles, this book provides stimulating and thoughtful ideas about the repertoire, in addition to incredibly useful practical applications. The book has collected a vast amount of information that touches upon all the key elements of being a successful singer. Chapters on vocal physiology, healthy singing, and pedagogy provide a foundation for technical health that is crucial to a lasting musical life as a singer. Martha provides a succinct and engaging historical context with which to approach this repertoire, and then delves astutely into the stylistic touchstones of the music which allow for great performance. She also provides the singer with an invaluable toolbox to build both musicianship and technique within the repertoire. The book is made that much more accessible by her inclusion of both concrete examples and general principles to guide the singer. Young singers and coaches trying to do justice to a Handel da capo aria regularly ask me how to approach ornamentation. I'm thrilled to be able to refer them to this book as a resource which so closely aligns with everything I believe based on my experience and my taste. So often, early music is considered a stuffy sector of the classical world, full of conventions and constraints. Martha sets the music free in her entertaining and illuminating account of how to approach it and provides the means to ensure that this music remains vibrant, dramatic, and engaging. The book is a resource I am thrilled to have not only for my personal use and the use of developing singers but for the joy it will bring to audiences lucky enough to benefit from the performances it informs.

ACKNOWLEDGMENTS

I love going to National Association of Teachers of Singing (NATS) conferences because even if you think you know what sessions you will attend or who you will meet, you always end up having wonderfully unexpected interactions with new and old friends and colleagues. That is exactly what happened at the Chicago conference in 2016 when I had a lovely conversation with Matthew Hoch during a coffee break, and a few weeks later, he called me up to ask me to contribute this volume to the "So You Want to Sing" series. I am grateful to both Matt and Allan Henderson for thinking of me for this project and to the NATS organization as a whole for championing this valuable series. Matt has been an unending source of positive energy and sensible advice. I also offer heartfelt thanks to Natalie Mandziuk and the team at Rowman and Littlefield. They have truly been a pleasure to work with.

I also would like to thank my many colleagues in the Princeton University Music Department for all the varied help they contributed: Gabriel Crouch and Jamie Reuland for their wonderful appendices; Wendy Heller for the extraordinary example of her book *Music in the Baroque*, its companion website, and her always wise and sensible suggestions; Wendy Young and Nancy Wilson for inside info on matters small and large; Sara Hagenbuch for a tour through all the library resources with which I was not familiar; John Burkhalter for his vast knowledge of the early music world; John Ahern for taking on the responsibility of the index; and Annika Socolofsky for her attention to detail in making the music examples (Sara and John can also be seen in the cover photo). I also have to thank Daniel Claro of the digital learning lab at the Mc-Graw Center for Teaching and Learning at Princeton for his patient help with online music examples, and Matt Pilsner, lighting and stage supervisor at the Lewis Center for the Arts, for his help with lighting the cover photo session. I am also grateful to John Orluck and Judith Klotz for their participation in the cover photo and to Judith for facilitating the contribution of Appendix B by La Spirita.

When I saw Matthew Hoch at the ICVT meeting in Stockholm the following summer (in 2017), he invited me to start working on the cover image. For this project, I must thank Jane Hines, Sergio De Iudicibus, Stephanie Tubiolo, Solène LeVan, Jennifer Borghi, and Aryeh Nussbaum Cohen for their help with that quest. David Kelly Crow, the photographer, ultimately made that magic "happen."

I am ever in debt to my many students who have brought in early music repertoire to their lessons, giving me the opportunity to teach details of style or score reading. Special mention goes to Madeline Kushan, Rebecca Singer, Daniel Pinto, Solène LeVan, and Candus Hedberg, in particular, for the examples they provided. I am also thankful to Adam Dillon from the Historical Performance Institute at Indiana University and Diana Cooley from the University of North Texas for additional information about their vocal degree programs. Ryan Brandau and Michael Manning provided enjoyable conversations that led to new bits of information.

And I could not have completed this project without the help of my cousin, Sarah Freiberg, distinguished baroque cellist and editor at *Strings Magazine*, who has been rewriting my sentences and adding invaluable points to my writing for almost fifteen years. I am ever so grateful for the support of my daughter Emily and, finally, my husband Michael, who has waited patiently as I disappeared into my writing nook, listened attentively as I thought out loud, and commented wisely after reading every chapter. His unfailing support is a boundless source of confidence and strength, and I can never thank him enough.

INTRODUCTION

What exactly is early music? Johannes Tinctoris, a fifteenth-century theorist, thought that any music composed more than forty years in the past was "early music" and, therefore, was not worth hearing.[1] *The New Grove Dictionary of Music and Musicians* includes a far broader definition: "a term once applied to music of the baroque and earlier periods, but now commonly used to denote any music for which a historically appropriate style of performance must be reconstructed on the basis of surviving scores, treatises, instruments and other contemporary evidence."[2] Since this covers almost one thousand years of repertoire from the eleventh to the early twentieth century, it is too much for one book to tackle. Instead, we will try to find a happy compromise between these two extremes. We will focus on baroque era music, putting its repertoire and style in context by examining medieval and Renaissance trends.

For classically trained singers, the core of early music might bring to mind Bach and Handel, and perhaps Purcell and Monteverdi. They are certainly the giants of the baroque period. However, there are many more seventeenth- and eighteenth-century composers, and they also produced a wealth of magnificent vocal repertoire. In fact, a great majority of European music written before 1750 was for voices: music for solo voices and groups of voices, with or without accompanying instruments;

music for the church and the theatre; music for the court and the chamber; music for public and private consumption; and music in many different languages and national styles. In this book, we will explore beyond the most familiar composers to expand your knowledge of the repertoire and the wide variety of singing styles.

We will also dive into the wealth of information now available that gives us an idea as to how these compositions might have been originally performed. Since the 1980s, and the explosion of interest in early music and historical performance practice, performances of music from the baroque period and earlier now reflect a wide variety of styles and approaches. Will your performance have a "modern" style, or a more "historically informed" one? Neither is right or wrong, but it is helpful to know the difference and what choices result in one approach or the other. We will look at stylistic issues including ornamentation and articulation, working with period instruments, and managing vibrato. We will also discuss reading manuscripts and choosing scores and editions. You don't need a degree in musicology to sing this repertoire, but it is helpful and interesting to know a bit about the development of music notation and music printing and publication. It is also fascinating to learn what singers and voice teachers of earlier periods had to say about vocal technique, training, and hygiene, as well as performance traditions and audience reception.

While the main emphasis of this book is repertoire from the seventeenth and eighteenth centuries, it is extremely valuable to know what styles and trends helped produce it. By looking at music from the medieval and Renaissance periods, we can better understand the context in which baroque music came to be, how notation evolved, or why ornamentation developed the way it did. We will also see a tremendous variety of singing styles and vocal repertoire. Perhaps you are a solo singer who has worked primarily on opera. You may discover sacred chamber music that really speaks to you, or small vocal ensembles that you didn't know existed. If you started out primarily singing in choruses, you might discover solo lute songs or secular cantatas that are very manageable technically and reveal your solo potential. Have you ever had the opportunity to sing in a five- or six-part consort with one voice on a part? It demands the technique of a solo singer and the sensibilities of a choral singer all in one. And of course, the seventeenth century saw the beginnings of opera and the rise of virtuoso singing celebrities. The *da capo* aria from this period demands both vocal and compositional skill for improvising dazzling ornaments and variations.

After we expand our repertoire horizons and learn a bit about the stylistic approach needed for this music, we will look at possibilities for practicing and performing early music. This will include suggestions for workshops, festivals, student and professional competitions, degree programs, and professional organizations, as well as online resources for finding scores and manuscripts. As a special bonus, my colleague at Princeton, Gabriel Crouch, who is director of the early music ensemble Gallicantus and a former member of The King's Singers, will talk about what is needed to be a consort singer; Princeton musicologist Jamie Reuland will reveal some secrets for understanding medieval notation; and members of the viol consort La Spirita will share advice for singers working with early music instrumentalists.

NOTES

1. Stanley Sadie and Howard Mayer Brown, eds. *Performance Practice: Music Before 1600* (New York, NY: W.W. Norton & Co, 1990), ix.

2. Harry Haskell, "Early Music," *The New Grove Dictionary of Music and Musicians*, edited by Stanley Sadie (London: Macmillan, 2001), 831.

ONLINE SUPPLEMENT NOTE

So You Want to Sing Early Music features an online supplement courtesy of the National Association of Teachers of Singing. Visit the link below to discover additional exercises and examples, as well as links to recordings of the songs referenced in this book.

http://www.nats.org/So_You_Want_To_Sing_Book_Series.html

A musical note symbol, denoted by a (♪) in this book, will mark every instance where there is corresponding online supplement material.

1

HISTORICAL OVERVIEW
OF THE REPERTOIRE

"Music for a while, shall all your cares beguile."

—Purcell, *Oedipus* (1692)

Many music history textbooks begin with music from ancient Greece and Rome and then move on to medieval Christian chant. While this is certainly not a music history textbook, I want to establish a context for the core of our baroque repertoire by exploring some of the traditions that began in the medieval and Renaissance periods. I'd like to create a continuum of developing practices and styles to understand specific composers and works. Whether student or professional, you will find it invaluable to place baroque music into such a context, even if you don't have much to do with the earlier periods or repertoire. What follows is a historical overview, with listening suggestions, that will clarify our discussion of the later repertoire and, hopefully, pique your interest in even earlier repertoire.

THE MEDIEVAL PERIOD

Plainchant

In early Christian church services in the fifth and sixth centuries, Latin texts were sung to unaccompanied, unison melodies called chants. The texts came from the church liturgy, and the melodies were passed along orally for generations. Texts and melodies varied depending on where they occurred in the service and whether they were for daily services or special church holidays and festivals. Chants could be syllabic and speech-like, almost declaimed, as in recitative, or more flowing and melismatic, containing more than one pitch per syllable. The style of chant and style of performance was related to the function of the chant in the liturgy. Monks in medieval monasteries might sing more than six hours a day during their regular schedule of worship. Even in modern-day monasteries, stories are told of novice monks who lose their voices in the first few months of training before they learn how to pace themselves and develop the ease and endurance necessary for singing the Divine Office.[1]

Gregorian Chant and Early Notation

Members of the Frankish Empire revised and standardized the texts of the church liturgy in the middle of the ninth century. The chants became known as Gregorian, a reference to either Pope Gregory I (r590–604) or Pope Gregory II (r715–731).[2] Eventually, the medieval chants were written down and copied by hand, and the manuscripts were preserved in the libraries of the great monasteries. The earliest surviving examples of these manuscripts date from around 900.[3] This early music notation was very primitive, using combinations of dots and squiggles called neumes, sometimes in different shapes and colors, to indicate the length or grouping of notes.[4] Representation of the rising and falling of pitches was very rudimentary as well, with a staff of only four lines. Aligning syllables with particular pitches didn't seem to be a priority, and sometimes the text was written separately from the music, making decisions about underlay problematic.

Thus, we see the beginning of a long and difficult journey in deciphering what the notation on the page really means. We need to search for answers into how rhythms and pitches should be performed and how text should be phrased and coordinated with pitches. Scholars of this very early repertoire wrestle with the ambiguities of the materials and often disagree about fine points of interpretation. Most do agree, however, that there are no definitive answers to how this music was performed, or how it originally sounded. As music notation developed over the next 900 years, it has become easier to answer these kinds of questions, but as we shall see, scholars continue to disagree about notation intricacies when it comes to questions of performance practice.

Solfège

In the early eleventh century, an Italian monk named Guido of Arezzo (991–after 1033) developed a more precise system of music notation and a helpful system for teaching singers to sight-read. He used the first syllable of each line of a Latin text and the corresponding pitch in a familiar chant to help singers remember the pattern of whole and half steps in the scale. Rodgers and Hammerstein recreated this helpful aid in the familiar "Do, Re, Mi" song from *The Sound of Music*, also known as "Doe, a Deer." Guido's syllables—*ut, re, mi, fa, sol*, and *la*—have become the foundation of solmization, or solfège.

Hildegard of Bingen (1098–1179)

Hildegard of Bingen entered a German Benedictine monastery at age fourteen and wrote poetry and musical settings to describe her mystical visions. Eventually, she helped found a convent for young women who wished to enter the order, and ultimately, she became the abbess there. Her monophonic (single-line) chants explored the deeper meaning of her visionary texts through their musical settings. These beautiful vocal pieces are haunting and inspiring and certainly worth hearing and singing. If you want to listen to a representative sample of her works, try "Alleluia! O Virga Mediatrix" (online example 1-1) or "Canticles of Ecstasy" (online example 1-2). Hildegard also wrote a liturgical drama, another common form of medieval sacred vocal music. Many other liturgical plays of the time, including the Play of Daniel, are anonymous. ♪

Secular Monody

Songs with one line of melody found their way into many areas of medieval secular life. Most were used for entertainment, in public and in private, by both upper and lower classes. Originally, the songs, written in the vernacular, were passed on orally; only later were the texts written down, and still later, the barest sketch of a melody was notated. In the twelfth and thirteenth centuries, these songs were written and performed by professional singer-songwriters known as troubadours and trouvères in French regions and Minnesingers in German areas. These performers often sang in large halls or open spaces filled with a variety of activities including juggling, dancing, wrestling, eating, and the like. Their songs were usually strophic and told stories of courtly love and adventure and were intended to capture the imagination of the audience and compete for their attention. Artwork of the period suggests that a singer may have been accompanied by other singers or instruments, but it is unclear what the actual accompaniment would have been. Here is another issue where scholars disagree on exactly what the sources indicate for performance practice. Many of these songs exist in modern editions and facsimiles.

Organum

By the thirteenth century, polyphony found its way into both sacred and secular music. The earliest examples of sacred polyphonic vocal music are called organum. In its most basic form, organum takes an existing chant melody and adds another melody above or below it as another layer. Often the two melody lines move in parallel motion, favoring perfect fourths, fifths, and octaves. Later on, the lines became more independent while still following the rules to maintain the preferred consonant intervals of octaves, unisons, fourths, and fifths. Sometimes, the existing chant would move more slowly while the newly added upper line would be more florid. The more slowly moving lower part was called the tenor, from the Latin *tenere*, which means "to hold."[5] The choir usually sang the tenor part in unison while soloists sang the more demanding polyphony. The rhythm was not usually notated, as everyone would know how to sing together in unison and soloists could figure out how to sing together based on free movement or the text. As additional lines were added to make more complex three- and four-part polyphony, composers started to devise new ways to indicate rhythm in an attempt to avoid chaos.

The Motet

A still more complex treatment of an existing chant became the motet. Composers took a section of organum, added a new text to the top part, and even added new lines of polyphony. The new text might be in Latin or French, secular in subject matter, and intended for non-liturgical use. The borrowed tenor part from the original organum, or chant, became known as the *cantus firmus*, a Latin term designating the plainchant line. Composers used some of these well-known tenor lines, or *cantus firmi*, to create numerous new motets. Since the new compositions often sported vernacular texts in the upper parts, the original Latin text of the tenor part became unnecessary and was often played by an instrument. As the rhythms of these new works became more complex, composers continued to develop new kinds of rhythmic notation. Since each line of the polyphony had a different text as well as varying numbers of syllables and notes, composers saved both space and valuable parchment by writing out each line separately, instead of in a full score. This new approach was called "choirbook format" and remained popular until the sixteenth century.

Ars Nova

In the fourteenth century, composers developed a new system of music notation allowing for a wider variety of rhythmic and metric possibilities. Now they could clearly indicate rhythmic flow and text underlay for the ever more complex polyphony. This new style was called ars nova and gave rise to some standard formal structures known as *formes fixes*, or "fixed forms." There were three varieties of fixed forms: the ballade, virelai, and rondeau. These fixed forms provided a predictable architecture, often a verse with a refrain, that also allowed flexibility for each individual piece. The subject matter for these pieces became more secular, often including love songs and political satire in addition to devotional liturgical texts. While the manuscripts contain little information about instrumentation, artwork and literature from this period show and describe singers and instrumentalists performing together. Performances probably varied and depended on availability, but harps, lutes, flutes, recorders, shawms, sackbuts, drums, bells, and cymbals may well have been included in vocal polyphony. Also, national styles of composition became more distinct, particularly between France and Italy, during this time. The development of this contrast in national styles continues as the centuries progress.

Musica Ficta

Literally meaning false or feigned music, term *musica ficta* refers to the accidentals that were added to the music to make cadences come out sounding "right" according to the rules of counterpoint. As polyphony became more complex, performers would alter certain pitches to maintain the preferred consonant intervals as they approached a cadence. Usually, these adjusted half-step intervals were not notated in the manuscripts. These accidentals are often corrected in modern editions, but beware, as there may be more than one workable solution. Not only will editors suggest possible choices, but performers cognizant of the complexities of this type of music will do so as well. You should just be aware that this is an issue that needs to be addressed.

Guillaume de Machaut (1300–1377)

Guillaume de Machaut was the most important poet and composer of the fourteenth century, and he was the leading composer of French ars nova. His reputation as a poet equaled that of Chaucer, author of *The Canterbury Tales*. Machaut was the first significant composer of vocal polyphony to be known by name. He also wrote about creating and performing music, and he took great care to preserve his works in illuminated manuscripts, which he presented as gifts to friends. This may be why he is still known today. His *Messe de Nostre Dame* (online example 1-3) was the first complete mass text to be set in four-part polyphony by one composer, thus setting a precedent for many other complete settings to follow. He also wrote twenty-three motets and dozens of settings of secular monody and polyphony. ♪

John Dunstable (1390–1453)

John Dunstable (sometimes written as Dunstaple), a leading English composer of the fifteenth century, wrote masses, motets, and other liturgical settings in the polyphonic style, as well as secular polyphonic songs. Listen to his motet *Veni Sancte Spiritus,* based on the hymn *Veni Creator* (online example 1-4). You might also find a mass based on the chant "Ave Maris Stella" (online example 1-5). ♪

Guillaume Dufay (1397–1474)

Guillaume Dufay (sometimes written as Du Fay) was one of the leading composers of his day. He spent time in Italian and French capitals and synthesized a new international style of composition. His music was performed and copied all over Europe. He composed masses, motets, chant settings, and secular songs in the popular polyphonic style of his time, which remained relatively stable throughout his career. Modern editions of his works appeared in the 1930s, and a critical edition of his complete works was completed in the 1960s. Listen to his motet *Nuper Rosarum Flores* (online example 1-6). He also wrote a mass based on the chant "Ave Maris Stella" as well as one based on another well-known and much-used chant "L'homme armé." ♪

THE RENAISSANCE

New Trends

Following Dufay's death, music changed rapidly. The next generation of composers developed many new musical trends and styles. The term Renaissance, which was coined in the mid-nineteenth century, usually refers to the 150 years from 1450–1600 and the resurgence of interest in ancient Greek and Roman culture. This "general cultural movement and state of mind" emphasized human values and the pleasures of the senses as opposed to spiritual values in the service of God.[6] A rebirth or flowering of interest in arts and sciences produced an explosion of new architecture and arts including painting, sculpture, and music. Music-making thrived in the courts and cathedrals of major cities while aristocratic families also supported and maintained their own staff of professional musicians for social and religious occasions.

Sacred polyphony continued to flourish and evolve through the upheavals of the Reformation and Counter-Reformation, and new secular forms, including madrigals and solo songs, gained popularity and importance. Poets and composers collaborated to coordinate text and music that would more closely reflect the phrasing and punctuation of the poetry. Composers became more careful about aligning musical notes and syllables to capture the natural rhythms of speech. Tuning systems were changing as well, allowing for more use of thirds and sixths and more complex rules about consonance, dissonance, and counterpoint. The arrival of printing and movable type at the beginning of the sixteenth century transformed musical culture completely, allowing for a greater distribution of scores and part books to use in the chapel, at court, or in private homes.

Johannes Ockeghem (c. 1410–1497)

Johannes (or Jean) Ockeghem, considered one of the greatest composers of the fifteenth century, spent most of his career in the service of the French royal court. He most likely started out as a choirboy at a cathedral in Antwerp and later sang for Charles I, Duke of Bourbon. As singer and composer for the court of the king of France, he composed masses, motets, and secular songs, known as *chansons*. In his masses, he developed ingenious forms of imitation and canon. His *Missa Prolationum* (online example 1-7) is full of complex canons. He also wrote a mass on "L'homme armé." His secular *chansons* were based on the traditional conventions of the *formes fixes* of courtly poetry and used two- and three-part counterpoint. ♪

Josquin des Prez (c. 1450–1521)

Josquin des Prez (also des Près, de Prés), another Franco-Flemish composer, is widely regarded as the greatest composer of his generation. He also had a profound influence on the music of the sixteenth century and beyond. He trained as a choirboy in northern France and worked as a singer and composer in the chapels of Aix-en-Provence and King Louis XI. He also held positions at the courts of the Sforza family in Milan and the Pope in Rome. Over his fifty-year career, he composed works in all the major genres of his time: masses, motets, psalm settings, and secular French *chansons* for four to six voices. He developed innovations in fugal imitative polyphonic writing, but he also tried to set the Latin and French texts so the music would communicate the meaning of the words. He was also careful to fit the musical stresses with the accentuation of the syllables so the words could be clearly heard and understood. Critics observed that he was able to capture the full range of human emotions in his music. Near the end of his life, the Italian printer Ottaviano Petrucci produced collections of his music, which were hugely popular and successful. Try listening to his epitaph for Ockeghem *Nymphes des Bois* (online example 1-8) and don't miss his humorous madrigal "El Grillo" (online example 1-9). ♪

Giovanni Pierluigi da Palestrina (c. 1525–1594)

Giovanni Pierluigi da Palestrina, a towering musical figure of the late sixteenth century, ushered polyphony into the new world of the Catholic Counter-Reformation. He successfully combined the brilliance of polyphonic writing achieved by his Franco-Flemish predecessors with the Council of Trent's demands for less profane delight described as giving "empty pleasure to the ear."[7] Palestrina aimed to convey more textural clarity in his music, with appropriate emotional connection to the liturgy. Educated as a choirboy in Rome, he briefly joined the choir of the Sistine Chapel and held various posts elsewhere in Italy before becoming director of the Cappella Giulia for Pope Julius III. He composed music for the grand festivals and religious occasions at St. Peters. His output was enormous, including 104 masses, 300 motets, seventy-two hymns, thirty-five Magnificat settings, and over a hundred secular madrigals. If you want to listen to one representative composition, make it the *Missa Papae Marcelli* (online example 1-10). Many of his works were published in his lifetime, and two complete editions of his works were produced in the nineteenth and twentieth centuries. ♪

Orlando di Lasso (c. 1530–1594) and
Tomás Luis de Victoria (1548–1611)

Two important contemporaries of Palestrina are Orlando di Lasso, also known as Orlande de Lassus, and Tomás Luis de Victoria. The Spanish Victoria was educated in Rome and may have studied with Palestrina. He returned to Spain where he composed important sacred music, including the well-known motet *O Magnum Mysterium* (online example 1-11), and a mass based on melodies from the motet. Orlando di Lasso, a Franco-Flemish composer, was educated as a choirboy in Italy and worked as a tenor in a chapel in Munich. Greatly admired all over Europe, he was a hugely prolific composer, writing masses, five- and six-part motets, passions, over a hundred Magnificat settings, 150 French *chansons*, and even more Italian madrigals. For listening samples, try the motet *Timor et Tremor* (online example 1-12), or the groundbreaking *Prophetiae Sibyllarum*. His secular chanson *Dessus le marché d'Arras'* (online example 1-13) describes a secret assignation between a soldier and a prostitute in the midst of a busy marketplace. ♪

The Italian Madrigal

In the sixteenth century, a new form of secular polyphony emerged: the madrigal. The earlier thirteenth-century madrigal used three-part counterpoint to set a simple strophic song with a refrain. The new sixteenth-century madrigal treated longer, more complex poems in a through-composed style with each line of text receiving its own unique musical setting. Composers chose texts by major poets such as Petrarch and combined polyphonic and homophonic textures to capture the different dramatic and emotional qualities of the words. Popular at a variety of courtly social gatherings, madrigals could be performed by amateurs or professional singers. Typically written in four or five parts, sixteenth-century madrigals were conceived as vocal chamber music rather than choral music, with one voice to a part. Some lines could be played or doubled by instruments, and by the end of the sixteenth century, madrigals might be performed by one solo voice on the top part with multiple instruments or a lute playing the remaining lines.

English Composers

Three major English composers of the Renaissance, Thomas Tallis (c. 1505–1585), William Byrd (c. 1540–1623), and Thomas Morley (1557–1602), were educated as choirboys in English cathedrals and held important posts as singers, organists, and composers at the Chapel Royal in London. Each was the leading musical figure of his generation, building on what he learned from his predecessor. Tallis and Byrd were both brought up Catholic but adapted their compositional styles to suit the new mid-century demands of the Anglican Church. Tallis began his career writing elaborate polyphonic works in Latin for church festivals and royal functions. Later on, he became the first composer to set English texts in the more preferred chordal and syllabic style demanded by the new Protestant church service.[8] He composed in all the major genres required by the church throughout the turbulent and dramatic changes of the early sixteenth century. His *Gaude Gloriosa* is an example of a grand motet, and the amazing *Spem in alium* (online example 1-14) for eight choirs of five voices each is not to be missed. Byrd also composed for the new Protestant Anglican Church and managed to include variety, novelty, and experimentation in his works, as well as influences of the Italian style. Listen to "Sing Joyfully" (online example 1-15) as an example of an Anglican anthem infused with virtuosic madrigal style. In addition to his religious works, Byrd also set English poetry in five-part polyphony. These secular consort songs for solo voices and viols were similar to Italian madrigals. ♪

Morley was a respected church musician and composer of sacred choral works, remembered more for his English madrigals and solo songs. In the late sixteenth century, he reinvented the Italian madrigal to suit popular taste, setting English texts that were narrative and light in tone. As we have seen with French *chansons* and Italian madrigals, these polyphonic compositions could be performed by a single voice to a part, with or without instruments, or by one solo voice singing the top part accompanied by multiple instruments or a single lute. In addition to a very popular and easily accessible treatise called *A Plaine and Easie Introduction to Practicall Musicke* (London 1597/R1971), Morley also wrote a book of solo lute songs, published in 1600, which includes the very famous setting of Shakespeare's "It Was a Lover and His Lass" (online example 1-16). ♪

THE EARLY BAROQUE

Seventeenth-Century Innovations

Music historians typically describe the baroque period as the years from 1600 to 1750, or from the publication of the first opera to the death of J. S. Bach. Of course, these boundaries are not entirely fixed in stone. Many trends that began in the late sixteenth century continued to inform the developments of the seventeenth century, or what we now call the early baroque period. The ideals of the Counter-Reformation, to uplift the heart and inspire the soul, continued into the new century as composers aimed to arouse the affections of their listeners and convey universal human emotions, both in sacred and secular music. Intelligibility of the text continued to be of utmost importance. Composers began to favor a solo vocal line with a simple accompaniment of a bass line and chords called the continuo. New rules for harmony and counterpoint governed the use of melodic dissonance to convey a heightened expression of the text. However, composers also continued to write complex polyphony and florid vocal lines, now anchored by a bass line and chordal structure.

Seventeenth-century notation became more precise. As dance forms influenced many kinds of vocal music, composers began to add bar lines to indicate rhythmic structure. At the same time, the new recitative style allowed the rhythm to follow more closely the natural declamation of the words. Composers also started writing music in a full-score format instead of separate part books. While most Renaissance music didn't specify particular voices and/or instruments, early baroque composers started indicating instruments and solo voice parts. This is not to say that seventeenth-century scores looked like twentieth-century ones. To work with early scores, twenty-first-century performers need to deal with issues of notation, rhythm, instrumentation, articulation, and ornamentation. Luckily, there are scholars and modern editors to help. We will talk much more about this in the chapters on ornamentation and scores.

The courts of kings and noble families continued to be major centers of patronage and music-making. The great cathedrals and smaller churches also gave employment to many singers, composers, and instrumentalists, producing important works of sacred music. Opera and chamber music, and other forms of secular entertainment, grew in both popularity and importance, inspiring composers to create new forms of vocal music. If you want to sing early music, this is definitely an important place to start.

Solo Song and Opera

While solo singing had been popular all through the Renaissance,[9] it really came into its own in the seventeenth century thanks, in part, to the members of the Florentine Camerata. This group of scholars and artists, including Giovanni de' Bardi (1534–1612) and Vincenzo Galilei (late 1520s–1591), father of the famous astronomer and physicist Galileo Galilei, met in Florence to discuss trends in the arts and sciences and perform new music. Participating artists included poet Ottavio Rinuccini (1562–1621), composer Jacopo Peri (1561–1633), and singer and composer Giulio Caccini (1551–1618). Both Peri and Caccini composed theatrical settings of Rinuccini's poem *Euridice*, using a new recitative style that combined a natural declamation of the text with lyric solo singing. The publication of both works in 1600 introduced the new form of opera.

Caccini and *Le nuove musiche*

Caccini was born in Rome and educated as a singer there. He later moved to Florence, where, in addition to participating in Bardi's Camerata, he worked for the Medici family as a celebrated tenor and voice teacher. After publishing and producing his operatic setting of *Euridice*, he published a book of songs in 1602 entitled *Le nuove musiche*, or *The New Music*. This volume included declamatory solo songs with simple accompaniments in the new recitative style. One of the songs, "Amarilli mia bella," known in an earlier five-voice setting, became popular as a solo song and, thanks to the ever reprinted Schirmer edition of *24 Italian Songs and Arias*, is still well-known to this day. Caccini's 1602 collection also included an invaluable introduction with specific instructions on how to sing this music in the new style. We will look at his recommendations in more depth in later chapters. The music of Palestrina, Lasso, and Byrd was becoming known as the *stile antico*, or old style, and would continue to be practiced and revered for church music throughout the seventeenth century. However, the *stile modern,* or modern style, of declamatory solo song would influence the development of vocal music for the rest of the baroque period and beyond.

Dowland and English Lute Songs

In England, the modern style of solo song grew in popularity as well, with John Dowland (1563–1626) as its most famous proponent. After being passed over for a position in Elizabeth's court in 1594, Dowland traveled through Germany and Italy, settling in Denmark as court lutenist to the Danish king. In 1612, he finally achieved a coveted position in the English court. He created a new kind of English song for solo voice and lute by combining elements from dance music, ballads, madrigals, and consort music. His innovative compositions balanced "poetic meter and musical rhythm, line and phrase length, rhyme scheme, and dance structure, creating a number of flawless masterpieces"[10] including "I Saw My Lady Weep," "Flow My Tears," and "In Darkness Let Me Dwell" (online example 1-17). He also devised a new printing format that differed from the familiar part book style and allowed the performers to sit around a table and read from one score (online example 6-3). He composed three books of lute songs, published in 1597, 1600, and 1603, as well as solo lute music and consort songs in the more familiar five-part setting for multiple voices and/or instruments. These beautiful songs that flourished in the transition from Renaissance to baroque should be part of any early music singer's repertoire. ♪

Claudio Monteverdi (1567–1643)

Claudio Monteverdi was the most important musician in late-sixteenth- and early-seventeenth-century Italy. A master and innovator in most all the major musical genres of his time, he bridged the transition between the culmination of Renaissance polyphony and the new developments of the early baroque. Born and educated in Cremona, he started composing sacred and secular music in his teens and published his first two books of madrigals in his early twenties. He began his career in the service of the Duke of Mantua, and eventually, he gained the most prestigious position of *maestro di cappella* at St

Mark's in Venice. He composed three major collections of liturgical and devotional music, in both Latin and Italian. His eight books of madrigals include both polyphonic vocal ensembles in the older Renaissance style, as well as instrumentally accompanied songs for one or more voices in the more homophonic and declamatory new style. His operas, including *Orfeo* (1607), *The Return of Ulysses* (1640), and *The Coronation of Poppea* (1643), laid the foundation for all operas to follow and earned for him the reputation of "one of the greatest musical dramatists of all time."[11] His influence on subsequent generations of theater composers is immeasurable.

Listening examples include his *Vespers* (online example 1-18), "Lamento de la Ninfa" from *Madrigals Book VIII* (online example 1-19), *Laudate Dominum* (online example 5-8), "Zefiro torna" (online example 6-6), *Orfeo* (online examples 6-7 and 6-16), *Poppea* (online example 6-9), *Ulysses* (online example 6-10), and *Lamento d'Arianna* (online example 7-23). ♪

Francesco Cavalli (1602–1676)

In the generation that followed Monteverdi, Francesco Cavalli became Italian opera's leading composer. He started as a soprano in the choir of St. Mark's in Venice, where he may have studied with Monteverdi, and he became well-known as a singer, organist, and composer. While he wrote sacred music in the traditional polyphonic style, Cavalli was most celebrated for his operas, which featured engaging, dramatic plots and tuneful, memorable arias. The difference between declamatory recitative and lyrical melodious aria became more distinct by the mid-seventeenth century. The aria would become the most central feature in all vocal genres of baroque music. Cavalli composed over forty operas, and many of the twenty-seven that survive have enjoyed modern productions, including *La Calisto* (online example 1-20). ♪

The Italian Cantata

Opera was all the rage in early seventeenth-century Venice, but vocal chamber music was the more popular secular offering in the rest of Italy. The cantata, a setting of dramatic poetry for solo voice and continuo, usually containing a combination of arias and recitatives, found its way into the homes of average folk as well as the courts of noble families and kings. Arias started out as lyric strophic songs and later developed into the now familiar ABA da capo form. Barbara Strozzi (1619–1677) was well-known as a composer and singer who performed at private gatherings of intellectuals and artists known as Academies. Unusual for a woman at the time, Strozzi published eight collections of motets, madrigals, arias, and cantatas, well worth exploring. Try listening to "L'amante segreto" (online example 1-21). Other composers of early Italian cantatas include Giacomo Carissimi (1605–1674), who also wrote sacred oratorios, and Antonio Cesti (1623–1669), who also composed operas. Later in the seventeenth century, Alessandro Scarlatti (1660–1725) composed over 600 secular cantatas of the highest quality, mostly for soprano and strings, as well as seventy operas. Listen to his cantatas "Bella dama di nome Santa" (online example 1-22) or "Ardo è ver, per te d'amore." Agostino Steffani (1654–1728) was another well-known opera composer who brought Italian opera to the German courts. He also wrote delightful chamber duets for two voices and continuo that influenced Handel (online example 1-23). ♪

German Composers

Heinrich Schütz (1585–1672) was the leading composer of sacred vocal music in seventeenth-century Germany. He began as a chorister in Kassel and later studied in Venice with Italian masters Gabrieli and Monteverdi. As Kapellmeister at the royal chapel in Dresden, Schütz introduced the Italian style of baroque music to Germany. A prodigious vocal composer, he supervised the publication of all thirteen printed collections of his vocal music. While these volumes include some Italian madrigals, most are sacred compositions, including large polyphonic choral works, German motets, and psalm settings, and two sets of *Kleine geistliche Konzerte* (1636 and 1639) for smaller forces and solo voices (online example 1-24). ♪

Danish-born Dietrich Buxtehude (c. 1637–1707) spent his career as organist at the Marienkirche in Lübeck, Germany. He composed a wide variety of sacred vocal works for a series of concerts at his church called *Abendmusik*, or evening music. These concerts included everything from compositions for solo voice and continuo to works for six choirs. Buxtehude had an innovative way of constructing a church cantata that combined aria and arioso passages with chorale sections. The resulting semi-dramatic religious work paved the way for later oratorios to come. Buxtehude composed in four different languages but mostly used German and Latin texts of Biblical prose or strophic poetry. Listen to his "Dixit Dominus Domino Meo" (online example 1-25). ♪

Lully and the Court of Louis XIV

While opera was becoming more and more popular in most parts of Europe, dance and theater were the preferred forms of entertainment at the French court of Louis XIV. The king himself was an accomplished dancer and liked to participate in grand productions that combined ballet and tragic drama. Jean-Baptiste Lully (1632–1687) trained as a violinist and organist, and he first arrived at court as an instrumentalist. He came to the attention of the king for his dancing, however, particularly his skill with comedic parts and mime. Eventually, he rose to the most important position of *surintendant de la musique de la chamber du roi* and began composing instrumental and ballet music. By the 1660s, when Cavalli brought his Italian operas to the French court, Lully provided additional ballet music. He also collaborated with dramatists and crafted incidental music for a 1670 production of Molière's *Le Bourgeois gentilhomme*.

Later in the 1670s, Lully started composing a new form of French opera, adapting Italian recitative to the specific demands of the French language by imitating the declamation of celebrated French stage actors. The stresses of his music mirrored the necessary stresses in the poetry. Boundaries between recitatives and airs were less distinct than in Italian opera and flowed more seamlessly from one to the other. Familiar dance forms provided a rhythmic framework. *Alceste* (1674) and *Armide* (1686) paved the way for the French operas of the eighteenth and nineteenth centuries (online examples 1-26, 6-8, and 6-12). Lully also composed large-scale sacred music. ♪

Other notable composers of French sacred and secular music of this period include Marc-Antoine Charpentier (1634–1704), Michel Richard de Lalande (1657–1726), and François Couperin (1668–1733).

Couperin is more associated with his instrumental music, but his *Troisième leçons de ténèbres* (1714) for two solo voices and continuo are not to be missed (online example 1-27). ♪

Purcell and Other English Composers

Henry Lawes (1596–1662) was an important song composer of the early seventeenth century. Trained as a singer and composer, he composed church anthems and psalm settings, as well as over 400 songs to high-quality poetry of the time, including "Go, Lovely Rose" and "A Complaint against Cupid" (online example 1-28). He provides a link in the song tradition that began with Morley and Dowland and culminated with Purcell. ♪

Henry Purcell (1659–1695) was one of England's most important seventeenth-century composers and, arguably, one of the greatest English composers of all time. A gifted composer as a child, he was trained as a chorister at the Chapel Royal and, eventually, succeeded John Blow (1648/9–1708) as organist and choirmaster at Westminster Abby. He wrote choral anthems with organ for church services, sometimes including parts for soloists and instruments. For formal occasions, he penned grand odes on celebratory texts for large forces of voices and instruments. He also wrote much secular vocal music. As in France, English audiences preferred theater to opera, and composers often wrote incidental music to plays that included songs inserted at appropriate moments. Purcell's *Dido and Aeneas* (1689), which was composed for a girl's boarding school, was unusual in that it was sung throughout (online example 1-29). While John Blow's *Venus and Adonis* (1684 or 1685; online example 1-30) was also sung throughout, *Dido* has remained one of the most important English operas of any century, ending with the justifiably famous "Dido's Lament." ♪

Purcell also composed many songs intended for amateur and professional singers. The two posthumously published volumes of *Orpheus Britannicus* (London 1698 and 1702) contain works of vocal chamber music as well as larger odes and songs that were originally intended as sections of staged works, including pieces from *King Arthur* (1691) and *The Fairy Queen* (1692).

THE HIGH BAROQUE

Standardization and Internationalization

In the first half of the eighteenth century, composers were standardizing and perfecting all the forms that had been developed in the early baroque period, including mass, motet, oratorio, cantata, and opera. There were five brilliant composer/performers who dominated the high baroque: Vivaldi, Telemann, Rameau, Bach, and Handel. All enjoyed success and fame. Each found a way to synthesize old and new trends, including contrapuntal and homophonic writing, intimate emotional expression, and grand theatrical display. Their compositions were heard in all the traditional venues of church, theater, and chamber, including courts of rulers and noble families and in the private homes of the upper and lower classes. Public concerts and performances became more popular as well, and the general public had a growing appetite for published music of all sorts.

During this period, national styles became even more distinct, and great rivalries arose, particularly between the Italian and French styles. At the same time, French and Italian music and musician traveled to international cities and courts, showcasing the cosmopolitan tastes of their patrons, and encouraging a new international musical style. Celebrity performers were in high demand all over Europe as well, and singers, in particular, developed great virtuosity to please their adoring public. If you want to sing early music, you will definitely want to explore the wide and fantastic repertoire created during the climax of the baroque period.

Antonio Vivaldi (1678–1741)

Antonio Vivaldi was most famous in his time as a violinist and composer of instrumental music, particularly for his hundreds of concertos for violin and other solo instruments, but he also wrote plenty of vocal music. By the 1720s, he was successfully writing operas in Venice and Rome, some twenty of which survived. In the 1730s, he traveled to Vienna, Prague, and Amsterdam where he most likely oversaw productions of his operas. He also composed sacred vocal music, including grand choral settings of liturgical texts. Many of these works show a significant influence of both the operatic and concerto style, including elaborate solo sections and lengthy instrumental ritornellos. Vivaldi also wrote solo motets for voice and instruments, including *Nulla in Mundo Pax Sincera* (online example 1-31). These virtuosic works are similar to concertos for the voice. He wrote dozens of Italian solo cantatas for the popular combination of voice and continuo. These more modest works usually contain several *da capo* arias punctuated by short recitatives. Listen to *Alla caccia dell'alme e de'cori* (online example 1-32). ♪

Georg Philippp Telemann (1681–1767)

Georg Philipp Telemann had a long and prolific career as a composer of all the usual forms of his time, including operas, masses, cantatas, passions, secular vocal chamber music, and songs, as well as instrumental works. A gifted child performer, studying composition, voice, organ, violin, and recorder, he started his career in Leipzig and, eventually, held positions as Kapellmeister, first in Frankfurt and then in Hamburg. He applied for the position of Kantor at St. Thomas's Church in Leipzig, but he withdrew his application when he received a raise in Hamburg, thus leaving the spot open for J. S. Bach. In both Frankfurt and Hamburg, Telemann was responsible for the musical activities at numerous churches, and he composed multiple cycles of church cantatas for weekly services, as well as passions and other oratorios for major holidays and festivals throughout the church calendar. Of the hundreds of sacred solo cantatas that survive, some are scored for large forces, including chorus, soloists, brass, and timpani, but most are for a solo voice, one solo instrument, and continuo, usually consisting of two *da capo* arias in German separated by a recitative. Listen to "Lauter Wonne, lauter Freude," "Ich hebe meine Augen auf," or "Seele, lerne dich erkennen" (online example 1-33). Telemann also wrote many secular cantatas in German for private and civic occasions. These vary in size and style depending on the situation for which they were intended: some for small forces such as the church cantatas, and some with more elaborate scoring. He also composed over forty operas, only a few of which survived, and helped revive interest in the Lied form of German song during the 1730s and 1740s. ♪

Rameau and Other French Composers

By the beginning of the eighteenth century, Paris welcomed Italian performers and composers, and the public could enjoy new entertainments from home and abroad. Court patronage continued, but other wealthy patrons sponsored both large public performances and smaller private musical gatherings. Jean-Philippe Rameau (1683–1764), known for his 1722 treatise on harmony, was introduced and championed by one of these noble patrons. Early in his career, he wrote a handful of French secular cantatas for solo voice and instruments, including *Orphée* (online example 1-34) and *Le berger fidèle*, as well as sacred motets in Latin, both grand and petite, for voices and various instrumental forces. It was not until he was in his fifties, however, that he composed his most celebrated stage works, including *Hippolyte et Arcie* (1733), *Les Indes galantes* (1735), and *Castor et Pollux* (1737). These tragic opera-ballets included music for dance, orchestral interludes, grand choruses, exotic stage spectacle, and, of course, recitatives and airs. Rameau introduced many reforms to the traditions of French opera established by Lully, and the public either loved him or hated him for it. Still, he had a profound impact on the future course of French music and opera. ♪

The secular cantata had a robust life in the salons of early-eighteenth-century Paris. Inspired by the Italian solo cantata, French composers were drawn to this form in which they could set flowery poetry describing a mythological or allegorical scene, complete with amorous entanglements and a concluding moral. Most cantatas were scored for a solo voice, usually soprano or tenor, and continuo, with various additional solo obbligato instruments, including violin and flute. They were performed by both amateur and professional musicians and were featured at small private gatherings and larger events in fashionable society.

André Campra (1660–1744) composed cantatas and airs as well as sacred motets. Listen to his cantata *Arion* and his sacred motet *Jubilate Deo* (online examples 1-35 and 1-36). Nicolas Bernier (1665–1734) wrote numerous books of cantatas and motets for one to three voices and instruments. Listen to his cantata *Médée* (online example 1-37). Michel Pignolet de Montéclair (1667–1737) wrote twenty French and four Italian cantatas that had an important impact on Rameau's operatic music. His cantata *La Mort de Didon* presents the tragic story of Dido as a dramatic solo scene, and his *Pan et Syrinx* (online example 1-38) features characters from mythology cavorting in Arcadia. Louis-Nicolas Clérambault (1676–1749), the most famous of all the cantata composers, wrote five books of cantatas that masterfully achieved a union of French and Italian style. His cantata *La Muse de l'Opéra* includes familiar operatic conventions in miniature, and his *L'Isle de Délos* (online example 1-39) is an island of delights. You may not be familiar with any of these composers, but it is well worth exploring their rich contribution to this corner of the repertory. ♪

Johann Sebastian Bach (1685–1750)

Johann Sebastian Bach is undoubtedly one of the most celebrated composers of all time. Except for opera, he developed every genre and style of music popular in his day to new levels of genius, and he left us with a wealth of instrumental and vocal repertoire that exceed the depth and complexity of any composer before him. Born to a large and well-known family of musicians, he spent most of his life in Germany. Even though he didn't travel internationally as many of his contemporaries did, he became familiar with the music of other composers by copying and arranging their compositions. He was particularly interested in works by Vivaldi and heard the older master Buxtehude play the organ on a trip to Lübeck. In his early career in Arnstadt, Weimar, and Cöthen, Bach composed mainly keyboard and instrumental music. In 1723, he became director of music at St. Thomas's School in Leipzig and devoted the rest of his life there to composing vocal music.

In Leipzig, Bach was responsible for teaching the boys at the school and providing music for the services at St. Thomas's and St. Nicholas's churches. This included daily services, weekly Sunday services, and festivals and special holidays throughout the church calendar. For the weekly Sunday services, Bach composed approximately 200 church cantatas in four yearly cycles. The German text of each cantata provided commentary on the Gospel reading for that week. Many of the cantatas begin with an opening chorus based on a chorale melody that is restated in a more simple form in the final movement. In between, there can be arias and duets interspersed with recitatives. Arias can be accompanied by smaller forces, including just continuo, perhaps with one or two obbligato instruments, or by a larger instrumental complement. Some cantatas use only solo singers and don't need a chorus at all. Bach also composed secular cantatas for social occasions, including the wonderful *Phoebus and Pan* (BWV 201), *Wedding Cantata* (BWV 202), and *Coffee Cantata* (BWV 211) (online example 1-40). You may find yourself singing in a Bach church cantata as part of a church service, but complete cantatas or arias from the cantatas can certainly be performed out of context on concert programs. ♪

While in Leipzig, Bach also composed larger choral works for special church holidays, including two Passion settings, a Magnificat, and the *Mass in B minor*, which was mostly compiled from earlier smaller works. The *St. Matthew Passion* (BWV 244) and the *St. John Passion* (BWV 245) are most often performed today as complete works in concert, but solo arias from these masterpieces can always be taken out of context and included on smaller concert programs. The same is true for the *Magnificat* (BWV 243) and *B minor Mass* (BWV 232). As singers, there are probably few of us who have not sung some of Bach's choral music in some form or other. If you want to sing early music as a solo singer, Bach should certainly hold a central place on your plate, and your diet of baroque repertoire would not be complete without a healthy portion, or at least a taste, of Bach arias in German.

Listening examples throughout this book include arias from the *Magnificat* (online example 5-2), *St. Matthew Passion* (online example 5-15), *Coffee Cantata* (online examples 5-16 and 6-19), and *St. John Passion* (online example 6-18). I hope you will explore beyond these examples to find arias and duets that suite your voice.

George Frideric Handel (1685–1759)

It is probably fair to say that almost every singer reading this book has sung, or is at least familiar with, *Messiah* by George Frideric Handel. Performed every year since it was first heard in 1742, it is one of the most recognizable and beloved vocal works from the baroque era. Handel produced a tremendous amount of magnificent vocal music in his illustrious career, and as a singer of early music, you should definitely explore beyond his most familiar works.

Born in Germany and educated as a keyboard player, Handel left an early job as a church musician to travel in Italy and pursue his interest in writing opera. While visiting Rome, Florence, Naples, and Venice, he met many Italian composers who had an important impact on him, including Alessandro Scarlatti. During this period, Handel wrote many secular Italian cantatas for solo voice and continuo. He also wrote chamber duets and trios and larger dramatic cantatas with multiple soloists and orchestral accompaniment. Listen to his "O numi eterni," also known as *La Lucrezia* for solo voice and continuo (online example 1-41). ♪

After returning briefly to Germany, he moved to London in 1710 where his opera *Rinaldo* met with great success and assured his reputation as an opera composer. Starting in 1720, Handel composed some of his greatest operas, including *Radamisto* (1720), *Ottone* (1723), *Giulio Cesare* (1724), and *Rodelinda* (1725), for an opera company called the Royal Academy of Music. He hired and wrote for internationally renowned Italian singers, including the castrato Senesino and sopranos Cuzzoni and Faustina. The London public went wild. The competition of another opera company in town featuring the Italian composer Nicola Porpora (1686–1768) and the legendary castrato Farinelli inspired vocal performances that reached new heights of virtuosity and showmanship. Throughout thirty-five years of composing and producing operas, Handel crafted over forty operatic works, each featuring four to six leading singers, with six to eight arias each. That's a huge number of opera arias available to us, and they are accessible in many editions. Transplanting and transposing arias was a common practice in Handel's day and is still permissible today. With such a great variety of arias, it is possible to find selections that fit your voice and personality.

By 1739, the London public was becoming saturated with Italian opera, and Handel turned to the composition of an innovative new form, the English oratorio. His twenty-six oratorios, including *Saul, Samson, Semele, Judas Maccabaeus, Israel in Egypt*, and, of course, *Messiah*, are full of wonderful choruses and operatic solo arias that the public could understand in their native language. While the twentieth century saw renewed interest in Handel's Italian operas, many of his English oratorios never fell out of favor. Throughout his career, Handel also composed anthems and liturgical works for the church and court chapels, not to mention his festive instrumental and orchestral works. Handel's vocal repertoire is a wealth of riches just waiting to be explored.

Listening examples throughout this book include excerpts and full productions of *Ottone* (online example 5-10), *Orlando* (online example

5-11), *Alcina* (online examples 6-14 and 6-15), *Acis and Galatea* (online example 6-17), *Theodora* (online example 6-20), and *Messiah* (online example 6-21). I hope these few examples will inspire you to search off the beaten path for many more wonderful Handel arias and ensembles awaiting you.

NOTES

1. Ross W. Duffin, ed. *A Performer's Guide to Medieval Music* (Bloomington, IN: Indiana University Press, 2000), 16.

2. Barbara Russano Hanning, *Concise History of Western Music: Based on Donald Jay Grout & Claude V. Palisca A History of Western Music,* Second Edition (New York, NY: W.W. Norton & Company, 2002), 16.

3. James W. McKinnon, *Gregorian Chant*, Vol. 10 in *The New Grove Dictionary of Music and Musicians*, edited by Stanley Sadie (London, Macmillan, 2001), 373.

4. Anthony Pryer, *Notation*, Vol. 2 in *The New Oxford Companion to Music*, edited by Denis Arnold (Oxford: Oxford University Press, 1984), 1247.

5. Hanning, 49.

6. Ibid, 102.

7. Ibid, 163.

8. Denis Arnold and John Milsom, *Thomas Tallis*, Vol. 2 in *Oxford Companion*, 1797.

9. Jeffery Kite-Powell, ed. *A Performer's Guide to Renaissance Music*, Second Edition (Bloomington, IN: Indiana University Press, 2007), 3.

10. Peter Holman and Paul O'Dette, *John Dowland*, Vol. 7 in *New Grove*, 531.

11. Arnold, *Claudio Monteverdi*, Vol. 2 in *Oxford Companion*, 1200.

ADDITIONAL RESOURCES

Arlt, Wulf. 2001. *Guillaume de Machaut.* Vol. 15 in *The New Grove Dictionary of Music and Musicians*, edited by Stanley Sadie, 478–90. London: Macmillan.

Arnold, Denis. 1984. *Agostino Steffani.* Vol. 2 in *The New Oxford Companion to Music*, edited by Denis Arnold, 1747. Oxford: Oxford University Press.

———. 1984. *Antonio Vivaldi.* Vol. 2 in *The New Oxford Companion to Music*, edited by Denis Arnold, 1936–38. Oxford: Oxford University Press.

———. 1984. *Claudio Monteverdi.* Vol. 2 in *The New Oxford Companion to Music*, edited by Denis Arnold, 1196–1200. Oxford: Oxford University Press.

————. 1984. *Francesco Cavalli.* Vol. 1 in *The New Oxford Companion to Music*, edited by Denis Arnold, 324–25. Oxford: Oxford University Press.

————. 1984. *Giulio Caccini.* Vol. 1 in *The New Oxford Companion to Music*, edited by Denis Arnold, 292. Oxford: Oxford University Press.

————. 1984. *Henry Purcell.* Vol. 2 in *The New Oxford Companion to Music*, edited by Denis Arnold, 1510–12. Oxford: Oxford University Press.

————. 1984. *Palestrina.* Vol. 2 in *The New Oxford Companion to Music*, edited by Denis Arnold, 1384–87. Oxford: Oxford University Press.

————. 1984. *Thomas Morley.* Vol. 2 in *The New Oxford Companion to Music*, edited by Denis Arnold, 1201–3. Oxford: Oxford University Press.

Arnold, Denis, and John Milsom. 1984. *Thomas Tallis.* Vol. 2 in *The New Oxford Companion to Music*, edited by Denis Arnold, 1797–98. Oxford: Oxford University Press.

Bent, Ian D., and Marianne Pfau. 2001. *Hildegard of Bingen.* Vol. 11 in *The New Grove Dictionary of Music and Musicians*, edited by Stanley Sadie, 493–99. London: Macmillan.

Bent, Margaret. 2001. *John Dunstaple.* Vol. 7 in *The New Grove Dictionary of Music and Musicians*, edited by Stanley Sadie, 711–17. London: Macmillan.

————. 2001. *Musica ficta.* Vol. 17 in *The New Grove Dictionary of Music and Musicians*, edited by Stanley Sadie, 441–51. London: Macmillan.

Carter, Tim, and Geoffrey Chew. 2001. *Claudio Monteverdi.* Vol. 17 in *The New Grove Dictionary of Music and Musicians*, edited by Stanley Sadie, 29–60. London: Macmillan.

de La Gorce, Jerome. 2001. *Jean-Baptiste Lully.* Vol. 15 in *The New Grove Dictionary of Music and Musicians*, edited by Stanley Sadie, 292–308. London: Macmillan.

Doe, Paul, and David Allison. 2001. *Thomas Tallis.* Vol. 25 in *The New Grove Dictionary of Music and Musicians*, edited by Stanley Sadie, 36–47. London: Macmillan.

Duffin, Ross W., ed. 2000. *A Performer's Guide to Medieval Music.* Bloomington, IN: Indiana University Press.

Elliott, Martha. 2006. *Singing in Style: A Guide to Vocal Performance Practices.* New Haven, CT: Yale University Press.

Fallows, David. 2001. *Ars Nova.* Vol. 2 in *The New Grove Dictionary of Music and Musicians*, edited by Stanley Sadie, 80–81. London: Macmillan.

Haar, James. 2001. *Orlande de Lassus.* Vol. 14 in *The New Grove Dictionary of Music and Musicians*, edited by Stanley Sadie, 295–322. London: Macmillan.

Hanning, Barbara Russano. 2002. *Concise History of Western Music: Based on Donald Jay Grout & Claude V. Palisca A History of Western Music, sixth edition*, Second Edition. New York, NY: W.W. Norton & Company.

Haskell, Harry. 2001. "Early Music." *The New Grove Dictionary of Music and Musicians*, Second Edition: 831–834.

Heller, Wendy. 2014. *Music in the Baroque: Western Music in Context*. New York: Norton.

Hicks, Anthony. 2001. *Georg Friderick Handel*. Vol. 10 in *The New Grove Dictionary of Music and Musicians*, edited by Stanley Sadie, 747–813. London: Macmillan.

Holman, Peter and Paul O'Dette. 2001. *John Dowland*. Vol. 7 in *The New Grove Dictionary of Music and Musicians*, edited by Stanley Sadie, 531–38. London: Macmillan.

Holman, Peter and Robert Thompson. 2001. *Henry Purcell*. Vol. 20 in *The New Grove Dictionary of Music and Musicians*, edited by Stanley Sadie, 604–30. London: Macmillan.

Hughes, Andrew. 2001. *Solmization*. Vol. 23 in *The New Grove Dictionary of Music and Musicians*, edited by Stanley Sadie, 644–49. London: Macmillan.

Kerman, Joseph. 2001. *William Byrd*. Vol. 4 in *The New Grove Dictionary of Music and Musicians*, edited by Stanley Sadie, 714–31. London: Macmillan.

Kite-Powell, Jeffery, ed. 2007. *A Performer's Guide to Renaissance Music*, Second Edition. Bloomington, IN: Indiana University Press.

Levy, Kenneth, et al. 2001. *Plainchant*. Vol. 19 in *The New Grove Dictionary of Music and Musicians*, edited by Stanley Sadie, 825–26. London: Macmillan.

Lockwood, Lewis, et al. 2001. *Palestrina*. Vol. 18 in *The New Grove Dictionary of Music and Musicians*, edited by Stanley Sadie, 937–57. London: Macmillan.

Macey, Patrick, et al. 2001. *Josquin des Prez*. Vol. 13 in *The New Grove Dictionary of Music and Musicians*, edited by Stanley Sadie, 220–66. London: Macmillan.

McKinnon, James W. 2001. *Gregorian Chant*. Vol. 10 in *The New Grove Dictionary of Music and Musicians*, edited by Stanley Sadie, 373–74. London: Macmillan.

Milsom, John. 1984. *Josquin des Prez*. Vol. 1 in *The New Oxford Companion to Music*, edited by Denis Arnold, 1004–6. Oxford: Oxford University Press.

Palisca, Claude V. 2001. *Guido of Arezzo*. Vol. 10 in *The New Grove Dictionary of Music and Musicians*, edited by Stanley Sadie, 522–26. London: Macmillan.

Perkins, Leeman L. 2001. *Jean de Ockeghem*. Vol. 18 in *The New Grove Dictionary of Music and Musicians*, edited by Stanley Sadie, 312–26. London: Macmillan.

Planchart, Alejandro Enrique. 2001. *Guillaume Du Fay*. Vol. 7 in *The New Grove Dictionary of Music and Musicians*, edited by Stanley Sadie, 647–64. London: Macmillan.

Pryer, Anthony. 1984. *Guillaume de Machaut.* Vol. 2 in *The New Oxford Companion to Music*, edited by Denis Arnold, 1110–12. Oxford: Oxford University Press.

Pryer, Anthony. 1984. *Notation.* Vol. 2 in *The New Oxford Companion to Music*, edited by Denis Arnold, 1247–68. Oxford: Oxford University Press.

Reckow, Fritz et al. 2001. "Organum." *The New Grove Dictionary of Music and Musicians*, Second Edition: 671–95.

Sadie, Stanley, and Howard Mayer Brown, eds. 1990. *Performance Practice: Music Before 1600.* New York, NY: W.W. Norton & Company.

Sadler, Graham, and Thomas Christensen. 2001. *Jean-Philippe Rameau.* Vol. 20 in *The New Grove Dictionary of Music and Musicians*, edited by Stanley Sadie, 778–806. London: Macmillan.

Smallman, Basil. 1984. *Heinrich Schütz.* Vol. 2 in *The New Oxford Companion to Music*, edited by Denis Arnold, 1649–52. Oxford: Oxford University Press.

Snyder, Kerala J. 2001. *Dietrich Buxtehude.* Vol. 4 in *The New Grove Dictionary of Music and Musicians*, edited by Stanley Sadie, 695–710. London: Macmillan.

Talbot, Michael. 2001. *Antonio Vivaldi.* Vol. 26 in *The New Grove Dictionary of Music and Musicians*, edited by Stanley Sadie, 817–43. London: Macmillan.

Thomas, Wendy. 1984. *Allessandro Scarlatti.* Vol. 2 in *The New Oxford Companion to Music*, edited by Denis Arnold, 1627–29. Oxford: Oxford University Press.

Thompson, Wendy, and Basil Smallman. 2017. *Dietrich Buxtehude*, edited by Denis Arnold. Accessed June 2, 2017. www.oxfordmusiconline.com.

Thompson, Wendy. 1984. *Henry Lawes.* Vol. 2 in *The New Oxford Companion to Music*, edited by Denis Arnold, 1052. Oxford: Oxford University Press.

Tunley, David. 2001. *Louis-Nicolas Clérambault.* Vol. 6 in *The New Grove Dictionary of Music and Musicians*, edited by Stanley Sadie, 47-49. London: Macmillan.

Walker, Thomas and Irene Alm. 2001. *Francesco Cavalli.* Vol. 5 in *The New Grove Dictionary of Music and Musicians*, edited by Stanley Sadie, 302–13. London: Macmillan.

Wilson, Christopher. 1984. *John Dowland.* Vol. 1 in *The New Oxford Companion to Music*, edited by Denis Arnold, 573–74. Oxford: Oxford University Press.

Wolff, Christoph et al. 2001. *Johann Sebastian Bach.* Vol. 2 in *The New Grove Dictionary of Music and Musicians*, edited by Stanley Sadie, 309–75. London: Macmillan.

Zohn, Steven. 2001. *Georg Philipp Telemann.* Vol. 25 in *The New Grove Dictionary of Music and Musicians*, edited by Stanley Sadie, 199–232. London: Macmillan.

❷

SINGING AND VOICE SCIENCE

Scott McCoy

This chapter presents a concise overview of how the voice functions as a biomechanical, acoustic instrument. We will be dealing with elements of anatomy, physiology, acoustics, and resonance. However, don't panic: The things you need to know are easily accessible, even if it has been many years since you last set foot in a science or math class!

All musical instruments, including the human voice, have at least four things in common: a power source, sound source (vibrator), resonator, and a system for articulation. In most cases, the person who plays the instrument provides power by pressing a key, plucking a string, or blowing into a horn. This power is used to set the sound source in motion, which creates vibrations in the air that we perceive as sound. Musical vibrators come in many forms, including strings, reeds, and human lips. The sound produced by the vibrator, however, needs a lot of help before it becomes beautiful music—we might think of it as raw material, like a lump of clay that a potter turns into a vase. Musical instruments use resonance to enhance and strengthen the sound of the vibrator, transforming it into sounds we identify as a piano, trumpet, or guitar. Finally, instruments must have a means of articulation to create the nuanced sounds of music. Let's see how these four elements are used to create the sounds of singing.

PULMONARY SYSTEM: THE POWER SOURCE OF YOUR VOICE

The human voice has a lot in common with a trumpet: both use flaps of tissue as a sound source, both use hollow tubes as resonators, and both rely on the respiratory (pulmonary) system for power. If you stop to think about it, you quickly realize why breathing is so important for singing. First and foremost, it keeps us alive through the exchange of blood gases—oxygen in, carbon dioxide out. However, it also serves as the storage depot for the air we use to produce sound. Most singers rarely encounter situations in which these two functions are in conflict, but if you are required to sustain an extremely long phrase, you could find yourself in need of fresh oxygen before your lungs are totally empty.

Misconceptions about breathing for singing are rampant. Fortunately, most are easily dispelled. We must start with a brief foray into the world of physics in the guise of Boyle's law. Some of you no doubt remember this principle: the pressure of a gas within a container changes inversely with changes of volume. If the quantity of a gas is constant and its container is made smaller, pressure rises. However, if we make the container bigger, pressure goes down. Boyle's law explains everything that happens when we breathe, especially when we combine it with another physical law: nature abhors a vacuum. If one location has reduced pressure, air flows from an area of higher pressure to equalize the two, and vice versa. Therefore, if we can create a zone of reduced air pressure by expanding our lungs, air automatically flows in to restore balance. When air pressure in the lungs is increased, it has no choice but to flow outward.

As we all know, the air we breathe goes in and out of our lungs. Each lung contains millions and millions of tiny air sacs, called alveoli, where gases are exchanged. The alveoli also function like ultra-miniature versions of the bladder for a bagpipe, storing the air that will be used to set the vocal folds into vibration. To get the air in and out of them, all we need to do is make the lungs larger for inhalation and smaller for exhalation. Always remember this relationship between cause and effect during breathing: we inhale because we make ourselves large; we exhale because we make ourselves smaller. Unfortunately, the lungs are organs, not muscles, and have no ability on their own to accomplish this feat. For this reason, your body came from the factory with special muscles designed to enlarge and compress your entire thorax (rib cage), while simultaneously moving your lungs. We can classify these muscles in two main categories: any muscle that has the ability to increase the volume capacity of the thorax serves an inspiratory function; any muscle that has the ability to decrease the volume capacity of the thorax serves an expiratory function.

Your largest muscle of inspiration is called the diaphragm (figure 2.1). This dome-shaped muscle originates from the bottom of your sternum (breastbone) and completely fills the area from that point around your ribs to your spine. It's the second-largest muscle in your body, but you probably have no conscious awareness of it or ability to control it directly.

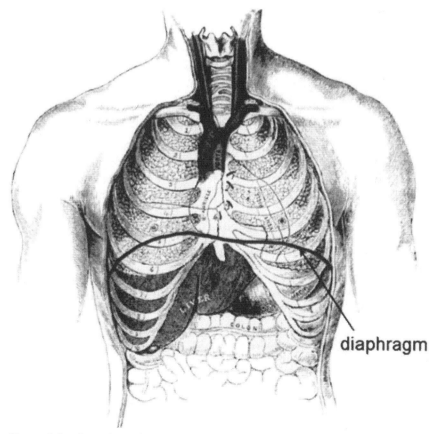

diaphragm

Figure 2.1.   Location of the diaphragm. *Courtesy of Dr. Scott McCoy*

When we take a deep breath, the diaphragm contracts and the central portion flattens out and drops downward a couple inches into your abdomen, pressing against all of your internal organs. If you release tension from your abdominal muscles as you inhale, you will feel a gentle bulge in your upper or lower belly, or perhaps in your back, resulting from the displacement of your innards by the diaphragm. This is a good thing and can be used to let you know you have taken a good inhalation.

The diaphragm is important, but we must remember that it cannot function in isolation. After you inhale, it relaxes and gently returns to its resting position through an action called elastic recoil. This movement, however, is entirely passive and makes no significant contribution to generating the pressure required to sustain phonation. Therefore, it makes no sense at all to try to "sing from your diaphragm"—unless you intend to sing while you inhale, not exhale!

Eleven pairs of muscles assist the diaphragm in its inhalation efforts, which are called the external intercostal muscles (figure 2.2). These muscles start from ribs one through eleven and connect at a slight angle downward to ribs two through twelve. When they contract, the entire thorax moves up and out, somewhat similar to moving a bucket handle. With the diaphragm and intercostals working together, you are able to increase the capacity of your lungs by about three to six liters, depending on your gender and overall physical stature; thus, we have quite a lot of air available to power our voices.

Eleven additional pairs of muscles are located directly under the external intercostals, which, not surprisingly, are called the internal intercostals (figure 2.2). These muscles start from ribs two through twelve and connect upward to ribs one through eleven. When they contract, they induce the opposite action of their external partners: the thorax is made smaller, inducing exhalation. Four additional pairs of expiratory muscles are located in the abdomen, beginning with the rectus (figure 2.2). The two rectus abdominis muscles run from your pubic bone to your sternum and are divided into four separate portions, called bellies of the muscle (lots of muscles have multiple bellies; it is coincidental that the bellies of the rectus are found in the location we colloquially refer to as our belly). Definition of these bellies results in the so-called ripped abdomen or six-pack of bodybuilders and others who are especially fit.

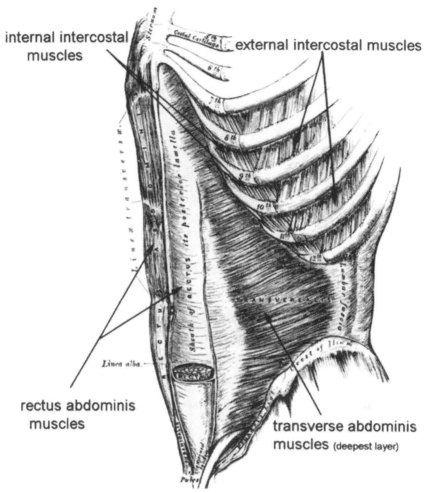

internal intercostal muscles

external intercostal muscles

rectus abdominis muscles

transverse abdominis muscles (deepest layer)

Figure 2.2. Intercostal and abdominal muscles. *Courtesy of Dr. Scott McCoy*

The largest muscles of the abdomen are called the external obliques (figure 2.3), which run at a downward angle from the sides of the rectus, covering the lower portion of the thorax, and extend all the way to the spine. The internal obliques lie immediately below, oriented at an angle that crisscrosses the external muscles. They are slightly smaller, beginning at the bottom of the thorax, rather than extending over it. The deepest muscle layer is the transverse abdominis (figure 2.2), which is oriented with fibers that run horizontally. These four muscle pairs com-

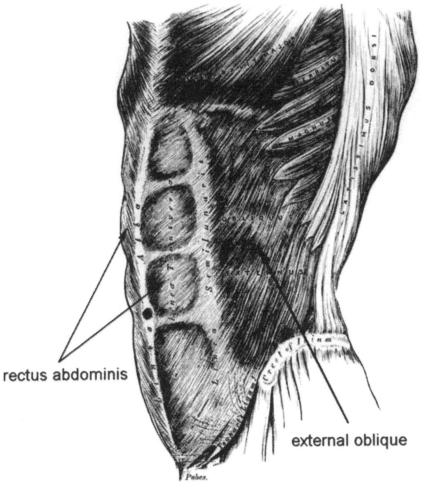

rectus abdominis

external oblique

Figure 2.3. External oblique and rectus abdominis muscles. *Courtesy of Dr. Scott McCoy*

pletely encase the abdominal region, holding your organs and digestive system in place while simultaneously helping you breathe.

Your expiratory muscles are quite large and can produce a great deal of pulmonary or air pressure. In fact, they easily can overpower the larynx. Healthy adults generally can generate more than twice the pressure that is required to produce even the loudest sounds; therefore, singers must develop a system for moderating and controlling airflow and breath pressure. This practice goes by many names, including breath support, breath control, and breath management, all of which rely on the principle of muscular antagonism. Muscles are said to have an antagonistic relationship when they work in opposing directions, usually pulling on a common point of attachment, for the sake of increasing stability or motor control. You can see a clear example of muscular antagonism in the relationship between your biceps (flexors) and triceps (extensors) when you hold out your arm. In breathing for singing, we activate inspiratory muscles (e.g., diaphragm and external intercostals) during exhalation to help control respiratory pressure and the rate at which air is expelled from the lungs.

One of the things you will notice when watching a variety of singers is that they tend to breathe in many different ways. You might think that voice teachers and scientists, who have been teaching and studying singing for hundreds, if not thousands of years, would have come to an agreement on the best possible breathing technique. However, for many reasons, this is not the case. For one, different musical and vocal styles place varying demands on breathing. For another, humans have a huge variety of body types, sizes, and morphologies. A breathing strategy that is successful for a tall, slender woman might be completely ineffective for a short, robust man. Our bodies actually contain a large number of muscles beyond those we've already discussed that are capable of assisting with respiration. For example, consider your latissimus dorsi muscles. These large muscles of the arm enable us to do pull-ups (or pull-downs, depending on which exercise you perform) at the fitness center. However, because they wrap around a large portion of the thorax, they also exert an expiratory force. We have at least two dozen such muscles that have secondary respiratory functions, some for exhalation and some for inhalation. When we consider all these possibilities, it is no surprise at all that there are many ways to breathe that can produce beautiful singing. Just remember to practice some muscular antagonism—maintaining a degree of inhalation posture during exhalation—and you should do well.

LARYNX: THE VIBRATOR OF YOUR VOICE

The larynx, sometimes known as the voice box or Adam's apple, is a complex physiologic structure made of cartilage, muscle, and tissue.

Biologically, it serves as a sphincter valve, closing off the airway to prevent foreign objects from entering the lungs. When firmly closed, it also is used to increase abdominal pressure to assist with lifting heavy objects, childbirth, and defecation. However, if we gently close this valve while we exhale, tissue in the larynx begins to vibrate and produce the sounds that become speech and singing.

The human larynx is a remarkably small instrument, typically ranging from the size of a pecan to a walnut for women and men, respectively. Sound is produced at a location called the glottis, which is formed by two flaps of tissue called the vocal folds (aka vocal cords). In women, the glottis is about the size of a dime; in men, it can approach the diameter of a quarter. The two folds are always attached together at their front point but open in the shape of the letter V during normal breathing, an action called abduction. To phonate, we must close the V while we exhale, an action called adduction (just as the machines you use at the fitness center to exercise your thigh and chest muscles).

Phonation only is possible because of the unique multilayer structure of the vocal folds (figure 2.4). The core of each fold is formed by muscle, which is surrounded by a layer of gelatinous material called

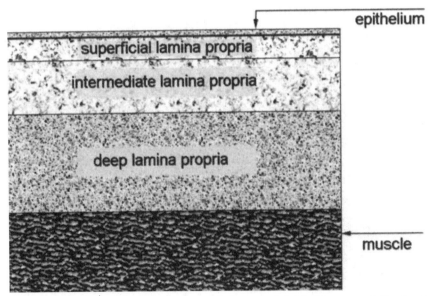

Figure 2.4. The layered structure of the vocal fold. *Courtesy of Dr. Scott McCoy*

the lamina propria. The vocal ligament also runs through the lamina propria, which helps to prevent injury by limiting how far the folds can be stretched for high pitches. A thin, hairless epithelial layer that is constantly kept moist with mucus secreted by the throat, larynx, and trachea surrounds all of this. During phonation, the outer layer of the fold glides independently over the inner layer in a wavelike motion, without which phonation is impossible.

We can use a simple demonstration to better understand the independence of the inner and outer portions of the folds. Explore the palm of your hand with your other index finger. Note that the skin is attached quite firmly to the flesh beneath it. If you poke at your palm, that flesh acts as padding, protecting the underlying bone. Now explore the back of your hand. You will observe that the skin is attached quite loosely— you easily can move it around with your finger. Moreover, if you poke at the back of your hand, it is likely to hurt; there is very little padding between the skin and your bones. Your vocal folds combine the best attributes of both sides of your hand. They provide sufficient padding to help reduce impact stress while permitting the outer layer to slip similar to the skin on the back of your hand, enabling phonation to occur. When you are sick with laryngitis and lose your voice (a condition called aphonia), inflammation in the vocal folds couples the layers of the folds tightly together. The outer layer no longer can move independently over the inner, and phonation becomes difficult or impossible.

The vocal folds are located within the five cartilaginous structures of the larynx (figure 2.5). The largest is called the thyroid cartilage, which is shaped like a small shield. The thyroid connects to the cricoid cartilage below it, which is shaped like a signet ring—broad in the back and narrow in the front. Two cartilages that are shaped like squashed pyramids sit atop the cricoid, called the arytenoids. Each vocal fold runs from the thyroid cartilage in front to one of the arytenoids at the back. Finally, the epiglottis is located at the top of the larynx, flipping backward each time we swallow to prevent food and liquid from entering our lungs. Muscles connect between the various cartilages to open and close the glottis and to lengthen and shorten the vocal folds for ascending and descending pitch, respectively. Because they sometimes are used to identify vocal function, it is a good idea to know the names of the muscles that control the length of the folds. We've already mentioned that a muscle forms

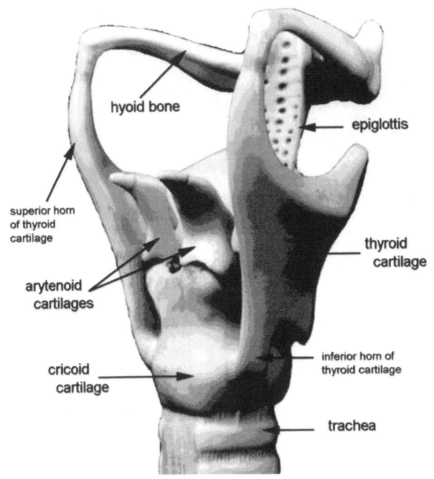

Figure 2.5. Cartilages of the larynx, viewed at an angle from the back.
Courtesy of Dr. Scott McCoy

the core of each fold. Because it runs between the thyroid cartilage and an arytenoid, it is named the thyroarytenoid muscle (formerly known as the vocalis muscle). When the thyroarytenoid, or TA, muscle contracts, the fold is shortened, and the pitch goes down. The folds are elongated through the action of the cricothyroid, or CT, muscles, which run from the thyroid to cricoid cartilage.

Vocal color (timbre) is created by the combined effects of the sound produced by the vocal folds and the resonance provided by the vocal tract. While these elements can never be completely separated, it is

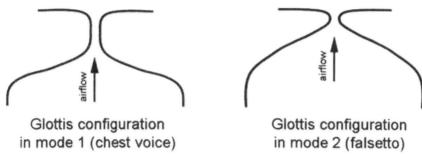

Glottis configuration   Glottis configuration
in mode 1 (chest voice)   in mode 2 (falsetto)

Figure 2.6. Primary modes of vocal fold vibration. *Courtesy of Dr. Scott McCoy*

useful to consider the two primary modes of vocal-fold vibration and their resulting sound qualities. The main differences are related to the relative thickness of the folds and their cross-sectional shape (figure 2.6). The first option depends on short, thick folds that come together with nearly square-shaped edges. Vibration in this configuration is given a variety of names, including mode 1, thyroarytenoid (TA) dominant, chest mode, or modal voice. The alternate configuration uses longer, thinner folds that only make contact at their upper margins. Common names include mode 2, cricothyroid (CT) dominant, falsetto mode, or loft voice. Singers vary the vibrational mode of the folds according to the quality of sound they wish to produce.

Before we move on to a discussion of resonance, we must consider the quality of the sound that is produced by the larynx. At the level of the glottis, we create a sound not unlike the annoying buzz of a duck call. That buzz, however, contains all the raw material we need to create speech and singing. Vocal or glottal sound is considered to be complex, meaning it consists of many simultaneously sounding frequencies (pitches). The lowest frequency within any tone is called the fundamental, which corresponds to its named pitch in the musical scale. Orchestras tune to a pitch called A-440, which means it has a frequency of 440 vibrations per second, or 440 Hertz (abbreviated Hz). Additional frequencies are included above the fundamental, which are called overtones. Overtones in the glottal sound are quieter than the fundamental. In voices, the overtones usually are whole number multiples of the fundamental, creating a pattern called the harmonic series (e.g., 100 Hz, 200 Hz, 300 Hz, 400 Hz, 500 Hz, etc. or G2, G3, D4, G4, B4—note that

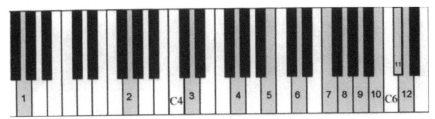

Figure 2.7. Natural harmonic series, beginning at G2. *Courtesy of Dr. Scott McCoy*

pitches are named by the international system in which the lowest C of the piano keyboard is C1; middle-C, therefore, becomes C4, the fourth C of the keyboard) (figure 2.7).

Singers who choose to make coarse or rough sounds, as might be appropriate for rock or blues, often add overtones that are inharmonic, or not part of the standard numerical sequence. Inharmonic overtones also are common in singers with damaged or pathological voices.

Under most circumstances, we are completely unaware of the presence of overtones—they simply contribute to the overall timbre of a voice. In some vocal styles, however, harmonics become a dominant feature. This is especially true in throat singing or overtone singing, as is found in places like Tuva. Throat singers tune their vocal tracts so precisely that single harmonics are highlighted within the harmonic spectrum as a separate, whistle-like tone. These singers sustain a low-pitched drone and then create a melody by moving from tone to tone within the natural harmonic series. You can learn to do this too. Sustain a comfortable pitch in your range and slowly morph between the vowels [i] and [u]. If you listen carefully, you will hear individual harmonics pop out of your sound.

The mode of vocal fold vibration has a strong impact on the overtones that are produced. In mode 1, high-frequency harmonics are relatively strong; in mode 2, they are much weaker. As a result, mode 1 tends to yield a much brighter, brassier sound.

VOCAL TRACT: YOUR SOURCE OF RESONANCE

Typically, resonance is defined as the amplification and enhancement (or enrichment) of musical sound through supplemental vibration. What does this really mean? In layman's terms, we could say that resonance makes instruments louder and more beautiful by reinforcing the original vibrations of the sound source. This enhancement occurs in two primary ways, which are known as forced and free resonance (there is nothing pejorative in these terms: free resonance is not superior to forced resonance). Any object that is physically connected to a vibrator can serve as a forced resonator. For a piano, the resonator is the soundboard (on the underside of a grand or on the back of an upright); the vibrations of the strings are transmitted directly to the soundboard through a structure known as the bridge, which also is found on violins and guitars. Forced resonance also plays a role in voice production. Place your hand on your chest and say [a] at a low pitch. You almost certainly felt the vibrations of forced resonance. In singing, this might best be considered your private resonance; you can feel it and it might impact your self-perception of sound, but nobody else can hear it. To understand why this is true, imagine what a violin would sound like if it were encased in a thick layer of foam rubber. The vibrations of the string would be damped out, muting the instrument. Your skin, muscles, and other tissues do the same thing to the vibrations of your vocal folds.

By contrast, free resonance occurs when sound travels through a hollow space, such as the inside of a trumpet, an organ pipe, or your vocal tract, which consists of the pharynx (throat), oral cavity (mouth), and nasal cavity (nose). As sound travels through these regions, a complex pattern of echoes is created; every time sound encounters a change in the shape of the vocal tract, some of its energy is reflected backward, much like an echo in a canyon. If these echoes arrive back at the glottis at the precise moment a new pulse of sound is created, the two elements synchronize, resulting in a significant increase in intensity. All of this happens very quickly—remember that sound is traveling through your vocal tract at more than 700 miles per hour.

Whenever this synchronization of the vocal tract and sound source occurs, we say that the system is in resonance. The phenomenon occurs at specific frequencies (pitches), which can be varied by changing the position of the tongue, lips, jaw, palate, and larynx. These resonant frequencies, or areas in which strong amplification occurs, are called formants. Formants provide the specific amplification that changes the raw, buzzing sound produced by your vocal folds into speech and singing. The vocal tract is capable of producing many formants, which are labeled sequentially by ascending pitch. The first two, F1 and F2, are used to create vowels; higher formants contribute to the overall timbre and individual characteristics of a voice. In some singers, especially those who train to sing in opera, formants three through five are clustered together to form a super formant, eponymously called the singer's formant, which creates a ringing sound and enables a voice to be heard in a large theater without electronic amplification.

Formants are vitally important in singing, but they can be a bit intimidating to understand. An analogy that works really well for me is to think of formants similar to the wind. You cannot see the wind, but you know it is present when you see leaves rustling in a tree or feel a breeze on your face. Formants work in the same manner. They are completely invisible and directly inaudible. However, just as we see the rustling leaf, we can hear, and perhaps even feel, the action of formants through how they change our sound. Try a little experiment. Sing an ascending scale beginning at B♭3, sustaining the vowel [i]. As you approach the D♯ or E♭ of the scale, you likely will feel (and hear) that your sound becomes a bit stronger and easier to produce. This occurs because the scale tone and formant are on the same pitch, providing additional amplification. If you change to a [u] vowel, you will feel the same thing at about the same place in the scale. If you sing to an [o] or [e] and continue up the scale, you'll feel a bloom in the sound somewhere around C5 (an octave above middle C); [a] is likely to come into its best focus at about G5.

To remember the approximate pitches of the first formants for the main vowels, [i]-[e]-[a]-[o]-[u], just think of a C-major triad in first inversion, open position, starting at E4: [i] = E4, [e] = C5, [a] = G5, [o] = C5, and [u] = E4 (figure 2.8). If your music theory isn't strong, you could use the mnemonic "every child gets candy eagerly." These pitches might vary by as much as a minor third higher and lower but no farther: Once a formant changes by more than that interval, the vowel that is produced must change.

Formants have absolutely no preference for what they amplify—they are indiscriminate lovers, just as happy to bond with the first harmonic as the fifth. When men or women sing low pitches, there almost always will be at least one harmonic that comes close enough to a formant to produce a clear vowel sound. The same is not true for women with high

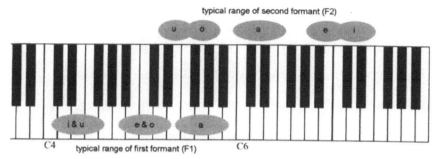

Figure 2.8. Typical range of first and second formants for primary vowels. *Courtesy of Dr. Scott McCoy*

voices, especially sopranos, who routinely must sing pitches that have a fundamental frequency higher than the first formant of many vowels. Imagine what happens if she must sing the phrase, "and I'll leave you forever" with the word "leave" set on a very high, climactic note. The audience won't be able to tell if she is singing "leave" or "love"; the two will sound identical. This happens because the formant that is required to identify the vowel [i] is too far below the pitch being sung. Even if she tries to sing "leave," the sound that comes out of her mouth will be heard as some variation of [a].

Fortunately, this kind of mismatch between formants and musical pitches rarely causes problems for anyone but opera singers, choir sopranos, and perhaps ingénues in classic music theater shows. Almost everyone else generally sings low enough in their respective voice ranges to produce easily identifiable vowels.

Second formants also can be important but more so for opera singers than everyone else. They are much higher in pitch, tracking the pattern [u] = E5, [o] = G5, [a] = D6, [e] = B6, [i] = D7 (you can use the mnemonic "every good dad buys diapers" to remember these pitches; figure 2.8). Because they can extend so high, into the top octave of the piano keyboard for [i], they interact primarily with higher tones in the natural harmonic series. Unless you are striving to produce the loudest unamplified sound possible, you probably never need to worry about the second formant; it will steadfastly do its job of helping to produce vowel sounds without any conscious thought or manipulation on your part.

If you are interested in discovering more about resonance and how it impacts your voice, you might want to install a spectrum analyzer on your computer. Free (or inexpensive) programs are readily available for download over the Internet that will work with either a PC or Mac computer. You don't need any specialized hardware—if you can use Skype or FaceTime, you already have everything you need. Once you've installed something, simply start playing with it. Experiment with your voice to see exactly how the analysis signal changes when you modify the way your voice sounds. You'll be able to see how harmonics change in intensity as they interact with your formants. If you sing with vibrato, you'll see how consistently you produce your variations in pitch and amplitude. You'll even be able to see if your tone is excessively nasal for the kind of singing you want to do. Other programs are available that will help you improve your intonation (how well you sing in tune) or enhance your basic musicianship skills. Technology truly has advanced sufficiently to help us sing more beautifully.

MOUTH, LIPS, AND TONGUE: YOUR ARTICULATORS

The articulatory life of a singer is not easy, especially when compared to the demands placed on other musicians. Like a pianist or brass player, we must be able to produce the entire spectrum of musical articulation, including dynamic levels from hushed pianissimos to thunderous fortes, short notes, long notes, accents, crescendos, diminuendos, and so on. We produce most of these articulations the same way instrumentalists do, which is by varying our power supply. However, singers have another layer of articulation that makes everything much more complicated; we must produce these musical gestures while simultaneously singing words.

As we learned in our brief examination of formants, altering the resonance characteristics of the vocal tract creates the vowel sounds of language. We do this by changing the position of our tongue, jaw, lips, and, sometimes, palate. Slowly say the vowel pattern [i]-[e]-[a]-[o]-[u]. Can you feel how your tongue moves in your mouth? For [i], it is high in the front and low in the back, but it takes the opposite position for [u]. Now, slowly say the word "Tuesday," noting all the places your tongue comes into contact with your teeth and palate and how it changes shape as you produce the vowels and diphthongs. There is a lot going on in there—no wonder it takes so long for babies to learn to speak!

Our articulatory anatomy is extraordinarily complex, in large part because our bodies use the same passageway for food, water, air, and sound. As a result, our tongue, larynx, throat, jaw, and palate are all interconnected with common physical and neurologic points of attachment. Our anatomical Union Station, in this regard, is a small structure called the hyoid bone. The hyoid is one of only three bones in your entire body that does not connect to other bones via a joint (the other two are your patellae, or kneecaps). This little bone is suspended below your jaw, freely floating up and down every time you swallow. It is a busy place, serving as the upper-suspension point for the larynx, the connection for the root of the tongue, and the primary location of the muscles that open your mouth by dropping your jaw.

Good singing—in any genre—requires a high degree of independence in all these articulatory structures. Unfortunately, nature conspires against us to make this difficult to accomplish. From the time we are born, our body relies on a reflex reaction to elevate the palate and raise the larynx each time we swallow. This action becomes habitual: palate goes up, larynx also lifts. However, depending on the style of music we are singing, we might need to keep the larynx down while the palate goes up (opera and classical) or the palate down with the larynx up (country and bluegrass). As we all know, habits can be very hard to change, which is one of the reasons that it can take a lot of study and practice to become an excellent singer. Understanding your body's natural reflexive habits can make some of this work a bit easier.

There is one more significant pitfall to the close proximity of all these articulators: tension in one area is easily passed along to another. If your jaw muscles are too tight while you sing, that hyperactivity will likely be transferred to the larynx and tongue—remember, they all are interconnected through the hyoid bone. It can be tricky to determine the primary offender in this kind of chain reaction of tension. A tight tongue could just as easily be making your jaw stiff, or an elevated, rigid larynx could make both the tongue and the jaw suffer.

Neurology complicates matters even further. You have sixteen muscles in your tongue, fourteen in your larynx, twenty-two in your throat and palate, and another sixteen that control your jaw. Many of these are very small and lie directly adjacent to each other, and you often are required to contract one quite strongly while its next-door neighbor must remain totally relaxed. Our brains need to develop laser-like control, sending signals at the right moment with the right intensity to the precise spot where they are needed. When we first start singing, these brain signals come more like a blast from a shotgun, spreading the neurologic impulse over a broad area to multiple muscles, not all of which are the intended target. Again, with practice and training, we learn to refine our control, enabling us to use only those muscles that will help, while disengaging those that would get in the way of our best singing.

FINAL THOUGHTS

This brief chapter has only scratched the surface of the huge field of voice science. To learn more, you might want to visit the websites of the National Association of Teachers of Singing (NATS), the Voice Foundation (TVF), or the National Center for Voice and Speech (NCVS). You can easily locate the appropriate addresses through any Internet search engine. Remember: knowledge is power. Occasionally, people are afraid that if they know more about the science of how they sing, they will become so analytical that all spontaneity will be lost or they will become paralyzed by too much information and thought. In my forty-plus years as a singer and teacher, I've never encountered somebody who actually suffered this fate. To the contrary, the more we know, the easier—and more joyful—singing becomes. ♪

3

VOCAL HEALTH FOR THE EARLY MUSIC SINGER

Wendy LeBorgne

GENERAL PHYSICAL WELL-BEING

All singers, regardless of genre, should consider themselves as "vocal athletes." The physical, emotional, and performance demands necessary for optimal output require that the artist consider training and maintaining their instrument as an athlete trains for an event. With increased vocal and performance demands, it is unlikely that a vocal athlete will have an entire performing career completely injury-free. This may not be the fault of the singer, as many injuries occur due to circumstances beyond the singer's control, such as singing through an illness or being on a new medication seemingly unrelated to the voice. ♪

Vocal injury has often been considered taboo to talk about in the performing world as it has been considered to be the result of faulty technique or poor vocal habits. In actuality, the majority of vocal injuries presenting in the elite performing population tend to be from overuse and/or acute injury. From a clinical perspective, over the past seventeen years, younger, less experienced singers with fewer years of training (who tend to be quite talented) generally are the ones who present with issues related to technique or phonotrauma (nodules, edema, contact ulcers, etc.), while more mature singers with professional performing careers tend to present with acute injuries (hemorrhage) or overuse and misuse injuries (muscle tension dysphonia, edema, GERD, etc.) or injuries following an illness. There are no current studies documenting use and training in correlation to laryngeal pathologies. However, there are studies that document that somewhere between 35 and 100 percent of professional vocal athletes have abnormal vocal fold findings on stroboscopic evaluation. Many times, these "abnormalities" are in singers who have no vocal complaints or symptoms of vocal problems. From a performance perspective, uniqueness in vocal quality often leads to one being hired, and perhaps a slight aberration in the way a given larynx functions may become quite marketable. Regardless of what the vocal folds may look like, the most integral part of performance is that the singer must maintain agility, flexibility, stamina, power, and inherent beauty (genre appropriate) for their current level of performance taking into account physical, vocal, and emotional demands.

Unlike sports medicine and the exercise physiology literature where much is known about the types and nature of given sports injuries, there is no common parallel for the vocal athlete model. However, because the vocal athlete utilizes the body systems of alignment, respiration, phonation, and resonance with some similarities to physical athletes, a parallel protocol for vocal wellness may be implemented/considered for vocal athletes to maximize injury-prevention knowledge for both the singer and teacher. This chapter aims to provide information on vocal wellness and injury prevention for the vocal athlete.

CONSIDERATIONS FOR WHOLE BODY WELLNESS

Nutrition

You have no doubt heard the saying "You are what you eat." Eating is a social and psychological event. For many people, food associations and eating have an emotional basis resulting in either overeating or being malnourished. Eating disorders in performers and body image issues may have major implications and consequences for the performer on both ends of the spectrum (obesity and anorexia). Singers should be encouraged to reprogram the brain and body to consider food as fuel. You want to use high-octane gas in your engine, as pouring water in your car's gas tank won't get you very far. Eating a poor diet or a diet that lacks appropriate nutritional value will have negative physical and vocal effects on a singer. Effects of poor dietary choices for the vocal athlete may result in physical and vocal effects ranging from fatigue to life-threatening disease over the course of a lifetime. Encouraging and engaging in healthy eating habits from a young age will potentially prevent long-term negative effects from poor nutritional choices. It is beyond the scope of this chapter to provide a complete overview of all the dietary guidelines for pediatrics, adolescents, adults, and the mature adult; however, a listing of additional references to help guide your food and beverage choices for making good nutritional choices can be found online at websites such as Dietary Guidelines for Americans, Nutrition. gov Guidelines for Tweens and Teens, and Fruits and Veggies Matter. See the online companion web page on the NATS website for links to these and other resources. ♪

Hydration

"Sing wet, pee pale." This phrase was echoed in the studio of Van Lawrence regarding how his students would know if they were well-hydrated. Generally, this rule of pale urine during your waking hours is a good indicator that you are well-hydrated. Medications, vitamins, and certain foods may alter urine color despite adequate hydration. Due to the varying levels of physical and vocal activity of many performers, to maintain adequate oral hydration, the use of a hydration calculator based on activity level may be a better choice. These hydration calculators are easily accessible online and take into account the amount and level of activity the performer engages in on a daily basis. In a recent study of the vocal habits of musical theater performers, one of the findings indicated a significantly underhydrated group of performers.[1]

Laryngeal and pharyngeal dryness as well as "thick, sticky mucus" are often complaints of singers. Combating these concerns and maintaining an adequate viscosity of mucus for performance has resulted in some research. As a reminder of laryngeal and swallowing anatomy, nothing that is swallowed (or gargled) goes over or touches the vocal folds directly (or one would choke). Therefore, nothing that a singer eats or drinks ever touches the vocal folds, and to adequately hydrate the mucous membranes of the vocal folds, one must consume enough fluids for the body to produce a thin mucus. Therefore, any "vocal" effects from swallowed products are limited to potential pharyngeal and oral changes, not the vocal folds themselves.

The effects of systemic hydration are well-documented in the literature. There is evidence to suggest that adequate hydration will provide some protection of the laryngeal mucosal membranes when they are placed under increased collision forces as well as reducing the amount of effort (phonation threshold pressure) to produce voice. This is important for the singer because it means that with adequate hydration and consistency of mucus, the effort to produce voice is less and your vocal folds are better protected from injury. Imagine the friction and heat produced when two dry hands rub together and then what happens if you put lotion on your hands. The mechanisms in the larynx to provide appropriate mucus production are not fully understood, but there is enough evidence at this time to support oral hydration as a vital component of every singer's vocal health regime to maintain appropriate mucosal viscosity.

Although very rare, overhydration (hyperhidrosis) can result in dehydration and even illness or death. An overindulgence of fluids essentially makes the kidneys work "overtime" and flushes too much water out of the body. This excessive fluid loss in a rapid manner can be detrimental to the body.

In addition to drinking water to systemically monitor hydration, there are many nonregulated products on the market for performers that lay claim to improving the laryngeal environment (e.g., Entertainer's Secret, Throat Coat Tea, Grether's Pastilles, Slippery Elm, etc.). Although there may be little detriment in using these products, quantitative research documenting change in laryngeal mucosa is sparse. One study suggests that the use of Throat Coat when compared to a placebo treatment for pharyngitis did show a significant difference in decreasing the perception of a sore throat.[2] Another study compared the use of Entertainer's Secret to two other nebulized agents and its effect on phonation threshold pressure (PTP).[3] There was no positive benefit in decreasing PTP with Entertainer's Secret.

Many singers use personal steam inhalers and/or room humidification to supplement oral hydration and aid in combating laryngeal dryness.

There are several considerations for singers who choose to use external means of adding moisture to the air they breathe. Personal steam inhalers are portable and can often be used backstage or in the hotel room for the traveling performer. Typically, water is placed in the steamer, and the face is placed over the steam for inhalation. Because the mucous membranes of the larynx are composed of a saltwater solution, one study looked at the use of nebulized saline in comparison to plain water and its potential effects on effort or ease to sound production in classically trained sopranos.[4] Data suggested that perceived effort to produce voice was less in the saline group than in the plain-water group. This indicated that the singers who used the saltwater solution reported less effort to sing after breathing in the saltwater than singers who used plain water. The researchers hypothesized that because the body's mucus is not plain water (rather it is saltwater—think about your tears), when you use plain water for steam inhalation, it may actually draw the salt from your own saliva, resulting in a dehydrating effect.

In addition to personal steamers, other options for air humidification come in varying sizes of humidifiers from room-size to whole-house humidifiers. When choosing between a warm-air or cool-mist humidifier, considerations include both personal preference and needs. One of the primary reasons warm-mist humidifiers are not recommended for young children is due to the risk of burns from the heating element. Both the warm-mist and cool-air humidifiers act similarly in adding moisture to the environmental air. External air humidification may be beneficial and provide a level of comfort for many singers. Regular cleaning of the humidifier is vital to prevent bacteria and mold buildup. Also, depending on the hardness of the water, it is important to avoid mineral buildup on the device, and distilled water may be recommended for some humidifiers.

For traveling performers who often stay in hotels, fly on airplanes, or are generally exposed to other dry-air environments, there are products on the market designed to help minimize drying effects. One such device is called a Humidflyer, which is a face mask designed with a filter to recycle the moisture of a person's own breath and replenish moisture on each breath cycle.

For dry nasal passages or to clear sinuses, many singers use neti pots. Many singers use this homeopathic flushing of the nasal passages regularly. Research supports the use of a neti pot as a part of allergy relief and chronic rhinosinusitis control when utilized properly, sometimes in combination with medical management.[5] Conversely, long-term use of nasal irrigation (without taking intermittent breaks from daily use) may result in washing out the "good" mucus of the nasal passages, which naturally help to rid the nose of infections. A study presented at the 2009 American College of Allergy, Asthma, and Immunology (ACAAI) annual scientific meeting reported that when a group of individuals who were using twice-daily nasal irrigation for one year discontinued using it, they had an increase in acute rhinosinusitis.[6]

Tea, Honey, and Gargle to Keep the Throat Healthy

Regarding the use of general teas (which many singers combine with honey or lemon), there is likely no harm in the use of decaffeinated tea (caffeine may cause systemic dryness). The warmth of the tea may provide a soothing sensation to the pharynx, and the act of swallowing can be relaxing for the muscles of the throat. Honey has shown promising results as an effective cough suppressant in the pediatric population.[7] The dose of honey given to the children in the study was two teaspoons. Gargling with salt or apple cider vinegar and water are also popular home remedies for many singers with the uses being from soothing the throat to curing reflux. Gargling plain water has been shown to be efficacious in reducing the risk of contracting upper respiratory tract infections (URTI). I suggest that when gargling, the singer only "bubble" the water with air and avoid engaging the vocal folds in sound production. Saltwater as a gargle has long been touted as a sore throat remedy and can be traced back to 2700 BCE in China for treating gum disease. The science behind a saltwater rinse for everything from oral hygiene to a sore throat is that salt (sodium chloride) may act as a natural analgesic (painkiller) and may also kill bacteria. Similar to the effects that not enough salt in the water may have on drawing the salt out of the tissue in the steam inhalation, if you oversaturate the water solution with excess salt and gargle it, it may act to draw water out of the oral mucosa, thus reducing inflammation.

Another popular home remedy reported by singers is the use of apple cider vinegar to help with everything from acid reflux to sore throats. Dating back to 3300 BCE, apple cider vinegar was reported as a medicinal remedy, and it became popular in the 1970s as a weight-loss-diet cocktail. Popular media reports apple cider vinegar can improve conditions from acne and arthritis to nosebleeds and varicose veins. Specific efficacy data regarding the beneficial nature of apple cider vinegar for the purpose of a sore throat, pharyngeal inflammation, and/or reflux has not been reported in the literature at this time. Of the peer-reviewed studies found in the literature, one discussed possible esophageal erosion and inconsistency of actual product in tablet form.[5] Therefore, at this time, strong evidence supporting the use of apple cider vinegar is not published.

Medications and the Voice

Medications (over the counter, prescription, and herbal) may have resultant drying effects on the body and, often, the laryngeal mucosa. General classes of drugs with potential drying effects include: antidepressants, antihypertensives, diuretics, ADD/ADHD medications, some oral acne medications, hormones, allergy drugs, and vitamin C in high doses. The National Center for Voice and Speech (NCVS) provides a listing of some common medications with potential voice side effects including laryngeal dryness. This listing does not take into account all medications, so singers should always ask their pharmacist of the potential side effects of a given medication. Due to the significant number of drugs on the market, it is safe to say that most pharmacists will not be acutely aware of "vocal side effects," but if dryness is listed as a potential side effect of the drug, you may assume that all body systems could be affected. Under no circumstances should you stop taking a prescribed medication without consulting your physician first. As every person has different body chemistry and reaction to medication, just because a medication lists dryness as a potential side effect, it does not necessarily mean you will experience that side effect. Conversely, if you begin a new medication and notice physical or vocal changes that are unexpected, you should consult with your physician. Ultimately, the goal of medical management for any condition is to achieve the most benefits with the least side effects. Please see the companion page on the NATS website for a list of possible resources for the singer regarding prescription drugs and herbs. ♪

In contrast to medications that tend to dry, there are medications formulated to increase saliva production or alter the viscosity of mucus. Medically, these drugs are often used to treat patients who have had a loss of saliva production due to surgery or radiation. Mucolytic agents are used to thin secretions as needed. As a singer, if you feel that you need to use a mucolytic agent on a consistent basis, it may be worth considering getting to the root of the laryngeal dryness symptom and seeking a professional opinion from an otolaryngologist.

Reflux and the Voice

Gastroesophageal reflux (GERD) and/or laryngopharyngeal reflux (LPR) can have a devastating impact on the singer if not recognized and treated appropriately. Although GERD and LPR are related, they are considered as slightly different diseases. GERD (Latin root meaning "flowing back") is the reflux of digestive enzymes, acids, and other stomach contents into the esophagus (food pipe). If this backflow is propelled through the upper esophagus and into the throat (larynx and pharynx), it is referred to as LPR. It is not uncommon to have both GERD and LPR, but they can occur independently.

More frequently, people with GERD have decreased esophageal clearing. Esophagitis, or inflammation of the esophagus, is also associated with GERD. People with GERD often feel heartburn. LPR symptoms are often "silent" and do not include heartburn. Specific symptoms of LPR may include some or all of the following: lump in the throat sensation, feeling of constant need to clear the throat/postnasal drip, longer vocal warm-up time, quicker vocal fatigue, loss of high-frequency range, worse voice in the morning, sore throat, and bitter/raw/brackish taste in the mouth. If you experience these symptoms on a regular basis, it is advised that you consider a medical consultation for your symptoms. Prolonged, untreated GERD or LPR can lead to permanent changes in both the esophagus and/or larynx. Untreated LPR also provides a laryngeal environment that is conducive for vocal fold lesions to occur as it inhibits normal healing mechanisms.

Treatments of LPR and GERD generally include both dietary and lifestyle modifications in addition to medical management. Some of the dietary recommendations include: elimination of caffeinated and carbonated beverages, smoking cessation, no alcohol use, and limiting tomatoes, acidic foods, drinks, and raw onions or peppers, to name a few. Also, avoidance of high-fat foods is recommended. From a lifestyle perspective, suggested changes include not eating within three hours of lying down, eating small meals frequently (instead of large meals), elevating the head of your bed, avoiding tight clothing around the belly, and not bending over or exercising too soon after you eat.

Reflux medications fall into three general categories: antacids, H2 blockers, and proton pump inhibitors (PPIs). There are now combination drugs that include both an H2 blocker and PPI. Every medication has both associated risks and benefits, and singers should be aware of the possible benefits and side effects of the medications they take. In general terms, antacids (e.g., Tums, Mylanta, Gaviscon) neutralize stomach acid. H2 (histamine) blockers, such as Axid (nizatidine), Tagamet (cimetidine), Pepcid (famotidine), and Zantac (ranitidine), work to decrease acid production in the stomach by preventing histamine from triggering the H2 receptors to produce more acid. Then there are the PPIs: Nexium (esomeprazole), Prevacid (lansoprazole), Protonix (pantoprazole), AcipHex (rabeprazole), Prilosec (omeprazole), and Dexilant (dexlansoprazole). PPIs act as a last line of defense to decrease acid production by blocking the last step in gastric juice secretion. Some of the most recent drugs to combat GERD/LPR are combination drugs (e.g., Zegrid [sodium bicarbonate plus omeprazole]), which provide a short-acting response (sodium bicarbonate) and a long release (omeprazole). Because some singers prefer a holistic approach to reflux management, strict dietary and lifestyle compliance is recommended and consultation with both your primary care physician and naturopath are warranted in that situation. Efficacy data on nonregulated herbs, vitamins, and supplements are limited, but some data does exist.

Physical Exercise

Vocal athletes, like other physical athletes, should consider how and what they do to maintain both cardiovascular fitness and muscular strength. In today's performance culture, it is rare that a performer stands still and sings, unless in a recital or choral setting. The range of physical activity can vary from light movement to high-intensity choreography with acrobatics. As performers are being required to increase their on-stage physical activity level from the operatic stage to the pop-star arena, overall physical fitness is imperative to avoid compromise in the vocal system. Breathlessness will result in compensation by the larynx, which attempts to regulate the air. Compensatory vocal behaviors over time may result in a change in vocal performance. The health benefits of both cardiovascular training and strength training are well-documented for physical athletes but relatively rare in the literature for vocal performers.

Mental Wellness

Vocal performers must maintain mental focus during performance and mental toughness during auditioning and training. Rarely during vocal performance training programs is this important aspect of performance addressed, and it is often left to the individual performer to develop their own strategy or coping mechanism. However, many performers are on antianxiety or antidepressant drugs (which may be the direct result of performance-related issues). If the sports world is again used as a parallel for mental toughness, there are no elite-level athletes (and few junior-level athletes) who don't utilize the services of a performance/sports psychologist to maximize focus and performance. I recommend that performers consider the potential benefits of a performance psychologist to help maximize vocal performance. Several references that may be of interest to the singer include: Joanna Cazden's *Visualization for Singers* (Joanna Cazden, 1992) and Shirlee Emmons and Alma Thomas's *Power Performance for Singers: Transcending the Barriers* (Oxford, 1998). ♪

Unlike instrumentalists, whose performance is dependent on the accurate playing of an external musical instrument, the singer's instrument is uniquely intact and subject to the emotional confines of the brain and body in which it is housed. Musical performance anxiety (MPA) can be career threatening for all musicians, but perhaps the vocal athlete is more severely impacted. The majority of literature on MPA is dedicated to instrumentalists, but the basis of definition, performance effects, and treatment options can be considered for vocal athletes. Fear is a natural reaction to a stressful situation, and there is a fine line between emotional excitation and perceived threat (real or imagined). The job of a performer is to convey to an audience through vocal production, physical gestures, and facial expression a heightened state of emotion. Otherwise, why would audience members pay top dollar to sit for two or three hours for a mundane experience? Not only is there the emotional conveyance of the performance but also the internal turmoil often experienced by the singers themselves in preparation for elite performance. It is well-documented in the literature that even the most elite performers have experienced debilitating performance anxiety. MPA is defined on a continuum with anxiety levels ranging from low to high and has been reported to comprise four distinct components: affect, cognition, behavior, and physiology. Affect comprises feelings (e.g., doom, panic, anxiety). Affected cognition will result in altered levels of concentration, while the behavior component results in postural shifts, quivering, and trembling. Finally, physiologically, the body's autonomic nervous system (ANS) will activate, resulting in the "fight-or-flight" response.

In recent years, researchers have been able to define two distinct neurological pathways for MPA. The first pathway happens quickly and without conscious input (ANS), resulting in the same fear stimulus as if a person was put into an emergent, life-threatening situation. In those situations, the brain releases adrenaline, resulting in physical changes of increased heart rate, increased respiration, shaking, pale skin, dilated pupils, slowed digestion, bladder relaxation, dry mouth, and dry eyes, all of which severely affect vocal performance. The second pathway that has been identified results in a conscious identification of the fear/threat and a much slower physiologic response. With the second neuromotor response, the performer has a chance to recognize the fear, process how to deal with the fear, and respond accordingly.

Treatment modalities to address MPA include psycho-behavioral therapy (including biofeedback) and drug therapies. Elite physical performance athletes have been shown to benefit from visualization techniques and psychological readiness training, yet within the performing arts community, stage fright may be considered a weakness or character flaw precluding readiness for professional performance. On the contrary, vocal athletes, like physical athletes, should mentally prepare themselves for optimal competition (auditions) and performance. Learning to convey emotion without eliciting an internal emotional response by the vocal athlete may take the skill of an experienced psychologist to help change ingrained neural pathways. Ultimately, control and understanding of MPA will enhance performance and prepare the vocal athlete for the most intense performance demands without vocal compromise.

VOCAL WELLNESS: INJURY PREVENTION

To prevent vocal injury and understand vocal wellness in the singer, general knowledge of common causes of voice disorders is imperative. One common cause of voice disorders is vocally abusive behaviors or misuse of the voice to include phonotraumatic behaviors such as yelling, screaming, loud talking, talking over noise, throat clearing, coughing, harsh sneezing, and boisterous laughing. Chronic or less than optimal vocal properties such as poor breathing techniques, inappropriate phonatory habits during conversational speech (glottal fry, hard glottal attacks), inept pitch, loudness, rate of speech, and/or hyperfunctional laryngeal-area muscle tone may also negatively impact vocal function. Medically related etiologies, which also have the potential to impact vocal function, range from untreated chronic allergies and sinusitis to endocrine dysfunction and hormonal imbalance. Direct trauma, such as a blow to the neck or the risk of vocal fold damage during intubation, can impact optimal performance in vocal athletes depending on the nature and extent of the trauma. Finally, external irritants ranging from cigarette smoke to reflux directly impact the laryngeal mucosa and can ultimately lead to laryngeal pathology.

Vocal hygiene education and compliance may be one of the primary essential components for maintaining the voice throughout a career. This section will provide the singer with information on prevention of vocal injury. However, just like a professional sports athlete, it is unlikely that a professional vocal athlete will go through an entire career without some compromise in vocal function. This may be a common upper respiratory infection that creates vocal fold swelling for a short time, or it may be a "vocal accident" that is career threatening. Regardless, the knowledge of how to take care of your voice is essential for any vocal athlete.

Train like an Athlete for Vocal Longevity

Performers seek instant gratification in performance, sometimes at the cost of gradual vocal building for a lifetime of healthy singing. Historically, voice pedagogues required their students to perform vocalises exclusively for up to two years before beginning any song literature. Singers gradually built their voices by ingraining appropriate muscle memory and neuromotor patterns through the development of aesthetically pleasing tones, onsets, breath management, and support. There was an intensive master-apprentice relationship and rigorous vocal guidelines to maintain a place within a given studio. Time off was taken if a vocal injury ensued or careers potentially were ended, and students were asked to leave a given singing studio if their voices were unable to withstand the rigors of training. Training vocal athletes today has evolved and appears driven to create a "product" quickly, perhaps at the expense of the longevity of the singer. Pop stars emerging well before puberty are doing international concert tours, yet many young artist programs in the classical arena do not consider singers for their programs until they are in their mid- to late twenties.

Each vocal genre presents with different standards and vocal demands. Therefore, the amount and degree of vocal training are varied. Some would argue that performing extensively without adequate vocal training and development is ill-advised, yet singers today are thrust onto the stage at very young ages. Dancers, instrumentalists, and physical athletes all spend many hours per day developing muscle strength, memory, and proper technique for their craft. The more advanced the artist or athlete, generally the more specific the training protocol becomes. Consideration of training vocal athletes in this same fashion is recommended. Generally, one would not begin a young, inexperienced singer on a Wagner aria without previous vocal training. Similarly, in non-classical vocal music, there are easy, moderate, and difficult pieces to consider pending level of vocal development and training.

Basic pedagogical training of alignment, breathing, voice production, and resonance are essential building blocks for the development of good voice production. Muscle memory and development of appropriate muscle patterns happen slowly over time with appropriate repetitive practice. Doing too much, too soon for any athlete (physical or vocal) will result in an increased risk for injury. When the singer is being asked to do "vocal gymnastics," they must be sure to have a solid basis of strength and stamina in the appropriate muscle groups to perform consistently with minimal risk of injury.

Vocal Fitness Program

Generally, one does not get out of bed first thing in the morning and try to do a split. However, many singers go directly into a practice session or audition without a proper warm-up. Think of your larynx similar to your knee, made up of cartilages, ligaments, and muscles. Vocal health is dependent upon appropriate warm-ups (to get things moving), drills for technique, and then cooldowns (at the end of your day). Consider vocal warm-ups a "gentle stretch." Depending on the needs of the singer, warm-ups should include physical stretching; postural alignment self-checks; breathing exercises to promote rib cage, abdominal, and back expansion; vocal stretches (glides up to stretch the vocal folds and glides down to contract the vocal folds); articulatory stretches (yawning, facial stretches); and mental warm-ups (to provide focus for the task at hand). Vocalises, in my opinion, are designed as exercises to go beyond warm-ups and prepare the body and voice for the technical and vocal challenges of the music they sing. They are varied and address the technical level and genre of the singer to maximize performance and vocal growth. Cooldowns are a part of most athletes' workouts. However, singers often do not use cooldowns (physical, mental, and vocal) at the end of a performance. A recent study looked specifically at the benefits of vocal cooldowns in singers and found that singers who used a vocal cooldown had decreased effort to produce voice the next day.[9]

Systemic hydration as a means to keep the vocal folds adequately lubricated for the amount of impact and friction that they will undergo has been discussed previously in this chapter. Compliance with adequate oral hydration recommendations is important and, subsequently, so is the minimization of agents that could potentially dry the membranes (e.g., caffeine, medications, dry air). The body produces approximately two quarts of mucus per day. If not adequately hydrated, the mucus tends to be thick and sticky. Poor hydration is similar to not putting enough oil in a car engine. Frankly, if the gears do not work as well, there is increased friction and heat, and the engine is not efficient.

Speak Well, Sing Well

Optimize the speaking voice utilizing ideal frequency range, breath, intensity, rate, and resonance. Singers generally are vocally enthusiastic individuals who talk a lot and often talk loudly. During a typical conversation, the average fundamental speaking frequency (times per second the vocal folds are impacting) for a male varies from 100 to 150 Hz and 180 to 230 Hz for women. Because of the delicate structure of the vocal folds and the importance of the layered microstructure vibrating efficiently and effectively to produce voice, vocal behaviors or outside factors that compromise the integrity of the vibration patterns of the vocal folds may be considered phonotrauma.

Phonotraumatic behaviors can include yelling, screaming, loud talking, harsh sneezing, and harsh laughing. Elimination of phonotraumatic behaviors is essential for good vocal health. The louder one speaks, the farther apart the vocal folds move from the midline, the harder they impact, and the longer they stay closed. A tangible example would be to take your hands, move them only six inches apart, and clap as hard and as loudly as you can for ten seconds. Now, move your hands two feet apart and clap as hard, loudly, and as quickly as possible for ten seconds. The farther apart your hands are, the more air you move and the louder the clap, and the skin on the hands becomes red and, ultimately, swollen (if you do it long enough and hard enough). This is what happens to the vocal folds with repeated impact at increased vocal intensities. The vocal folds are approximately 17 mm in length and vibrate at 220 times per second on A3, 440 on A4, 880 on A5, and more than 1,000 per second when singing a high C. That is a lot of impact for little muscles. Consider this fact when singing loudly or in a high tessitura for prolonged periods of time. It becomes easy to see why women are more prone than men to laryngeal impact injuries due to the frequency range of the voice alone.

In addition to the number of cycles per second (cps) the vocal folds are impacting, singers need to be aware of their vocal intensity (volume). One should be aware of the volume of the speaking and singing voice and consider using a distance of three to five feet (about an arms-length distance) as a gauge for how loud to be in general conversation. Using cell phones and speaking on a Bluetooth device in a car generally results in greater vocal intensity than normal, and singers are advised to minimize unnecessary use of these devices.

Singers should be encouraged to take "vocal naps" during their day. A vocal nap would be a short period of time (five minutes to an hour) of complete silence. Although the vocal folds are rarely completely still (because they move when you swallow and breathe), a vocal nap minimizes impact and vibration for a short window of time. A physical nap can also be refreshing for the singer mentally and physically.

Avoid Environmental Irritants: Alcohol, Smoking, Drugs

Arming singers with information on the actual effects of environmental irritants so that they can make informed choices about engaging in exposure to these potential toxins is essential. The glamour that continues to be associated with smoking, drinking, and drugs can be tempered with the deaths of popular stars, such as Amy Winehouse and Cory Monteith, who engaged in life-ending choices. There is extensive documentation about the long-term effects of toxic and carcinogenic substances, but here are a few key facts to consider when choosing whether to partake.

Alcohol, although it does not go over the vocal folds directly, does have a systemic drying effect. Due to the acidity of alcohol, it may increase the likelihood of reflux, resulting in hoarseness and other laryngeal pathologies. Consuming alcohol generally decreases one's inhibitions, and therefore, you are more likely to sing and do things that you would not typically do under the influence of alcohol.

Beyond the carcinogens in nicotine and tobacco, the heat at which a cigarette burns is well above the boiling temperature of water (water boils at 212°F; cigarettes burn at over 1400°F). No one would consider pouring a pot of boiling water on their hand, and yet the burning temperature for a cigarette results in significant heat over the oral mucosa and vocal folds. The heat alone can create deterioration of the lining, resulting in polypoid degeneration. Obviously, cigarette smoking has been well-documented as a cause for laryngeal cancer.

Marijuana and other street drugs are not only addictive but can cause permanent mucosal lining changes depending on the drug used and the method of delivery. If you or one of your singer colleagues is experiencing a drug or alcohol problem, research or provide information and support on getting appropriate counseling and help.

SMART PRACTICE STRATEGIES FOR SKILL DEVELOPMENT AND VOICE CONSERVATION

Daily practice and drills for skill acquisition are an important part of any singer's training. However, overpracticing or inefficient practicing may be detrimental to the voice. Consider practice sessions of athletes: they may practice four to eight hours per day broken into one- to two-hour training sessions with a period of rest and recovery in between sessions. Although we cannot parallel the sports model without adequate evidence in the vocal athlete, the premise of short, intense, focused practice sessions is logical for the singer. Similar to physical exercise, it is suggested that practice sessions do not have to be all "singing." Rather, structuring sessions so that one-third of the session is spent on warm-up; one-third on vocalises, text work, rhythms, character development, and so on; and one-third on repertoire will allow the singer to function in a more efficient vocal manner. Building the amount of time per practice session—increasing duration by five minutes per week, building to sixty to ninety minutes—may be effective (e.g., Week 1: twenty minutes three times per day; Week 2: twenty-five minutes three times per day, etc.).

Vary the "vocal workout" during your week. For example, if you do the same physical exercise in the same way day after day with the same intensity and pattern, you will likely experience repetitive strain–type injuries. However, cross-training or varying the type and level of exercise aids in injury prevention. Therefore, when planning your practice sessions for a given week (or rehearsal process for a given role), consider varying your vocal intensity, tessitura, and exercises to maximize your training sessions, building stamina, muscle memory, and skill acquisition. For example, one day you may spend more time on learning rhythms and translation and the next day you spend thirty minutes performing coloratura exercises to prepare for a specific role. Take one day a week off from vocal training and give your voice a break. This does not mean complete vocal rest (although some singers find this beneficial) but rather a day without singing and limited talking.

Practice Your Mental Focus

Mental wellness and stress management are equally as important as vocal training for vocal athletes. Addressing any mental health issues is paramount to developing the vocal artist. This may include anything from daily mental exercises/meditation/focus to overcoming performance anxiety to more serious mental health issues/illness. Every person can benefit from improved focus and mental acuity.

ADDITIONAL VOCAL WELLNESS TIPS

When working with singers across all genres, the most common presentation in my voice clinic relates to vocal fatigue, acute vocal injury, and loss of high-frequency range. Vocal fatigue complaints are generally related to the duration of their rehearsals, recording sessions, "meet and greets," performances, vocal gymnastics, general lack of sleep, and the vocal requirements to traverse their entire range (and, occasionally, outside of physiological comfort range). Depending on the genre performed, singing includes a high vocal load with the associated risk of repetitive strain and increased collision force injuries. Acute vocal injuries within this population include phonotraumatic lesions (hemorrhages, vocal fold polyps, vocal fold nodules, reflux, and general vocal fold edema/erythema). Often, these are not injuries related to problematic vocal technique, but rather they are due to "vocal accidents" and/ or overuse (due to required performance/contract demands). Virtually all singers are required to connect with the audience from a vocal and emotional standpoint. Physical performance demands may be extreme and, at times, highly cardiovascular and/or acrobatic. Both physical and vocal fitness should be foremost in the minds of any vocal performer, and these singers should be physically and vocally in shape to meet the necessary performance demands.

The advanced and professional singer must possess a flexible, agile, and dynamic instrument and have appropriate stamina. The singer must have a good command of their instrument as well as an exceptional underlying intention to what they are singing as it is about relaying a message, characteristic sound, and connecting with the audience. Singers must reflect the mood and intent of the composer requiring dynamic control, vocal control/power, and an emotional connection to the text.

Commercial music singers use microphones and personal amplification to their maximal capacity. If used correctly, amplification can be used to maximize vocal health by allowing the singer to produce voice in an efficient manner while the sound engineer is effectively able to mix, amplify, and add effects to the voice. Understanding both the utility and limits of a given microphone and sound system is essential for the singer both for live and studio performances. Using an appropriate microphone can not only enhance the singer's performance, but can also reduce the vocal load. Emotional extremes (intimacy and exultation) can be enhanced by appropriate microphone choice, placement, and acoustical mixing; thus saving the singer's voice.

Not everything a singer does is "vocally healthy," sometimes because the emotional expression may be so intense it results in vocal collision forces that are extreme. Even if the singer does not have formal vocal training, the concept of "vocal cross-training"—which can mean singing in both high and low registers with varying intensities and resonance options—before and after practice sessions and services is likely a vital component to minimizing vocal injury.

FINAL THOUGHTS

Ultimately, the singer must learn to provide the most output with the least "cost" to the system. Taking care of the physical instrument through daily physical exercise, adequate nutrition and hydration, and focused attention on performance will provide a necessary basis for vocal health during performance. Small doses of high-intensity singing (or speaking) will limit impact stress on the vocal folds. Finally, attention to the mind, body, and voice will provide the singer with an awareness when something is wrong. This awareness and knowledge of when to rest or seek help will promote vocal well-being for the singer throughout his or her career.

NOTES

1. Wendy LeBorgne et al., "Prevalence of Vocal Pathology in Incoming Freshman Musical Theatre Majors: A 10-Year Retrospective Study," Fall Voice Conference, New York, 2012.

2. Josef Brinckmann et al., "Safety and Efficacy of a Traditional Herbal Medicine (Throat Coat) in Symptomatic Temporary Relief of Pain in Patients with Acute Pharyngitis: A Multicenter, Prospective, Randomized, Double-Blinded, Placebo-Controlled Study," *Journal of Alternative and Complementary Medicine* 9, no. 2 (2003): 285–98.

3. Nelson Roy et al., "An Evaluation of the Effects of Three Laryngeal Lubricants on Phonation Threshold Pressure (PTP)," *Journal of Voice* 17, no. 3 (2003): 331–42.

4. Kristine Tanner et al., "Nebulized Isotonic Saline versus Water Following a Laryngeal Desiccation Challenge in Classically Trained Sopranos," *Journal of Speech Language and Hearing Research* 53, no. 6 (2010): 1555–66.

5. Christopher Brown and Scott Graham, "Nasal Irrigations: Good or Bad?" *Current Opinion in Otolaryngology, Head and Neck Surgery* 12, no. 1 (2004): 9–13.

6. T. M. Nsouli et al., "Long-Term Use of Nasal Saline Irrigation: Harmful or Helpful?" American College of Allergy, Asthma and Immunology Annual Scientific Meeting, Abstract 32, 2009.

7. Mahmood Shadkam et al., "A Comparison of the Effect of Honey, Dextromethorphan, and Diphenhydramine on Nightly Cough and Sleep Quality in Children and Their Parents," *Journal of Alternative and Complementary Medicine* 16, no. 7 (2010): 787–93.

8. Laura Hill et al., "Esophageal Injury by Apple Cider Vinegar Tablets and Subsequent Evaluation of Products," *Journal of the American Dietetic Association* 105, no. 7 (2005): 1141–44.

9. Renee O. Gottliebson, "The Efficacy of Cool-Down Exercises in the Practice Regimen of Elite Singers," PhD dissertation, University of Cincinnati, 2011.

4

GRANDFATHERS OF VOICE PEDAGOGY

"For this reason, it is necessary (among other virtues) to refer your-self to the judgement of a wise person in these matters."

—Bénigne de Bacilly, *Remarques curieuse sur l'art de bien chanter* (Paris, 1668)

The previous two chapters contain state-of-the-art information on vo-cal health, technique, and voice science by two of today's best-known authorities. Just to put those chapters in perspective, learned authorities have been writing about singing and performing for hundreds of years. In the past, such texts were often called treatises. In this chapter, we will examine some of the earliest treatises that focus on singing by writers I would like to call the grandfathers of modern voice pedagogy. Then you can compare the instructions from teachers in the sixteenth, seven-teenth, and eighteenth centuries with the information you just learned from twenty-first-century experts.

You may find that the suggestions made by earlier treatise writers are things that we mostly take for granted today, such as to sing beautifully or to make sure you sing the correct pitches and rhythms. However, some of these suggestions offer interesting and important glimpses into how to approach the vocal repertoire from earlier periods. Some of the teachings may no longer be relevant to modern singers, either because we now know more about anatomy and voice science, or we have worked out the problems of early notation. However, much of the information found in these early treatises is basic commonsense advice that is still valuable hundreds of years later and worth appreciating with the fresh understanding of our modern perspective. It is also worth revisiting this early advice so we can learn how best to sing the early repertoire, both technically and stylistically. We will delve into the stylistic issues in more detail in chapter 5.

In his book, *Historical Vocal Pedagogy Classics*, Berton Coffin starts with an Italian treatise from 1723 by Pier Francesco Tosi (c. 1653–1732). We will certainly get to Tosi, but I would like to begin with earlier treatises first. I'll follow Coffin's model and give some brief historical information on each writer, and then paraphrase or summarize the most important and relevant points in the treatise. I will also include some direct quotes to give you the flavor of the period. However, I want to offer some general cautions about reading these early documents: when scholars translate an early source, they are trying to make sense out of a foreign language that is many centuries old and that is from a different culture and historical context. Even in modern writing about singing, it is difficult to accurately describe in words the delicate physical sensations, sounds, or reactions to sounds that make up our subtle art. In writings from an earlier time, translated into modern English, we may come upon confusing use of terminology. For example, what is the difference between *tremolo* and *tremblement*, or *cadence* and trill, or trill and *tremolo*? Do these terms refer to vibrato or specific ornaments? What do the writers mean by head voice, feigned voice, or falsetto, or chest and throat? In the context of an early treatise, these terms may not mean exactly what they mean to us in the twenty-first century. Scholars have done their best to sort through the different possible meanings, but it remains a murky terrain with no easy path through it. There may be no final answers to these questions, but they can serve as valuable points of departure in our exploration of how to sing early music. ♪

BEFORE 1500

The earliest writings on singing are concerned with instructing members of a choir, most likely men and boys, on how to sing a chant together and find a comfortable blending of different vocal types and ranges. It was important to sing clear vowels with beautiful, steady tones and with an appropriate sense of devotion and religious observance. Soft, sweet sounds were prized over loud ones, particularly in the higher registers, and writers often colorfully compared bad singing to animal sounds.

Jerome of Moravia (died after 1271)

Jerome of Moravia was a musical theorist who worked in Paris in the late thirteenth century and joined the Dominican order. His *Tractus de musica* dealt with a wide range of topics having to do with the performance of church music. His twenty-fifth chapter concentrates on singing. A lot of Jerome's instructions deal with how to fit the syllables of the text to the melody of the chant. Remember, the early notation was not clear about this. He also gives recommendations on how and where to add ornaments. Some of these suggestions also seem to indicate something about vibrato: "Long ornaments are those whose vibration is steady and does not exceed a semitone. Open ornaments are those whose vibration is steady and does not exceed a whole tone."

He also offers five things that are important for several singers chanting together:

1. Everyone should know the chant and agree on the "harmonic time."
2. Everyone should be a good singer, and they should choose a conductor who they will all follow with diligent attention to all the notes and pauses.
3. Concerning voices with different ranges, head, chest, and throat, he advises that they each sing within a comfortable range for their voice. "They all must maintain their individuality during singing." He is most likely talking about men and boys.
4. It is important to choose a starting note for the chant that is neither too high nor too low, so all the different voices can sing together— "yet not too deep, which is to shout, or not too high, which is to shriek, but in between, which is to sing."
5. It is most important to sing beautifully from the heart: "However, the chief obstacle to producing beautiful notes is sadness of the heart . . . it comes indeed from the joyousness of the heart because melancholy persons can have beautiful voices but cannot indeed sing with beauty."[1]

Conrad von Zabern (died 1481)

Conrad von Zabern was a professor of music at the University of
Heidelberg around 1470. His treatise *De modo bene cantandi*, a method
of good singing, was published in 1474 and includes six rules for good
choir singing:

1. Start singing together without anticipating or holding back.
2. Everyone should sing the same rhythm.
3. Choose an appropriate starting pitch so everyone will be singing in
   a comfortable range, neither too high nor too low.
4. Choose appropriate tempos to suit the different church occasions.
5. Everyone should sing the same notes and sing with devotion.
6. Everyone should sing with beauty and refinement.

He then goes on to mention all the bad habits that are to be avoided:
Don't put "h's" on repeated vowels to make "ha, ha, or he, he." Don't sing
through the nose. Pronounce vowels clearly and correctly so the words
are understood. Don't let the pitch sag or wander on a sustained vowel.

He complains bitterly about what we might interpret as too much
vibrato: "A very common sign of poor training is the horrid wavering up
or down of the pitch . . . whoever has this shocking habit should desist
entirely from singing until he has procured relief."

An additional defect is singing with too much force and breath pressure: "Another common habit is the violent squeezing out or pushing
of the voice, which injures the beauty and sweetness of the singing in
the highest degree . . . A particularly striking crudity is that of singing
the high notes with a loud tone, indeed with full lung power. And truly,
if there is a person who, by nature, has a heavy, trumpet-like voice,
it makes a great disturbance in the whole choral song and appears as
though the voices of several oxen were mixed in with the choir."

Von Zabern talks about unifying the three registers of the voice:
"whoever sings well must use his voice in three degrees. The low notes
are to be sung entirely from the chest, the middle ones with moderate
strength, and the high ones with a soft voice. And the change from one
to the other must not be sudden, but gradual, according to the movement of the melody." He also urges singers to sing with life and emotion
but in the appropriate amount: "One must avoid both extremes: bawling

too loud and singing too faint-heartedly." And finally, he warns singers not to make unseemly movements of the body or head, nor to sway from side to side, raise the head too high up, make strange faces, or open the mouth either too wide or not wide enough.[2]

THE SIXTEENTH CENTURY

As in the previous centuries, treatise writers in the sixteenth century also discuss finding an appropriate range in which to sing and blending the different registers of the voice. They prefer soft, sweet singing, especially in the high range, and singers are warned not to force or strain. Appropriate physical presentation is necessary, and a steady, clear tone is better than a wavering, unsteady one. Expressing the text clearly and with appropriate emotion is important, but now the writers place more emphasis on developing agility for adding florid ornamentation. These elaborate additions were called divisions, passages, or coloratura. These terms came from the practice of taking a longer note value, such as a whole note or half note, and dividing it into smaller portions that moved more quickly, or coloring in a white note with a series of smaller black notes, thus the terms divisions or coloratura.

Hermann Finck (1527–1558)

Hermann Finck, a German composer and organist, taught at Wittenberg University. His treatise *Pratica musica* was published in 1556. In book five, "On the Art of Singing Elegantly and Sweetly," he gives advice for aspiring singers of polyphony:

1. Make sure an appropriate voice type sings each of the four or five parts, tender and soothing on the top part, sharper and heavier on the bottom part, with the middle voices adapting themselves to the outer voices. He is probably talking about men and boys.
2. Be sure everyone begins the piece securely, without being tense or tentative.
3. No one should strain their voice: "For many singers change their tone colors, becoming black in the face and come to the end of

their breath . . . become debased and deformed, with distorted and gaping mouths, with heads tossed back, and with bleating and barbaric cries . . . they ruin and deform the most beautiful music."

4. No roaring and screaming or bellowing with raucous sounds. "The higher a voice rises, the quieter and lovelier should the note be sung; the more it descends, the richer the sound . . . the high as well as the low, become soft, gentle, and clearly understood, whereby the hearts are filled with wonder and the mind is pleasantly affected."

Finck gives extensive advice on how and where to ornament polyphony so the voices don't conflict with each other and cause confusion and chaos. He talks about two different kinds of coloratura: that made with the tongue and that made with the throat.[3]

Adrian Petit Coclico (1499–1562)

Adrian Petit Coclico was a Flemish composer who also taught in Wittenberg, Germany, before settling in Frankfurt in 1550, where his treatise *Compendium musices* was published in 1552. He recommends that a German boy select a teacher who sings well himself, beautifully and smoothly, and who adds beautiful ornaments to his phrases so the student may imitate him. Coclico offers his own exercises for developing agility and advises that the boy must work hard to perfect these patterns so they may be executed clearly and correctly with the throat.[4]

Giovanni Camillo Maffei (1533–1603)

Giovanni Camillo Maffei, an Italian doctor of medicine and amateur singer, penned his work *Letter on Singing*, published in Naples in 1562. He talks about different types of voices—big and small, high and low, rough and smooth, rigid and flexible—as varied in his time as they are now. He tries to explain how the use of airflow can affect the different sounds a voice can make and how the mind can control the breath. He gives rules for how to add ornamentation to four voice polyphony, general recommendations for good singing, and magic potions and elixirs to cure various vocal ills. Here are his ten sensible rules for singing:

1. A singer should avoid any affectation.
2. Practice your vocal exercises in the morning before eating or four or five hours after a meal when the stomach is not full.
3. Find a quiet and solitary place to practice, such as some shady valley or rocky hollow.
4. Make no unnecessary movement of the body when singing, "those people appear ugly to us who, when they sing, shake their heads, tremble in their legs, or move their hands and feet."
5. Use a mirror when you practice so you can see any ugly expressions you might make when singing.
6. You should "extend the tongue so that the tip touches the base of the lower teeth."
7. Keep your mouth moderately open when singing.
8. Let out the breath a little at a time, taking care that it doesn't go out through the nose or palate.
9. Talk with people who sing easily "because listening to them leaves certain images in the memory that are no small help."
10. Practice diligently without giving up easily.

Maffei also provides several "recipes" to keep one's voice healthy:

when the voice is spoiled by too much humidity: take four dried figs, remove the skin, take half a dram of calamint [herb grown for medicinal purposes—still available today], and also a scruple of gum Arabic, and grinding everything up in a mortar, make balls, one of which you should keep in your mouth night and day.

Mix a dram of licorice, a dram of saffron, two of incense, with some wine or grape juice. Take a little at a time. Cabbage soup is also good for a humid throat.

For roughness of throat, he recommends gargling with a little sandarac and squill vinegar and some honey. [Sandarac is a resin from a cypress-like tree, still used today to make varnish. It could also refer to an arsenic-like substance. Squill is a bulb that can be dried and turned into a powder. Medicinally it is used as an expectorant for coughs but is also included in rat poison. Probably best to avoid this recipe, although apple cider vinegar and honey work well.]

For a dry throat "take oil of violet and mix it with sugar, so both together become like honey, then swallow this a little at a time, and especially when you go to bed . . . and chicken broth is good for this purpose and dried figs with lots of liquid.[5]

Vincenzo Giustiniani (1564–1637)

Vincenzo Giustiniani was a Roman nobleman who was very knowledgeable about the music of his day despite not being a professional musician. His 1628 *Discorso sopra la musica*, or *Discourse on Music*, describes the singing of the women at the courts of Ferrara and Mantua around 1575. His account gives us a rare glimpse into how the women of noble households sang secular polyphony:

> The ladies of Mantua and Ferrara were highly competent, and vied with each other not only in regard to timbre and training of their voices but also in the design of exquisite passages delivered at opportune moments, but not in excess. Furthermore, they moderated or increased their voices, loud or soft, heavy or light, according to the demands of the piece they were singing; now slow, breaking off with sometimes a gentle sigh, now singing long passages legato or detached . . . now with long trills, now with short, and again sweet running passages sung softly, to which sometimes one heard an echo answer unexpectedly. They accompanied the music and the sentiments with appropriate facial expressions, glances, and gestures, with no awkward movements of the mouth or hands or body which might not express the feeling of the song. They made the words clear in such a way that one could hear even the last syllable of every word, which was never interrupted or suppressed by passages and other embellishments.[6]

Lodovico Zacconi (1555–1627)

Lodovico Zacconi, a musician, theorist, and priest, worked primarily in Venice. While he wrote his treatise *Prattica di musica* over many years, Book I, from 1592, deals with singing and florid ornamentation. Zacconi talks about how and where to add florid ornaments to vocal polyphony and says that graces and ornaments make the music more beautiful. He describes how to develop the facility and agility necessary to execute florid ornaments with speed and clarity and says that some singers have this ability naturally and others must work diligently to perfect it. He warns that the singer with a naturally agile throat will always bring more delight, and if a singer can't learn to do the florid ornaments perfectly, he should leave them out.

"This manner of singing and these ornaments are called by the common people *gorgia*; this is nothing other than an aggregation or collection of many eighths and sixteenths gathered in any one measure . . . it is much better to learn by hearing it than by written examples. Two things are required for him who wishes to enter this profession: chest and throat; chest, to carry such a large number of notes to a correct end; throat, to produce them easily."

He cautions that the notes must be separated vigorously and enunciated clearly to be recognized as the florid ornaments known as *gorgia*. He also requires that all the Italian vowels be pronounced clearly and accurately. He advises singers not to show off if they are particularly good at *gorgia*, but rather be a supportive colleague and share the placement of ornaments: "The player of any game is not praised for playing alone, but for playing well and getting along with others." He also tells singers not to add too many ornaments, and to add them in the appropriate places: "That singer will always be praised who, with a few ornaments, makes them at the right moment."

His remarks about *gorgia* and *tremolo* raise questions about vibrato that are not easily answered: "I say also that the *tremolo*, that is the trembling voice, is the true gate to enter the passages and to become proficient in the *gorgia* . . . The *tremolo* should be short and beautiful, for if it is long and forceful, it tires and bores." However, Zacconi also warns that singers who shake their voices and move their heads may think that they are singing *gorgia*, but they are not.[7]

Many early writers about singing caution against the wavering or trembling voice. While it is not clear what kind of vibrato early singers used, it was probably not quite the same as what modern classical singers are trained to use today. Moreover, while we are not certain exactly what kind of throat articulation they may have used to execute *gorgia* or fast coloratura, modern singers must make the fast notes distinct and clear. We will talk much more about this in the chapter on style and ornamentation.

MOVING INTO THE SEVENTEENTH CENTURY

By the beginning of the seventeenth century, tastes had clearly changed, as critics complained about the excessive practice of adding florid ornamentation to vocal polyphony. With the development of the solo song, treatise authors emphasized expressing the emotions of the text and moving the listeners over showy coloratura. A solo singer could use rubato and be more flexible with the flow of tempo and rhythm. Soft, sweet singing was still prized, and writers talked about using an appropriately vibrating voice. In addition to boy trebles, grown male falsettists and castrati were singing in churches and theaters and treatise writers addressed the use of head voice or feigned voice in their discussions of vocal registers.

Giovanni de' Bardi (1534–1612)

Giovanni de' Bardi, an amateur musician, poet, and wealthy patron of the arts in Florence, was the founder of the Florentine Camerata that supported the development of solo song and opera. His *Discourse on Ancient Music and Good Singing* from around 1580 discussed the problems of vocal polyphony and the new innovations of solo song. He criticized ensemble singers who stretched out the rhythm and the time to insert long *melismas* and ornaments but allowed singers of solo song more rhythmic flexibility. He blasted singers who sang too loudly and didn't blend with their vocal or instrumental colleagues, whether in ensemble or solo settings. Moreover, he had strong words for performers who made excuses for not singing well. Some things never change.

> Let us now speak of the great distinction that should be made between singing alone and singing in company . . . that good part singing is simply joining one's voice with the voices of others and forming one body with these; the same may be said of those others who to complete their passages, disregard the time, so breaking and stretching it that they make it altogether impossible for their colleagues to sing properly. The singer ought also to take care to enter softly after a rest, not imitating those who enter so noisily that they seem to be finding fault with you for some mistake, or those others, who . . . sing so loudly in the high register that they seem like criers auctioning off the pledges of the unfortunate, like little snarling dogs . . .

When singing alone, whether to the lute or to some other instrument, the singer may contract and expand the time at will, seeing that it is his privilege to regulate the time as he thinks fit.

Besides this, it is necessary to sing accurately and well, to give each tone and semitone its proper place, and to connect the sounds exactly.

Finally, the nice singer will endeavor to deliver his song with all the suavity and sweetness in his power, rejecting the notion that music must be sung boldly . . .

When you sing you will take care to stand in a suitable posture . . . And you will not imitate those who, with much ado, begin tuning their voices and recounting their misfortunes, saying that they have caught cold, that they have not slept the night before, that their stomach is not right, and other things of this sort, so tedious that before they begin to sing they have canceled the pleasure with their exasperating excuses.[8]

Giulio Caccini (1551–1618)

Giulio Caccini, a member of Bardi's Florentine Camerata, revolutionized the development of Italian solo song and opera with his setting of *Euridice* in 1600 and the publication of his collection of solo songs *Le nuove musiche* in 1602. In the foreword of this collection, he discussed some of the difficulties that had developed with vocal polyphony, namely, that the popular custom of adding complex ornamental divisions and melismas to already complex counterpoint made it virtually impossible to understand the text. In reaction to the excesses of this practice, he wanted to offer simple solo songs in a declamatory style, allowing the singer to convey the meaning of the text in a clear and heartfelt way: "For unless the words were understood, they could not move the understanding." He also explained how he had set the text according to the meaning of the words, to capture the sentiment and emotion of the poetry with his harmonic settings.

Caccini, a tenor, accompanied himself on a simple stringed instrument, either a lute or theorbo, performing his new songs for noblemen in Florence and Rome. He recounted how "they had never before heard harmony of a single voice, accompanied by a single stringed instrument, with such power to move the passions of the mind." Since he was both singing and playing, a singer/songwriter in the same vein as James Taylor, and didn't have to "fit himself to others," he could bend the time and use what he called a "noble neglect of the song," or what we would call rubato, to "talk in harmony" and convey the passions of the text.

He suggested choosing a starting pitch that would allow the singer to use his clear and natural voice and avoid "feigned tunes of notes." We can't be exactly sure what this means, but it might indicate some sort of falsetto, or head voice. Since he was a tenor, he might have preferred not to sing notes in head voice or feigned voice "because for the most part they offend the ear . . . from a feigned voice can come no noble manner of singing." He said a singer must be in command of his breath so it can serve "to give the greater spirit to the increasing and diminishing of the voice, to exclamations and other passions." So, perhaps in modern language, if you choose a good key to sing in and have good breath support, you shouldn't need to resort to head voice for any notes. Caccini also trained women and castrati, but perhaps the emphasis on the natural spoken quality of the declamation favored what we might call a mixed middle voice, even in the soprano range.

He wanted singers to use the customary ornaments that gave singing its beauty and sweetness, including trills, groups, exclamations of increasing and abating of the voice, what we would call *messa di voce*, and some divisions. However, to assure that they were not misplaced or overused, he wrote out most of the ornaments he wanted in appropriate places. This was highly unusual and innovative, since most composers didn't write in any ornaments at all, and most singers just added them where they wanted to. We shall talk more about the specific ornaments in chapter 5.[9]

John Dowland (1563–1626)

John Dowland was the most famous composer of English solo lute songs at the start of the seventeenth century and was himself a virtuoso lutenist and singer. His treatise on singing, published in London in 1609, was a translation of Ornithoparcus's much earlier *Andreas Ornithoparcus His Micrologus*. One section, "Of the Divers Fashions of Singing, and of the Ten Precepts for Singing," seems to speak to both ensemble church singers and secular solo singers:

God doesn't like bellowing and braying, but "he rejoyceth more in sweetness than in noyse, more in the affection, than in the voice."

1. Sing the right notes.
2. Sing in the right key with the correct sharps and flats.
3. Conform your voice to the words: sad when the words are sad, and merry when the words are merry.
4. Keep the equality of the measure—don't add time or sing out of rhythm.
5. Balance the three registers of the voice: low, middle, and high.
6. Sing correct vowels and make them clear and understandable.
7. Don't sing too loud, "braying like an ass . . . for God is not pleased with loud cryes, but with lovely sounds."
8. Sing with the appropriate quality—solemn or joyous—for different Church holidays.
9. Don't make unsightly movements of body or mouth.
10. Sing to please God, not men, with devotion, not for worldly fame.[10]

Michael Praetorius (1571–1621)

Michael Praetorius was a composer and scholar who worked as Kapellmeister in Lüneberg and for the Duke of Brunswick. His treatise *Syntagma musicum*, written between 1614 and 1619, included a section with instructions for singers that was subtitled: "How to teach and inform the choir boys to sing in the new Italian style with particular pleasure and joy." He echoes Caccini, emphasizing a natural spoken declamation of the words with clear and correct pronunciation. "So must a musician not only sing but sing with art and grace, thereby moving the heart and affections of the auditors." He chastises singers who add too many diminutions, or put them in the wrong places, making the text difficult to understand. "Singing should not be spoiled by inappropriate diminutions . . . instead, each word and sentence should be properly understood by everyone."

He requires a singer to have a fine natural voice and a thorough knowledge of music. He also requires that "a singer must have a pleasantly vibrating voice (not, however, as some are trained to do in schools, but with particular moderation) and a smooth, round throat for singing diminutions; second, he must be able to maintain a steady long tone, without taking too many breaths; third, he must choose one voice, such as cantus, altus, or tenor, etc., that he can sustain with full and bright sound without falsetto (i.e., half and forced voice)." This may be similar to Caccini's disparagement of feigned voice. "The defects in the voice are: that some singers take too many breaths; some sing through the nose and hold the voice in the throat; others sing with the teeth closed. All these are not to be praised, rather they deform the harmony and do not please."[11]

Bénigne de Bacilly (1621–1690)

Bénigne de Bacilly was a French singing teacher and composer most well-known for his 1668 treatise *Remarques curieuses sur l'art de bien chanter*, or *A Commentary upon the Art of Proper Singing*. The treatise includes a wealth of information on early baroque singing style in general and seventeenth-century French declamation and ornamentation in particular. In his opening remarks, Bacilly praises singers with naturally beautiful and well-placed voices and says these gifts can only be perfected with training, never acquired. He describes proper vocal style as having the following:

> proper pitch, proper sustaining of the voice, good carriage and support, proper performance of *cadences* and *tremblement*, proper throat pulsation when necessary (and the omission of this technique when it is not called for; i.e., knowing when to slur over certain notes), the proper performance of *passages* and *diminutions* . . . proper pronunciation, expression, and emotional interpretation.

As I mentioned earlier, it is difficult to know exactly what the terms "cadence," "tremblement," and "throat pulsation" are referring to here. In a later section, the translator, Austin Caswell, substitutes "vibrato" for the French term *cadence*. Bacilly says that a pretty voice can be pleasing to the ear because of its clearness and sweetness and nice vibrato, but it might lack fire and expressiveness, while a big or strong voice might have an extremely errant vibrato. In this case, the singer needs to relax and not force the voice in order to correct this defect. Here again, we see an indication that seventeenth-century singers did sing with some vibrato, but it was probably much more subtle and varied than the consistent modern vibrato singers use today.

Bacilly recommends doing vocal exercises in the morning before eating, and he stresses the importance of good breathing and singing tones from the diaphragm. He says a good ear is necessary to know how to soften a loud tone, or steady a shaky tone, or know which tones need to be accented and which ones glided over. He stresses the importance of good taste and recommends listening to singers who have performed extensively and developed a good style. He also stresses the importance of choosing a good teacher who can demonstrate beautiful singing and the proper way to add ornaments to airs.

He talks at length about the importance of good disposition, or agility of the throat. This is needed to execute ornaments, or *agréments*, as they are called in French, and diminutions, or *passages*. He recommends that singers practice this technique in the morning, first by accenting the notes with solidity and then gradually increasing speed.

Most of Bacilly's instructions are aimed toward the performance of a type of solo song called *air de cour*. In these secular songs, as in songs of Dowland or Caccini, singers could accompany themselves, or be accompanied by a lute or theorbo. In the French form, the first verse is typically sung more simply, while the second verse receives more ornamentation. The choice and placement of the ornaments should be intimately connected to the meaning of the text. Poetic rules about long and short syllables also have an important impact on the placement of ornaments, as Bacilly explains in the second half of his treatise. He stresses that it is crucial to learn how to interpret the text and choose appropriate ornaments from the example of a good teacher.[12]

THE EIGHTEENTH CENTURY

In the first half of the eighteenth century, writers on singing continued to prefer soft, sweet high notes and steady, sustained notes without wavering or trembling. They did mention vibrato but mostly as a kind of ornament, used sparingly and in specific situations. They spoke about different vocal registers but mostly agreed that a good singer showed a smooth continuity of sound from the bottom to the top of their range. A singer's most important job was to communicate the emotions of the text, and the ornamentation they chose needed to reflect the meaning of the words. All the treatises from this period included extensive instructions for specific ornaments, both small decorations and longer divisions and cadenzas. Writers distinguished between the adagio and allegro style—for slow, introspective music, sometimes called "pathetic"—or energetic, bravura music, and they described the different approach to ornamentation needed for each. They discussed the specific requirements for different performance venues including church, chamber, and theater. They also compared the increasingly contrasting national styles of Italian, French, and German composers and performers.

Pier Francesco Tosi (1653–1732)

Pier Francesco Tosi was a soprano castrato who began his career in Italian churches and cathedrals. He performed opera in Genoa, and he later gave chamber music concerts in London where he taught voice and composed. His treatise *Opinioni dei cantori antichi e moderni* (1723) was translated into English by the musician and composer J. E. Galliard as *Observations on the Florid Song* (1742) and was both a summing up of late seventeenth-century vocal practices and a point of departure for later treatises. Tosi was, in Galliard's words, "a Singer of great Esteem and Reputation" and stressed the importance of study, dedication, and artistry for anyone embarking on a career in singing. Most of his advice is directed toward soprano voices, both female and male, boy trebles, or castrated adult men. Many of his general recommendations are similar to pieces of advice we have seen in earlier treatises.

A good singer must have a general knowledge of music and know all the keys, scales, and clefs. Sing the correct accidentals and always sing in tune, "for one that sings out of Tune losses all his other perfections." Tosi warns against singing tones that pass through the nose or are choked in the throat, which are "the two most horrible Defects in a Singer." You must be able to hold out sustained notes without shrillness or trembling, and he warns that it is important not to let the voice "become subject to a Flutt'ring in the Manner of all those that sing in a very bad taste." This may be a reference to too much vibrato.

He describes three different vocal registers: "*Voce di Petto* [chest voice] is a full Voice which comes from the Breast by Strength and is the most sonorous and expressive. *Voce di Testa* [head voice] comes more from the Throat, than from the Breast . . . *Falsetto* is a feigned Voice, which is entirely formed in the Throat." This adds a bit of clarification to the terms used by Caccini, but it is still not clear what the difference is between "head voice" and "falsetto." In any case, Tosi advises blending all the registers and uniting the natural and the feigned voice so that they are indistinguishable. He also advises singing higher notes more gently, "the higher the Notes, the more it is necessary to touch them with softness to avoid screaming." Indeed, later on in the treatise, he says being able to sing *piano* is the mark of a good singer.

Regarding demeanor, singers should have a noble bearing, good posture, and avoid grimaces or strange movements. Tosi recommends practicing with a mirror to "avoid those convulsive Motions of the Body, or of the Face." He also advises practicing in the morning and warns that one hour a day may not be enough. He cautions against holding your music in front of your face when you perform, and he recommends performing often in front of people of distinction to get over the fear that causes so many vocal problems, including difficulty with breath, choking, singing out of tune, unsteady tone, and poor rhythm.

Tosi disapproves of singers who make excuses for being sick or not in good voice, criticizes singers who sound as if they have asthma when they take a breath, and advises a singer to "manage his Respiration, that he may always be provided with more Breath than is needed." Singers should not breathe in the middle of a word unless it is during a long division, in which case taking a breath is allowed. Divisions should be fast and distinctly articulated, neither too marked, nor too joined together. You shouldn't use your head, chin, or tongue to help with agility, and you shouldn't use "ha ha ha" or "gha gha gha" to help with the articulation. Vowels must be sung clearly, and words must always be pronounced correctly without affectation and distinctly understood; otherwise, there is no difference between a human voice and an oboe. Communicating the meaning of the text is the "greatest Part of that Delight which vocal Musick conveys."

Tosi's chapters on specific ornaments including appoggiaturas, trills, divisions, and cadences, or cadenzas, are well worth reading. He also gives specific recommendations for singing recitative in the three different approaches needed for church, chamber, and theater. He gives extensive advice on ornamenting the return of da capo arias and the difference between the allegro and pathetic styles. I'll give more details in chapter 5. In general, Tosi councils that a student may listen to the example of his teacher or other good singers and imitate them but never copy directly. Ornaments must always seem natural and spontaneous, ideally newly invented for each performance. Moreover, they should not be too excessive or serve the vanity of the singer. The wise singer will continue to study and learn throughout his career and use all the tools of ornamentation to serve judgment, art, and taste and "give Delight to the Soul."[13]

Michel Pignolet de Montéclair (1667–1737)

Michel Pignolet de Montéclair, the composer of French cantatas, published *Principes de musique* in 1736. This treatise presents detailed and illustrated instructions for performing the principle ornaments in French baroque vocal music. We will revisit Montéclair's recommendations for specific ornaments in chapter 5, but I wanted to present some of his more general advice here.

"To sing French well . . . one must have taste, soul, vocal flexibility, and discernment to give the words the expression to their meaning."

Montéclair stresses the importance of communicating the words and their meanings with clear diction and appropriate expression. Agility is also important for clearly executing the various ornaments that give vocal music its charm and beauty. In French music, in particular, writers often speak of *le bon gout*, or good taste, when it comes to ornaments and style.

Montéclair clarifies the distinction between *cadence* and *tremblement*, explaining: "The *cadence* is an ending or conclusion of the melody which is to music what a period is to prose. There are *cadences* or conclusions of melodies without *tremblements*, just as there are *tremblements* without *cadences*." This seems to indicate that a *tremblement* is a gentle trill ornament that can be used at the conclusion of a phrase or elsewhere in a vocal line. It may be such a subtle trembling of the voice that it sounds similar to a gentle vibrato, but it is not used consistently throughout a phrase, rather as a specific ornamental gesture in a particular place. He describes another specific trembling ornament called *le flaté*, which the translators call vibrato: "Several small, gentle exhalations without raising or lowering the pitch . . . on a note of long duration or on a note of repose . . . If the *flaté* were used on all important notes it would become unbearable in that it would render the melody tremulous and too monotonous." Again we see instructions that discourage the use of our consistent modern vibrato and encourage a variety of delicate ornamental gestures that help shape and express the text.[14]

Johann Joachim Quantz (1697–1773)

Johann Joachim Quantz, flutist and composer in the court of Frederick the Great, was one of three instrumentalists who contributed important method books reflecting the musical practices of the high baroque period: Quantz's was on flute playing; Carl Philipp Emanuel Bach (1714–1788), second son of Johann Sebastian Bach, wrote a treatise on keyboard playing; and Leopold Mozart (1719–1787), father of Wolfgang Amadeus Mozart, contributed one on violin playing. All three works include important information on early eighteenth-century style in general, as well as specific recommendations for singers.

In his treatise, *Versuch einer Anweisung die Flöte traversière zu spielen* (Berlin, 1752), Quantz reiterates many requirements of a good singer that we have heard elsewhere. You must have a good, pure tone, without the defects of singing in the nose or throat. You should blend all the registers from bottom to top and know how to join the chest register to the falsetto with a smooth transition and no noticeable break. You should have a good ear and sing in tune. You must be able to sustain a steady, long note without trembling or screeching. You must also be able to use the *messa di voce* and *portamento* in an agreeable way. Your trill should be neither too slow nor too fast, and you should take care to distinguish between trills that should be a half step or a whole step.

Your enunciation must be clear so all the words may be understood. Your vowels should be accurate and steady, especially during divisions and other ornaments. You should express the appropriate emotion to go with the words and also choose ornaments that reflect the sentiments of the words being decorated. The adagio style demands "a moving, expressive, caressing, graceful, sustained manner . . . as well as in the addition or ornamentation in conformity with the words and melody." The allegro style demands "a lively, brilliant manner and with lightness," with clear and fast passage-work.

You should avoid a hard attack or forcible breath on high notes; "even less should he howl them out, for this changes the sweetness into brutality." You must know how to adapt your voice to the different demands of the theater and the chamber, or between strong and weak accompaniments, "so that his singing in the higher register does not change into a bawling." You must take breaths in appropriate places and be sure of your tempo so that taking a breath does not throw you off the beat. Your ornaments must be your own, never copied from someone else.[15]

Johann Friedrich Agricola (1720–1774)

Johann Friedrich Agricola was a scholar, organist, composer, and voice teacher who studied with Johann Sebastian Bach and Johann Joachim Quantz and worked in the court of Frederick the Great. In 1757, he published a German translation of Tosi's *Observations on the Florid Song* called *Anleitung zur Singkunst*, or *Introduction to the Art of Singing*. At this time, Italian singers were in great demand, and the Italian style of singing was wildly popular all over Europe. Agricola wanted to encourage the use of this style in Germany and improve the training of German singers. However, by 1757, many of Tosi's recommendations were thought old-fashioned. While the *Anleitung* faithfully preserved the translation of the original treatise, Agricola also updated Tosi's instructions with extensive commentary of his own that reflected the current taste and style of mid-eighteenth-century Berlin. He also addressed his treatise to both female and male voices of all ranges, as well as soloists and ensemble singers.

Some of the most notable additions to Tosi include the discoveries about vocal physiology by the French scientist Antoine Ferrein, published in the 1741 treatise *De la formation de la voix de l'homme*. Agricola presents a discussion of breathing and laryngeal function based on Ferrein's work that approaches our modern understanding. Agricola also writes extensively about the registers, in both male and female voices, and attempts to further clarify the confusing terminology of chest voice, head voice, and falsetto. While he disagrees with the Italian distinction between head voice and falsetto, he agrees that it is important for all voice types to unify the different registers so they are smoothly blended with no jarring breaks. He also advises higher female voices to be able to sing intermediate notes in both a high, "falsetto" position and a low, "natural voice" position. Then they may sing ascending notes in one way and descending notes in the other. He allows that not all voices are suited to this, but "it is the art and natural advantage of those whose voices sound the same throughout."

Agricola also writes extensively about ornamentation and the way it was practiced in the court of Frederick the Great. Italian singers were known for their elaborate improvised ornaments, particularly in the da capo of arias. By the mid-eighteenth century, this practice had gotten a bit out of hand and inspired some backlash. As we saw at the end of the sixteenth century, the reaction against the excessive florid ornamentation of polyphony inspired the development of solo song. In the early seventeenth century, Caccini notated the ornamentation he wanted in his compositions to discourage the tasteless excess of some singers. However, little by little throughout the seventeenth century, singers started adding more and more decoration until by the 1750s their dazzling feats of showmanship nudged the pendulum back in the other direction once again.

Frederick the Great, who was an avid amateur musician and supportive patron of the arts, was also a monarch who liked things his way. In the interest of good taste, and to exercise artistic control, he urged German composers to notate the ornamentation they wanted in the da capo of arias in their scores. Even though his teacher Quantz was in favor of improvised ornaments, Frederick wanted to discourage singers at the Berlin opera from improvising new and different ornaments for each performance and showing off their individual abilities. Agricola laid out specific rules for divisions and cadenzas that limited the creative freedom of singers but also discouraged tasteless excess.[16] We will look at the German approach to ornamentation in more detail in chapter 5.

NOTES

1. Jerome of Moravia, from *Tractus de musica*, quoted in Carol MacClintock, *Readings in the History of Music in Performance* (Bloomington, IN: Indiana University Press, 1979), 3–7.

2. Conrad von Zabern, from *De modo ben cantandi* (1474), quoted in MacClintock, *Readings*, 12–16.

3. Hermann Finck, from *Pratica musica* (Wittenberg, 1556) quoted in MacClintock, *Readings*, 61–67.

4. Adrian Petit Coclico, from *Compendium musices* (1552), quoted in MacClintock, *Readings*, 30–36.

5. Giovanni Camillo Maffei, from *Letter on Singing* (Naples, 1562), quoted in MacClintock, *Readings*, 37–61.

6. Vincenzo Giustiniani, from *Discorso sopra la musica* (1628), quoted in MacClintock, *Readings*, 27–29.

7. Ludovico Zacconi, from *Prattica di musica* (Venice, 1596), quoted in MacClintock, *Readings*, 68–75.

8. Giovanni de' Bardi, *Discourse on Ancient Music and Good Singing*, (Florence, 1580), quoted in Oliver Strunk, *Source Readings in Music History: The Renaissance* (New York: Norton, 1965), 100–11.

9. Giulio Caccini, Preface to *Le nuove musiche* (Florence, 1602), quoted in Oliver Strunk, *Source Readings in Music History: The Baroque Era* (New York: Norton, 1965), 17–32.

10. John Dowland, *Of the Divers Fashions of Singing, and of the Ten Precepts for Singing* (London, 1609), quoted in MacClintock, *Readings*, 159–62.

11. Michael Praetorius, from *Syntagma musicum*, quoted in MacClintock, *Readings*, 150–52.

12. Bénigne de Bacilly, *Remarques curieuse sur l'art de bien chanter* (Paris, 1668), translated by Austin B. Caswell as *A Commentary upon the Art of Proper Singing* (New York: Institute of Mediaeval Music, 1968).

13. Pier Francesco Tosi, *Opinioni de' cantori antichi e moderni* (Bologna, 1723), translated and edited by John Ernst Galliard as *Observations on the Florid Song* (London, 1743) (London: William Reeves, 1905).

14. Michel Pignolet de Montéclair, *Principes de musique* (Paris, 1736), translated in *Cantatas for One and Two Voices*, edited by James R. Anthony and Diran Akmajian (Madison, WI: A-R Editions, 1978), ii–xiii.

15. Johann Quantz, from *Versuch einer Anweisung die Flöte traversière zu spielen* (Berlin, 1752), quoted in MacClintock, *Readings*, 357-359.

16. Johann Friedrich Agricola, *Anleitung der Singkunst* (Berlin, 1757), translated by Julianne Baird as *Introduction to the Art of Singing* (Cambridge: Cambridge University Press, 1995.)

RESOURCES

Agricola, Johann Friedrich. 1995. *Anleitung zur Singkunst (Berlin 1757)*. Translated by Julianne Baird. Cambridge: Cambridge University Press.

Bach, Carl Philipp Emanuel. 1949. *Versuch über die wahre Art das Clavier zu spielen (Berlin 1753)*. Translated by W. J. Mitchell. New York: Norton.

Bacilly, Bénigne de. 1968. *Remarques curieuse sur l'art de bien chanter (Paris 1668)*. Translated by Austin B. Caswell. New York: Institute of Medaevil Music.

Bardi, Giovanni de'. 1965. "Discourse on Ancient Music and Good Singing." In *Source Readings in Music History: The Renaissance*, by Oliver Strunk, 100–11. New York, NY: W.W. Norton & Company.

Caccini, Giulio. 1965. "Le nuove musiche—Forward." In *Source Readings in Music History: The Baroque Era*, by Oliver Strunk, 17–32. New York, NY: W.W. Norton & Company.

Coclico, Adrian Petit. 1979. "Compendium musices." In *Readings in the History of Music in Performance*, by Carol MacClintock, 30–37. Bloomington, IN: Indiana University Press.

Coffin, Berton. 1989. *Historical Vocal Pedagogy Classics*. Metuchen, NJ: Scarecrow Press.

Dowland, John. 1979. "Of the Divers Fashions of Singing, and of the Ten Precepts for Singing." In *Readings in the History of Music in Performance*, by Carol MacClintock, 159–62. Bloomington, IN: Indiana University Press.

Finck, Hermann. 1979. "Pratica musica." In *Readings in the History of Music in Performance*, by Carol MacClintock, 61–65. Bloomington, IN: Indiana University Press.

Giustiniani, Vincenzo. 1979. "Discorso sopra la musica." In *Readings in the History of Music in Performance*, by Carol MacClintock, 27–29. Bloomington, IN: Indiana University Press.

Grant, Bonnie L. 2016. *Lesser Calamint Plants*. February 19. Accessed July 18, 2017. https://www.gardeningknowhow.com/edible/herbs/mint/growing-calamint-herbs.htm.

Grieve, M. 2017. *Squill*. July 18. http://www.botanical.com/botanical/mgmh/s/squill86.html.

Maffei, Giovanni Camillo. 1979. "Letter on Singing." In *Readings in the History of Music in Performance*, by Carol MacClintock, 37–61. Bloomington, IN: Indiana University Press.

Montéclair, Michel Pignolet de. 1978. "Principes de musique." In *Cantatas for One and Two Voices*, by Michel Pignolet de Montéclair, edited by James R. and Diran Akmajian Anthony, ii–xiii. Madison, WI: A-R Editions.

Moravia, Jerome of. 1979. "Tractus de musica." In *Readings in the History of Music in Performance*, by Carol MacClintock, 3–7. Bloomington, IN: Indiana University Press.

Mozart, Leopold. 1985. *Versuch einer gründlichen Violinschule (Augsburg, 1756)*, Second Edition. Translated by Editha Knocker. Oxford: Oxford University Press.

Praetorius, Michael. 1979. "Syntagma musicum." In *Readings in the History of Music in Performance*, by Carol MacClintock, 162–70. Bloomington, IN: Indiana University Press.

Quantz, Johann Joachim. 1979. "Versuch einer Anweisung die Flöte traversiere zu spielen (Berlin 1752)." In *Readings in the History of Music in Performance*, by Carol MacClintock, 357–59. Bloomington, IN: Indiana University Press.

———. 1985. *Versuch einer Anweisung die Flöte traversiere zu spielen (Berlin 1752)*. Translated by Edward R. Reilly. New York: Schirmer.

Tosi, Pier Francesco. 1905. *Opinioni de' cantori antichi e moderni, o sieno Osservazioni sopra il canto figurato (Bologna, 1723)*. Translated by Gaillard. London: William Reeves.

von Zabern, Conrad. 1979. "De modo bene cantandi." In *Readings in the History of Music in Performance*, by Carol MacClintock, 12–16. Bloomington, IN: Indiana University Press.

Wikipedia contributors. 2017. *Sandarac*. June 12. Accessed July 18, 2017. https://en.wikipedia.org/wiki/Sandarac.

Zacconi, Ludovico. 1979. "Prattica di musica." In *Readings in the History of Music in Performance*, by Carol MacClintock, 67–75. Bloomington, IN: Indiana University Press.

5

ELEMENTS OF BAROQUE STYLE

"The singer will always be praised who, with a few ornaments, makes them at the right moment."

—Lodovico Zacconi, *Prattica di musica* (Venice, 1596)

In this chapter, we will focus on music from the seventeenth and eighteenth centuries and look at issues of baroque style, including articulation, rhythm, phrasing, and ornamentation. We shall discuss elements that are not included in the score that the performer must add, such as tempo and dynamic markings, instrumentation and accompaniment, and, especially, ornamentation. We will look at differences in national styles, comparing Italy, England, France, and Germany and, particularly, the varying approaches to rhythm, ornamentation, and improvisation. How language impacts choices about rhythm, articulation, and phrasing will also be discussed, as well as how all these elements contribute to the rhetoric of baroque music.

We have already learned how vocal treatises from this period stressed the importance of conveying the affect, or mood of a piece, as well as moving the passions of the listeners. Once solo song and *seconda prattica* superseded polyphony as the preferred form of vocal music, a singer's most important job became communicating the appropriate meaning and emotions of the text and the music. Singers of this period knew all the necessary tools for achieving this goal and inflaming the hearts of their audiences. However, many of the tools they used were not notated in the score. In this chapter, you will learn the tools you need for persuasive singing in a baroque style.

RHETORICAL FIGURES IN BAROQUE MUSIC

Rhetoric, or the art of persuasive speech, was well-known to singers in the sixteenth and seventeenth centuries. Anyone who wanted to be a persuasive communicator—including lawyers, preachers, actors, and singers—was trained in the rules of rhetoric practiced and taught by ancient Greek and Roman orators. Many treatises on the subject explained how to use specific figures of speech to elevate normal daily language into something more lofty and inspiring. If you have ever heard an effective and moving public speaker, you've probably heard traditional rhetorical devices. These devices, or figures, could include carefully thought out places of emphasis and intensification, planned repetition—with increasing or decreasing energy—using contrast and contradiction, areas of pause and suspense, and, finally, sections that build to a climax.[1] These kinds of rhetorical figures found their way not only into the poetry of the early baroque period but also the musical compositions as well. It is not necessary for modern singers to know the specific Latin terms for all these particular devices, but it is helpful to know that they exist and to be on the lookout for them in baroque music.

The Text Leads the Way

Of course, in vocal music, the text has a big influence on the musical composition. The text has built-in punctuation and is constructed of distinct elements such as words, phrases, and sentences. Baroque music also has a discernable grammar. Small groups of notes or musical gestures work as syllables and fit together to form larger musical gestures similar to words, which then fit together to form musical phrases, sentences, paragraphs, and even larger forms. It might seem obvious to us that with spoken language, certain words or phrases require more or less emphasis. Pauses in certain places also help to make the meaning of the text clear. Similarly, it was obvious to baroque musicians that certain notes or groups of notes needed more or less emphasis and separating these distinct elements was helpful to make the syntax and grammar of the music clear. We will learn how to use articulation, dynamics, and ornamentation to highlight and clarify both the smaller and larger constructions of grammar in both text and music of baroque repertoire. The more you learn to recognize these elements in baroque music, the easier it will be to shape and highlight them appropriately.

This may sound complicated in an abstract context, so let us look at how it all works in a piece of music that you probably know. Antonio Caldara's aria "Sebben, crudele" from 1710 is included in the Schirmer collection of *Twenty-Four Italian Songs and Arias* in a nineteenth-century arrangement by Alessandro Parisotti. You can also find a more faithful version of the original aria in the 1991 John Glenn Paton edition of *26 Italian Songs and Arias*. We'll talk more about choosing editions in chapter 7. For now, let's just look at how the melody in the Schirmer collection is constructed and see if we can find the smaller and larger pieces used to construct rhetorical figures. The example here in the text (figure 5.1) is in the high key. The score in online example 5-1 is in D minor. ♪

In each of the first four bars of the vocal melody, we have distinctive groups of notes that fit together to form the musical phrase: the repeated

Figure 5.1.   Caldara: "Sebben, crudele," a) mm. 5–14, b) mm. 19–26.

notes on the word "Sebben," as well as the jump up of the fourth to the syllable "cru" in m. 5; the descending dotted quarter, eighth and quarter notes of "-dele" in m. 6; the rising two eighths and quarter note of "fai lan-" in m. 7; and the descending half step of "-guir" in m. 8. These small segments or figures are used again and again throughout the aria to build larger structures. In the second phrase, we see the same descending dotted quarter, eighth, and quarter-note figure from m. 6 used again for "-dele" in m. 10. In the completion of this second line of text, we can also see the rhetorical device of repetition and intensification as Caldara repeats the ascending quarter-note steps of "sempre fedele," builds to a climax on the syllable "ti" in m. 12, and then uses the combination of two eighth notes and a quarter note to complete the phrase with a full cadence in m.14. The repetition of the text here helps to emphasize its meaning: "always faithful, always faithful I will love you."

As he restates the first two lines of text in the next section of melody (figure 5.1b), Caldara creates suspense as he repeats ascending step-wise motion combined with a descending half step. Using contrast, the climactic tessitura and harmonic tension of "-guir" in m. 22, "languish," is released and resolved by the four bars of descending step-wise motion toward the full cadence of "-mar" in m. 26. Caldara also uses dissonant suspensions in this descending line to intensify the emotional yearning of the text. In fact, all of these musical gestures help convey the meaning and emotion of the text. It is perfectly acceptable to sing the notes and rhythms as they come, but it is much more fun, expressive, and stylistic if you recognize and bring out the separate building blocks of baroque musical grammar.

WHAT'S NOT IN THE SCORE

As you saw in chapter 1, the history of early music is also a history of music notation. By the beginning of the seventeenth century, notation had become more precise, and, over the course of the baroque period, notational practices developed even further. However, a baroque score is in no way a complete set of performance instructions. It is really just a sketch of the composition, a starting place for performers to add their own creative input. Composers knew that performers would be familiar with stylistic conventions and would fill in missing elements that were not indicated in the score. Often composers were performers themselves and could easily make decisions for their own performances. They also collaborated closely with performers and could decide what was needed in rehearsals. Choices were often flexible, depending on the space used for the performance or the personnel available. Performers could be creative and spontaneous depending on the specific performance situation. So let's see what was not included in the score and what kinds of decisions performers had to make.

Instrumentation and Accompaniment

Very often, instrumentation or even voice assignments were not indicated in the score. In late Renaissance and early baroque polyphony, different lines of counterpoint could be sung by individual voices or played by various instruments. The choice was very flexible depending on who was available. Performers decided what type of voice (or instrument) to use for a particular vocal line based on the range of the music and perhaps also on the clef used to notate that line. In vocal duets by Monteverdi, for example, you might use two sopranos or two tenors for two higher vocal lines, or soprano and tenor, soprano and alto, or tenor and bass depending on the range of the vocal lines and the voices available. In seventeenth-century solo song, you could probably transpose the vocal line to fit your range comfortably. You could also accompany yourself, or be accompanied by a variety of plucked stringed instruments, including a lute or theorbo.

The Continuo.   As the seventeenth century progressed, the most popular vocal accompaniment featured a combination of an instrument to play chords, such as a keyboard, along with an instrument to play a sustained bass line, such as a low-pitched, bowed-stringed instrument. A wide variety of instrument combinations was possible to form this team known as the continuo. Composers indicated what chords to play by placing numbers or figures over the bass notes. Continuo players knew how to improvise a complete accompaniment from this shorthand system known as thorough bass or figured bass. We will talk much more about choosing continuo instruments and working with figured bass in chapter 6.

Obbligato Instruments.   As composers added obbligato instrumental lines to their cantatas, they did not always indicate a specific instrument, such as violin, oboe, or flute. They tended to be more precise about this in the later baroque repertoire. However, it was also possible to interchange the instruments used for obbligato lines depending on the situation. When not indicated, editors of modern editions often make these choices for performers. However, just as a jazz combo or rock band can decide what combination of instruments and voices they want to cover the bass, chords, and solo lines, baroque musicians had a great deal of flexibility about these decisions. We'll talk more about this in chapter 6 as well.

Tempo

Tempo was not often indicated in baroque scores. Treatises recommended looking at the music itself, particularly the mood or affect, to determine a proper tempo. In vocal music, the text is certainly the best place to start to find the dramatic and emotional quality of the piece. The tempo should reflect this quality, be it lighthearted and joyful, or introspective and sad. In the recitative style of the early seventeenth century, the singer can also shape the phrases and the tempo based on the specific meaning and rhythm of the words. Remember that Caccini advised bending the time, using what he called the "noble neglect of the song," or what we would call rubato, to speak in harmony and convey the passions of the text. The way the bass line moves can give clues to tempo and rubato as well. If the bass line is static or moves slowly, the singer has more flexibility to push and pull the tempo. However, if the bass line has faster rhythms, this might indicate that the vocal line should coordinate with it more strictly. A singer's personal temperament and dramatic abilities, as well as the way their voice moves, can also contribute to a choice of tempo.

A great example of this is in the prologue of Monteverdi's *Coronation of Poppea* (figure 5.2). Virtue, in the middle of her opening scene, speaks in a declamatory style for several measures over a stationary C major harmony of whole notes in the bass. Then suddenly, mid-sentence, the bass line starts moving in quarter and eighth notes, and the harmony travels farther afield. Virtue is describing how she will teach

Figure 5.2. Monteverdi: prologue from *L'incoronazione di Poppea*, mm. 106–113.

the way to navigate the course to Olympia, and Monteverdi graphically illustrates this with movement in both the vocal and bass lines. The tempo for the first three bars of this section can be flexible and declamatory, but when the bass starts moving, the tempo should be steady and bright, even though there is no indication of this in the score.

Recitative and Aria.   In earlier baroque music, including all of Monteverdi's operas, declamatory, recitative sections and lyrical, tuneful sections flowed freely back and forth, varying moods and tempos. Therefore, for earlier baroque music, you should use the meaning of the text as well as the combination of the rhythms of the bass line and the vocal line to help guide your tempo choices. In later baroque music, the difference between recitative and aria became more distinct. In the recitative style, the mood of the text might change from line to line, and the tempo choice can reflect this. In arias, there is typically one mood in each section of music and one tempo per affect.

Mood and Meter.   In this era, composers sometimes added tempo indications, but these described moods rather than specified speeds: *allegro* = cheerful; *allegretto* = rather gaily but gracious; *andante* = walking comfortably; *adagio* = at ease; *grave* = serious. The meter marking could also indicate a kind of movement based on the number of strong beats per measure: for example, 3/4 was felt as three beats that had a very different character than 3/8, which was felt in one.

Dance Forms.   Baroque music was also often modeled after well-known dance forms. The meter marking, in combination with the familiar dance rhythms, gave a good idea of what the tempo should be. Finally, some wonderful advice from Leopold Mozart in his 1756 treatise on violin playing is useful for music of all periods: "Every melodious piece has at least one phrase from which one can recognize quite surely what sort of speed the piece demands."[2]

Figure 5.3.   J. S. Bach: Magnificat in D major BWV 243, a) "Et exulta-vit," mm. 1–14; b) "Quia fecit," mm. 1–6.

Let's see how this all works in two pieces from Bach's Magnificat in D major. The "Et exultavit" movement (figure 5.3a), which has no tempo indication, is a minuet in 3/8. The character of this classic French court dance has been described as noble with elegant simplicity. Tempo recommendations for the minuet range from lively to moderate with one strong beat per measure. The text of this piece is uplifting and joyful, which would seem to indicate a livelier tempo, but the thirty-second note figures scattered throughout the bass line, violin part, and vocal line put an upper limit on the speed and help keep it from becoming too hectic. Based on how your voice moves, you should pick a tempo that highlights the joyful yet elegant character of the music and text, and the one strong beat per measure rhythm of the dance. You can listen to a performance of this aria with a piano vocal score in online example 5-2. ♪

The "Quia fecit" bass aria from the Magnificat (figure 5.3b) is a gavotte, a dance form that starts on the upbeat and has two strong beats per measure. The character of a gavotte was usually described as graceful, and it could be joyful or serious in a range of moderate tempos. Bach gives no tempo indication for this aria, but it is important to bring out the gavotte phrasing and rhythm—an upbeat feeling on "quia" leading to a more stressed beat of "*fe*cit" with less emphasis on "mihi" leading to more emphasis for "*ma*gna." The choice of tempo should also highlight the solemn and grand quality of this text. You can see a full score of this aria in online example 5-3. ♪

Dynamics

Most of the time, baroque composers did not indicate dynamics in their scores. Modern editions often add dynamics, but these are just suggestions based on stylistic conventions. Performers can use dynamics to highlight the smaller and larger constructions of baroque rhetoric and musical grammar. This usually involves creating contrasting emphasis, between individual notes, measures, and whole phrases or sections of music. More important syllables in a text can be louder than unstressed syllables, as with the first syllable of "*fe*cit" or "*ma*gna" in the Bach example. Dissonant pitches, which were considered more expressive, can be louder than consonant ones, as with the first quarter note of "-guir" in

m. 22 of "Sebben crudele" (figure 5.1). Repeated phrases can be shaded with different dynamics: for example, the second statement of "sempre fedele" in m. 11 can have slightly more emphasis and be slightly louder than the first statement in the previous two measures. When the whole eight-bar phrase of mm. 19–26 is repeated in mm. 27–34, the dynamic can be either louder to build more excitement, or softer to create contrast. When new text and melody are introduced for the B section of the aria in m. 35, a different dynamic can highlight the contrasting material (see online example 5-1).

Terraced Dynamics. Using dynamics to build contrasting phrases or sections of music is sometimes called terraced dynamics. In some cases, rising sequences can get louder, and falling sequences can get softer, but no particular choice is right or wrong. More contrast is always more interesting and more stylistic. It is up to the performer to create a dramatic quality that will inspire and delight, while faithfully conveying the meaning of the text. Dynamics are one of the tools that can help achieve this.

Articulation

Articulation is another tool that helps create contrast and drama. In his treatise on flute playing, Quantz wrote:

> Musical ideas that belong together must not be separated; on the other hand, you must separate those ideas in which one musical thought ends and a new idea begins . . . You must know how to make a distinction in execution between the *principal* notes, ordinarily called *accented* or in the Italian manner, *good* notes, and those that pass, which some foreigners call *bad* notes. When it is possible, the principal notes always must be emphasized more than the passing.[3]

Heavy/Light. Some other writers of the period described notes as heavy and light, rather than good and bad. Treatises also instructed that the usual manner of playing and singing baroque music was detached and separated. Composers didn't typically include slur marks to indicate phrases or accent marks to indicate stress or emphasis. Musicians in the baroque period just knew that this kind of articulation was needed.

Agricola advised singers to make long melismas distinct and clear by gently repeating the vowel sound on each note. He also recommended emphasizing the first note in a group of three or four fast notes to maintain clarity and a steady tempo.[4] Dividing a long melisma into smaller pieces makes the passage easier to sing. It also highlights the stressed and unstressed contours of the music. You can decide which notes to emphasize based on how the shape of the melody interacts with the harmonic movement.

Legato

Some pieces of music demand a smooth and connected articulation, and instrumentalists were often advised to emulate the *cantabile* style of singers. The *cantabile* style could be used for slower, more introspective musical affects. This was also sometimes called the adagio or "pathetic" style. The use of legato articulation gained favor as the eighteenth century progressed. However, the legato articulation singers used in the baroque period was probably very different from our twenty-first-century conception of a consistently smooth, uninterrupted flow of sound. Highlighting slurred or connected notes could be used as another tool to convey the meaning of the text and add contrast and variety to the musical material.

Diction

Text and diction also help with articulation, and each language has its own distinct rhythms and character. German has many percussive consonant clusters and rules about separating words that begin with vowels. French has long and short syllables that are reflected in the complex rules governing poetry of this period. English has percussive consonants and a wide variety of syllable stresses. The grammar and syntax of early seventeenth-century poetry in English demand careful and thoughtful phrasing to reveal its meaning. Italian may seem the most legato of languages, but it is still necessary to emphasize certain syllables over others and highlight certain sounds in a stream of vowels to make the meaning of the text clear.

You may come across archaic forms or early spellings of words in some languages that may demand a historical form of pronunciation. Italian pronunciation, not including the many dialects, is much the same today as it was four hundred years ago, but that is not the case with French or even English. Here are some sources that have information on historical pronunciation for early music.[5]

Let's see how you can use diction and articulation in the two Bach arias mentioned earlier. In "Et exultavit" (figure 5.3a), considering the lively minuet tempo and joyous meaning of the text, you can sing short, separate syllables for "Et ex-ul" in the first measure, and then give more emphasis to "ta-" on the first beat of m. 14. Be careful not to accent the unaccented second syllable of "ta<u>vit</u>." The "ta" syllable is "heavy" and gets more emphasis; the "vit" syllable is "light" and gets less. The melisma on "spiritus" in the next measure (see online example 5-2) can be smoothly connected followed by a detached "me-us," with "me" being heavy and "us" being light. So in just four measures, you can use a wide variety of articulations to make the text clear, support the dance-like tempo, and bring contrast and interest to the phrases.

In the bass aria (figure 5.3b), the opening line of text, "Quia fecit mihi magna," has many smooth vowel sounds and fewer percussive consonants. You should still highlight the heavy and light syllables, as we mentioned earlier, to bring out the gavotte dance rhythms. In the long melisma on "potens" (see online example 5-3), you can emphasize the first sixteenth note in each group of four sixteenth notes and separate the downward-jumping eighth notes. You can slur the step-wise sixteenth notes in the first half of m. 12 and then separate the sixteenth and eighth notes with separate syllables in the second half of that measure. Once again, you can use many different kinds of articulations to bring shape and contrast to the phrases.

Rhythm

Just as baroque composers were often inconsistent in indicating instrumentation, tempo, and articulation, they were also inconsistent in their notation of rhythms. Performers in the baroque era knew that certain rhythms needed to be executed differently than the way they were written. Scholars who study this complex issue call it "Rhythmic Alteration." It is similar to jazz, in which musicians today see a series of even eighth notes and know to play them with a gentle lilt to make them "swing," or pop singers who adjust the rhythm of a melody to fit a more natural declamation of the text. In the early baroque era, particularly in French music, even eighth notes could be played with *inégalité* to make them slightly unequal, giving the music a graceful lilt. Dotted figures could be softened into triplets, or made extra dotted for a very crisp, snapped character. The choice depended on the affect and context of the music and, of course, the text.

In later baroque repertoire, dotted figures could be executed in a wide variety of ways, from very dotted, sometimes called "double-dotted," to very softened triplets, depending on the character of the music. If dotted and triplet figures, or triplets and even eighth notes, occurred simultaneously, performers might alter one of the rhythms to agree with the other, depending on the situation. Since it was unusual to have a two-against-three rhythm in the baroque era, it was more common to adjust contrasting rhythms so they would agree.

You can see an example of this in the cantata *Arion* from 1708 by the French composer André Campra (figure 5.4). This cantata for high

Figure 5.4.   Campra: "L'Onde et les Zephire," mm. 16–24, from *Arion*, Cantatas Book I (1708).

voice, flute, and continuo opens with a slowish aria in a triple meter, followed by a short recitative and an *ariette* in a faster duple meter. In this *ariette*, entitled "L'Onde et les Zephirs," we see triplets, dotted figures, and duple figures used simultaneously. In m. 20, the voice part is written with dotted eighths and sixteenths while the flute part has an eighth-note triplet. In m. 21, the flute part has two even eighth notes on the first beat. In m. 22, both parts are written with dotted figures, and in m. 24, the voice part has a dotted rhythm on the first beat and a triplet on the second beat. Because of the playful text and lively tempo, all these various rhythms should probably be adjusted to agree as gentle triplets throughout. It will feel quite natural and easy to do this. The affect should be as graceful and lovely as the waves of the breeze described in the text, and you should not try to make these different rhythms contrast.

Sometimes composers notated similar phrases in the same piece in a variety of rhythms. Perhaps Campra found it easier to notate three pitches in one beat as a triplet and two pitches in a similar kind of beat as a dotted figure. We can never really know if these notational practices were intentional, the result of idiosyncratic or sloppy penmanship, or scribal error. Each situation demands careful consideration and a choice by the performer. The dramatic and emotional quality of a work can dictate how gentle or energetic to make the dotted figures. The internal rhythm of long and short syllables of words can also suggest how to phrase notes together or reconcile inconsistent rhythms. Modern editors often make these decisions for performers, but scholars and editors don't always agree, and there are no easy answers to these questions. Modern singers should know that this issue exists and that some of the rhythms they see in baroque scores can be interpreted with a degree of flexibility.

Vibrato

This controversial subject has provoked four hundred years of passionate comments from scholars, teachers, and singers. As you saw in chapter 4, early writers on singing had conflicting opinions and used confusing terminology when referring to vocal vibrato. When historical performance practice became popular in the late twentieth century, many performances of baroque vocal repertoire were sung with a white, straight tone. This led to an angry backlash from some critics and vocal pedagogues. Most writers and singers today agree that vibrato is a natural part of healthy singing, and taste in early music singing has changed in favor of a more natural use of vibrato. However, it is important to consider certain key issues when deciding how to use vibrato in baroque repertoire.

Singers in the seventeenth and eighteenth centuries probably did sing with vibrato, but it was most likely narrow and shimmering. They may have used it as one of their many tools of communication, just as they used varied articulation, rhythm, tempo, and ornamentation. Just as you should not use a consistent and ever-present legato for baroque repertoire, you should not use vibrato as a consistent presence either. You need to be able to make different kinds of heavy and light articulations clear. You need to be able to make the difference between dissonant and consonant pitches clear. You need to be able to make all kinds of ornaments clear, including small decorations and fast passage work. All of this is more difficult with a large, uniform, and ongoing vibrato.

Vocal vibrato is caused by pressurized air flowing through the vocal tract. The size and speed of the vibrato are determined by the quality of air pressure as it relates to the degree of tension in the vocal apparatus. Modern singers have learned to sing louder to fill larger halls, carry over larger orchestras, and produce more penetrating high notes. A more forceful, consistent flow of air pressure and more muscular approach to tone production have led to the modern "operatic" vibrato, which can alter the pitch of a note anywhere from a half step to a major third, going both above and below the principal tone of the note. This kind of vibrato would make it very difficult to create the delicate contrasts we have been talking about for baroque style. Moreover, remember that the grandfathers of voice pedagogy recommended gentle and soft singing, with sweet, steady, and unforced tones. However, rather than just removing the vibrato altogether, which might lead to the tightening of the throat, modern singers should think about regulating and varying the speed and pressure of the airflow that supports the tone. This will hopefully result in a variety of kinds of vibrato, including some straight tones, which will be useful in many different kinds of situations.

Ornamentation

Another major component usually not notated in baroque scores was ornamentation. Baroque singers would have known how and where to add ornaments to the music they sang. However, over the course of 150 years from 1600–1750, fashions and taste in ornamentation changed dramatically, both over time and from place to place. Different performance situations also demanded different approaches to ornamentation. Music written for the church, for example, especially recitatives, could accept more ornamentation and flexibility of tempo. Opera recitatives were sung with little if any ornaments, while opera arias demanded much more elaborate and showy ornamentation. Music written for the chamber fell somewhere in between. In the following sections, we will look at different national styles of ornamentation from Italy, England, France, and Germany and see how they developed from the early to the later baroque period.

NATIONAL STYLES OF ORNAMENTATION

When you add ornaments to baroque music, you need to appreciate that one size does not fit all. Approaches to ornamentation varied widely from country to country. Writers of the time compared and contrasted singers and composers from different countries and concluded that the Italians favored dazzling passage work and vocal showmanship, while the French preferred good taste and a more spoken dramatic expression; early English composers combined elements of both Italian and French approaches, and the later German composers found a successful mix of the best of everything in a forward-thinking, universal style. Some composers preferred to write more of the ornamentation into their music, while other composers expected singers to add significant ornamentation and improvisation to complete the composition. I'll give you some basic ideas of where to start with baroque ornamentation, with the hope that you will continue to investigate this vast and fascinating topic on your own.

Italy

The two basic kinds of ornaments that early Italian writers talked about are graces and diminutions. Graces, or *accenti*, are small gestures that don't significantly alter the contours of the melody but rather adorn it with trills and decorative appoggiaturas. Diminutions, or divisions, are more florid decorations that divide larger note values into a series of smaller, faster notes. A singer can use diminutions to recompose a melody within an aria, or, more commonly, to embellish a cadence.

Early Italian Graces.   The small ornaments that Caccini talks about in *Le nuove musiche* include the *trillo, gruppo, messa di voce, esclamazione,* and *sprezzatura. Sprezzatura* is what Caccini called the noble neglect of the song. We would call it rubato: a gentle bending of the rhythm and the tempo to achieve a more expressive and declamatory delivery of the text. Tosi describes it as "stealing the time" and recommends it for use with a single instrument in music of a pathetic or tender nature. The bass must continue in exact time while the voice may delay or anticipate for the sake of the text. *Esclamazione* and *messa di voce* are ornaments in which the singer uses dynamics to add drama and expression: *messa di voce* is a crescendo and decrescendo on a single note, while *esclamazione* on one note is a soft entrance followed by a crescendo.

Of all the small graces, the trill is the most important. It can be used anywhere a small decoration is needed, particularly at cadences. Caccini describes two different trill ornaments, the *trillo* and the *gruppo* (figure 5.5), and instructs students to practice slowly and gradually increasing speed until the ornament is clearly articulated by the throat.

The *trillo,* also sometimes called *tremolo,* is an ornament on one note that was particularly popular in the early seventeenth century. Scholars disagree if the increasing note values in Caccini's example indicate how to perform the ornament or merely how to practice it. Singers today can use a variety of speeds, either steady, increasing, or decreasing, depending on the drama and the text; perhaps faster and lighter for a happy or

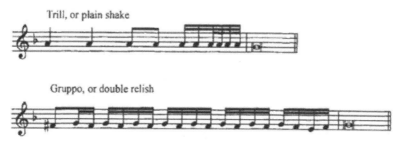

Figure 5.5.   Caccini: *trillo* and *gruppo* from *Le nuove musiche* (1602).

joyful effect, or slower and more sob-like to convey anguish or despair. You can try a combination of diaphragm and/or throat articulation for the *trillo* and experiment until you find what works for you.

The *gruppo* is an ornament in which two pitches alternate either a whole step or a half step. Later in the century, it was more widely used than the *trillo* and became known as the trill. It is important for modern singers to be able to make clear distinctions between notes that are rearticulated on one note, like the *trillo*, or on two notes, like the *gruppo* or trill. It is also essential to distinguish between a note that fluctuates with vibrato and an ornament in which pitches alternate.

Early Italian Divisions.   We have already mentioned that seventeenth-century singers were prized for their flexible throats and fast, clear passage work. We have also mentioned that simple declamatory melodies were favored over excessive diminutions. In the introduction to *Le nuove musiche*, Caccini explained that he had notated most of the ornaments he wanted in his music, and the singer only needed to add a few small things here and there. By looking at what Caccini has included in his songs, we can get an idea of the divisions that were typical of that time, and figure out similar gestures that we can add.

"Amarilli mia bella" was one of the most famous songs to come from Caccini's 1602 collection. It was well-known all over Europe and continued to be popular into the nineteenth century when it was included in a collection of *Arie antiche* published by Casa Ricordi in 1885. That version, which was significantly altered by Romantic-era editors, is included in G. Schirmer's *24 Italian Songs and Arias*. (Online example 5-4 shows the nineteenth-century score in the low key.) ♪ If you compare that version to the version in the John Glen Paton edition of *26 Italian Songs and Arias*, you will see a more fleshed out accompaniment and some romantic period ornaments added to the Schirmer score. If you sing this piece from either edition, consider using a gentle, soft tone, adding some rubato, incorporating some *esclamazione* or *messa di voce* on the long notes, and perhaps a *trillo* or *gruppo* at the cadences. Understand the fast notes, or diminutions, in the last few measures to be Caccini's ornamental flourish for the final cadence. Now listen to the YouTube performance by tenor Fernando Guimarães on the companion website and follow the bare-bones transcription that accompanies the audio (online example 5-5). Notice how Guimarães uses rubato, *messa di voce, esclamazione*, varied vibrato and straight tone, and some added ornaments in the second statement of the refrain in the style of Caccini's final flourish. ♪

Listen to Julianne Baird sing another Caccini song from his 1614 *Nuove Musiche* collection, "Amore ch'attendi" (online examples 5-6, the audio, and 5-7, the score). This song has a simple declarative melody, written mostly in quarter notes, with a few faster eighth-note flourishes. In the second and third verses of the song, Baird varies and recomposes the simple melody by adding faster passages to the slower rhythms. You can also hear her add delicately articulated *trillos* to some of the cadences. She is using both graces and divisions in the Italian seventeenth-century style. ♪

Monteverdi's music is full of examples of both small and more elaborate ornaments that we can use as models for our own early Italian ornaments. In the motet "Laudate Dominum" from 1641 (figure 5.6), Monteverdi has written an extensive cadential flourish that includes running passages, *trillos* on one pitch, and the option for more decoration on the penultimate measure. Listen to the dazzling clarity and precision in Catherine Bott's performance (online example 5-8). She sings with a very pure and clear tone that was favored in late-twentieth-century performances of this repertoire. She decides to leave the penultimate measure of the "omnis Spiritus" section plain. In contrast, Philippe Jaroussky (online example 5-9) sings with more vibrato in places and adds additional decorations to simple melodies and cadences. He also includes many more instruments in his accompanying band. ♪

In the prologue of Monteverdi's opera *Il ritorno d'Ulisse in patria*, you can see in Human Frailty's opening declaration (figure 5.7a) that some of the measures remain very plain with whole and half notes, while others have small dotted and moving eighth-note decorations. In the section that follows (figure 5.7b and c), the character Time sings elaborate florid passages at mm. 49–51 and at m. 60 near the final cadence. You can use these shapes and patterns as ideas for your own decorations for plainer measures. You certainly don't have to decorate every simple rhythm, but you should feel free to add some ornaments if you think they will enhance the text and the drama.

Figure 5.6. Monteverdi: "Laudate Dominum," mm. 68–75.

The best place to add ornaments is at a cadence, for example m. 62 in Time's section above, or m. 20 in Human Frailty's. Countertenor and stage director Drew Minter has suggested some possible decorative patterns for a typical cadence in *L'incoronazione di Poppea* (figure 5.8). You can use ideas from Monteverdi himself, from other singers, or make up your own ornaments based on the patterns you see in the music of the period.

Figure 5.7. Monteverdi: prologue from *Il ritorno d'Ulisse in patria*, a) Human Frailty: mm. 9–20; b) Time: mm. 48–53; c) Time: mm. 60–63.

Figure 5.8. Italian cadential ornaments by Drew Minter: final measures of "Disprezzata regina" from act I of Monteverdi's *L'incoronazione di Poppea*.

Later Italian Graces—Appoggiaturas.   The two most important graces in later Italian baroque repertoire are the appoggiatura and the trill. *Appoggiare* in Italian means "to lean," and an appoggiatura is made by leaning on an auxiliary note. This usually adds dissonance to a strong beat, creating more contrast between heavy and light and a feeling of tension and release. Sometimes appoggiaturas were notated into the music, either as a small ornamental note, or as a regular-size note. Remember in "Sebben crudele" how Caldara wrote dissonant suspensions in mm. 23 and 24 (see figure 5.1 and online example 5-1). These all act as written-out appoggiaturas. More often, however, appoggiaturas were not notated, and composers expected that singers would add them where appropriate. You can add appoggiaturas by using neighbor notes or passing notes. Neighbor notes, either upper or lower, can add dissonance to a strong beat. The appoggiatura should be sung on the beat and louder than the main note. It usually can take half the value of the main note or more. You may also add decoration by using passing note appoggiaturas to fill in thirds or larger leaps. Appoggiaturas are also expected at cadences of recitatives.

Let's see how this works in the last eight bars of "Comfort Ye My People" from Handel's *Messiah* (figure 5.9). Even though *Messiah* was composed in Dublin and the text is in English, this masterpiece of the high baroque showcases the best of Handel's Italian-opera style. You can add an upper neighbor note F♯ appoggiatura on the first syllable of "wilderness" in m. 32. Just replace the first dotted eighth note E with an F♯. On the downbeat of m. 34, you can add a passing note D♯ for the first quarter note of "Lord." In the next measure, you can add either a lower neighbor note appoggiatura by repeating the B on the first syllable of "desert" or sing a D♯ for an upper neighbor note appoggiatura. For the final cadence, you should add a passing note between the C♯ and A so you have a nice stressed and dissonant B on the downbeat of the last measure. A common convention is for the continuo to wait until the voice is finished before playing the last two chords, but some continuo players and conductors prefer to play them as written. These suggestions show the variety of possibilities for adding appoggiaturas.

Figure 5.9. Handel: "Comfort Ye My People," mm. 30–37, from *Messiah*.

Later Italian Graces—Trills.   The trill is the other essential Italian grace. Sometimes it was notated and sometimes not. By the late seventeenth and early eighteenth centuries, this ornament always used two pitches alternating and usually started on the upper note. It was expected at major cadences in arias but could also be added to decorate internal melodies as well. It could also be combined with appoggiaturas and other preceding and concluding figures. Remember that dissonant notes add more expression and get more emphasis, so it is best to start a trill on a dissonant upper neighbor note. In "Sebben crudele," (figure 5.1, online example 5-1) you can add a trill for the cadence in mm. 25–26, and since you are already singing the upper note on the first beat of m. 25, start the trill by reemphasizing the G on beat 2, alternate between G and F♯ on the second syllable of "voglio," and conclude on the E of "amar."

Later Italian Divisions and Improvised Variations. Italian singers in the late baroque were celebrated all over Europe for their virtuosic display of dazzling improvised variations. The da capo aria, whether in opera or cantata, was the place to show off vocal and compositional skills. There are a number of things you can do to embellish da capo arias: add a few small decorations, including trills and appoggiaturas, to the initial A section, add a few small things to the B section, including some recomposition of the melody, add extensive decorations and divisions to recompose the melodic material in the return of the A section, and finish with a thrilling cadenza for the final cadence.

As we learned before, divisions can be used to fill in slower rhythms with faster notes. You can also reshape the contours of a fast melody to vary the patterns and add variety. Your variations must go with the harmony and follow traditional voice leading rules.[6] You should also maintain the character of the piece and, as always, use the text for inspiration and guidance. Slow, introspective arias will benefit from certain kinds of ornaments while fast, bravura arias will demand others.

Let's look at two examples. We are fortunate to be able to see some ornaments for an aria by Handel that may have been written by the composer himself. Figure 5.10 shows an aria from his opera *Ottone*, transcribed from a manuscript with added embellishments. Many such ornamented manuscripts exist, and they are fascinating to study.[7] You can see both smaller and more extensive adjustments to the melodic shape and rhythm. Listen to a recording of this aria online by Iwona Sobotka singing with the period instrument orchestra The Academy of Ancient Music (online example 5-10), and compare her variations and ornaments to those in the manuscript. (The aria starts at 1'03", and the ornamented da capo starts at 5'10".) Sobotka sings this adagio-style aria with a modern operatic vocal production, but she adds graces, diminutions, varies her vibrato, and uses a variety of articulations to bring a baroque style to her performance. We will talk more about singing with period instruments in chapter 6. ♪

Listen online to countertenor Bejun Mehta sing the fast bravura aria "Fammi combattere" from *Orlando* (online example 5-11 is the video, and 5–12 is the score). In the initial A section of this allegro-style aria, he sings mostly what Handel wrote with some added trills at cadences.

Figure 5.10. Handel: "Affanni del pensier" from *Ottone* (1723), mm. 7–17, transcription of ornaments in *G. F. Handel: Three Ornamented Arias*, ed. Winton Dean, Oxford University Press, 1976.

Mehta also adds a few small decorations and variations and a small cadenza in the B section. The da capo is where he really shows off with exciting and unexpected variations that reveal his range and flexibility. ♪

Cadenzas. A cadenza is an extended flourish at the final cadence. We saw that in the early seventeenth century it was already popular to add something special at the final cadence. As the baroque era progressed, singers started adding more and more to their final flourishes until the entire orchestra had to stop and wait for them to finish. Treatises and critics of the time advised that cadenzas should be performed all in one breath on the penultimate syllable. At the least, you should remember to add a trill to the final cadence. In addition, you can include a few extra notes before the trill, perhaps showing off a higher part of your range. You can also include some thematic material from the aria itself, or add some new and unexpected notes that haven't been heard yet. As with other diminutions, your cadenza must follow voice-leading rules and follow the harmony. You should also maintain the character of the aria and use the text for inspiration.

The best way to learn how to ornament Italian baroque arias is to listen to and look at as many examples of this kind of ornamentation as you can from other singers, teachers, and historical sources. Some singers in the baroque era improvised different ornaments every time they performed. Others wrote out customized ornaments, and we are very lucky to be able to study surviving examples of these. Start small by copying a few things that you have seen or heard, and then try making up your own. Write out the ornaments that you want to try and practice them. You don't have to improvise ornaments on the fly, although if you sing multiple performances of *Messiah* every season, you may want to give it a shot. The more you experiment, the easier it will get.

England

At the beginning of the baroque era, England was known for Shakespeare and other illustrious poets and dramatists. More treatises about oration, gesture, and acting survive from this time than works about singing. However, by the mid-seventeenth century, Caccini's *Le nuove musiche* had been translated into English and was widely known.

British composers and singers incorporated Italian approaches to ornamentation and declamation. French dance forms were also popular
and influenced the approach to tempo, rhythm, and articulation in
English vocal music.

    English Graces. English ornaments, similar to the Italian ones,
fall into two basic categories: graces and divisions. Ornament tables of
graces, such as the one in figure 5.11,[8] list specific English names for
particular ornamental gestures. For modern singers, it is more important to recognize the musical figure and be able to execute it as an ornament than to keep track of what it is called. You will see these types of
gestures written into music in some cases, and you may also add them
to other passages that seem in need of further decoration.

    Figure 5.12a shows the beginning of Purcell's song "The Fatal Hour."
In figure 5.12b, I have provided a skeleton of the melody without the
ornamental decorations. If you compare Purcell's melody with the list
of graces in figure 5.11, you can see that Purcell has incorporated variations on the elevation, backfall, double backfall, and shaked backfall into
his composed melody. With these distinctions in mind, I would probably give more importance to the first G in m. 1, move lightly through
the sixteenth notes that follow, and make a strong arrival on the first F
in m. 2. That F is actually an appoggiatura to the E on beat 2 of m. 2,
so I would give it more weight and length than the sixteenth notes and
resolution that follows. I would also make sure my vibrato was small
enough to highlight the expressive dissonances: the G on beat 2 of the
first measure becomes dissonant on beat 3 as the bass note moves down
from E to D; the F on beat 1 of m. 2 is dissonant against the C in the
bass before it resolves to the E on beat 2. You can analyze the rest of
the melody in this way and make decisions on heavy/light articulation,
grammatical pauses, and use of vibrato, using the ornamental gestures
as a guide. Moreover, remember, all these decisions help to convey the
drama of the text.

Figure 5.11. Graces from later seventeenth-century English sources.

Figure 5.12. Purcell: a) "The Fatal Hour," mm. 1–7; b) "The Fatal Hour," mm. 1–5 skeleton melody.

English Divisions. We are also fortunate to have many ornamented manuscripts from the period that can provide great examples of added graces and divisions in early English songs. Figure 5.13 shows a transcription of the lute song "Why Stayes the Bridegroome" by Alfonso Ferrabosco from 1609. It includes both small added graces and longer florid divisions. The longer divisions seem to demand more time than the bass note underneath the original melody would allow. This probably indicated that the singer and lute player would use rubato and a flexible tempo in keeping with the Italian declamatory style. In contrast, figure 5.14 shows Purcell's song "Fly Swift, Ye Hours" in which the written-out divisions should be performed in a steady tempo and strictly coordinated with the bass line.

Ornaments written into scores and ornaments added to period manuscripts can give you great ideas about how to recognize and add your own ornaments to English baroque music. What we can't tell from

Figure 5.13. Ferrabosco: "Why Stayes the Bridegroome," manuscript source with ornaments.

manuscript sources, however, is whether the amount of added ornamentation was considered too much or too little. Reports from composers and critics of the time are conflicting. It is best for the modern singer to be familiar with what kinds of ornaments are possible and appropriate, and then make the choice of how much to add based on your own good taste. A simple melody in a slow to moderate tempo can probably benefit from a few small ornaments, while a more decorated melody in a faster tempo is probably fine as is. Remember that decorative embellishments that you add to the music or see written in the music are ornamental gestures. If you sing them this way, then you will be singing in a baroque style.

Figure 5.14. Purcell: "Fly Swift, Ye Hours," mm. 1–6.

France

French baroque composers and singers emphasized grace and beauty
over showy ornaments. They preferred precise pronunciation of the
poetry with elegance and good taste to what they thought of as vulgar
Italian bravura. Lovely phrasing and gentle rhythms inspired by court
dances give French music its distinct character. Florid diminutions
are much less common, and while some appoggiaturas are notated in
French scores, most ornaments are trills indicated by a simple "+" or
"t." The performer may decide the specific ornament to add based on
the needs of the text and drama.

Figure 5.15 shows a table of some of the most basic ornaments from
eighteenth-century sources, including Montéclair's *Principles of Music*,
Michel Corrette's *The Perfect Mastersinger*, and Bérard's treatise *On
the Art of Singing*.[9] (You can also see a manuscript of *Principes de musique* in online example 5-13.) ♪

Figure 5.15 examples a through e show various kinds of appoggiaturas that can be written as small notes, or added in similar kinds of
places when not notated. They can be performed stressed and on the
beat or lighter and before the beat depending on the meaning of the
word and length of the syllable. Examples f though j are trills, usually
written in scores as "+" or "t." These are most often started on the upper note and can be longer or shorter depending on the context. It is
important to distinguish a note that trembles with a gentle, short trill
from a note that fluctuates with vibrato.

French Ornaments in Recitatives. Figure 5.16 from Jean-
Philippe Rameau's *Le berger fidèle* shows how various ornaments can
function in a recitative. In the first measure, the trill on "Ber-*ger*" can
start on the C of the preceding syllable and be quite short. In this way,
you won't disturb the flow of the line to the half cadence on the downbeat of the second measure. Here, though no ornament is indicated,
you could add a *port de voix*, or rising appoggiatura (figure 5.15b), by
approaching the D on "pré-*sen*-te" from the C below. In m. 3, you can
give dramatic color to "fu-*ne*-ste" by starting the trill on the G of the
preceding note. At the full cadence in m. 4, you can add a *coulé*, or passing appoggiatura, on the beat. Because of the fermata, you can take your
time with the expressive dissonance of the F moving to the E♭. The trill
on the downbeat of m. 6 can start on G as it passes from the A of the

Figure 5.15. French ornaments from eighteenth-century sources.

Figure 5.16. Rameau: *Le berger fidèle*, recitative no. 5, from *Cantatas Book I* (1728).

preceding syllable. The length and speed of the trill should reflect the word "content." Likewise, in mm. 7 and 8 for "rare" and "beau," you can use prepared trills to highlight each word and fill in the elongated note values. Or you may decide to save a longer trill for "beau" and choose a different inflection for "rare."

French Ornaments in Arias. In Montéclair's cantata *Ariane et Bachus*, we can see how ornaments in an aria are notated using small notes and the "+" symbol (figure 5.17). The appoggiatura on the downbeat of m. 16 should be stressed and on the beat to add tension and anguish to the word "cru-*el*." The small note on the downbeat of m. 17 functions

Figure 5.17. Montéclair: *Ariane et Bachus,* a) mm. 11–19; b) mm. 27–31, from *Cantatas Book 3* (1728).

as the appoggiatura to a prepared trill on the syllable "Mi-no-*tau*-re." It should also come on the beat. The small note attached to the second beat of m. 17 should come slightly before the beat, forming a conclusion to the trill that leads to the unaccented silent syllable "Mi-no-tau-*re*." It could also be seen as a *coulé*, or passing appoggiatura, and is a common rhythmic gesture, particularly for setting a final mute "*e*." The trill on the downbeat of m. 18 is also prepared by a written appoggiatura. In contrast, the trill on the next downbeat for the second syllable of "dou-*leurs*" has no written appoggiatura but should be started on a dissonant B from the previous syllable.

You can vary the speed and length of these trills to go with the meaning and character of each word, perhaps shorter and crisper for "in-*grat*," and slower and sadder for "dou-*leurs*." You might also add a passing note, by itself or with a trill, between the C and A♯ in m. 18 before the half cadence at "douleurs." In fact, when the opening phrase is restated by the flute in m. 30, this ornament is included. For more ideas on how to execute specific ornaments, look at how ornaments are notated in other vocal and instrumental parts of a piece. You get to choose, based on how you want to color and inflect the text.

Rhythmic Alteration.   All the eighth-note rhythms in this triple-meter aria, both dotted and plain, should probably be gently uneven and performed more similar to triplets. All the downbeats should get slightly more stress while the second and third beats of each measure should lead to the next downbeat. The dance-like phrasing, gentle *inégalité*, and delicate ornaments will give your performance an appropriate French style. You can listen to a recording of this aria in online example 5-14. ♪

Germany

Music in seventeenth-century Germany was influenced by the Italian style, imported by Italian-trained composers and traveling Italian singers. In the early eighteenth century, German courts and noble households employed both Italian singers and French dancing masters to satisfy the aristocracy's desire for the latest musical fashions. As we learned in chapter 2, however, Frederick the Great discouraged the Italian practice of elaborate improvised ornamentation at his court in

Berlin, preferring that composers would write more ornamentation into their scores. Treatises by his court musicians explained his rules and restrictions. Appoggiaturas and trills were still the most important small ornaments written into music. Instructions in German treatises dealt mostly with how to execute the notations found in scores.

German Appoggiaturas.   The trickiest issue regarding appoggiaturas is their placement in relation to both the main note and the beat. Agricola, Quantz, Carl Philipp Emanuel Bach, and Leopold Mozart all translated appoggiatura as *Vorschlag*, which literally means "before the beat." This implies that the ornament comes before the main note. It would seem to indicate that the ornament should come before the beat, but this is not always the case. As with so many issues we have looked at, context is all-important. In most cases, appoggiaturas can be performed stressed and on the beat and take half the value of their main note (figure 5.18a). Passing appoggiaturas can be performed more lightly and come before the beat if they are filling in descending thirds (figure 5.18b). Agricola recommends that appoggiaturas before a rest can take the entire value of the main note, which then resolves on the rest (figure 5.18c).

German Slides.   Other ornaments that come before the main note are the *Schleifer* (slide) and the *Anschlag* (compound or double appoggiatura) (figure 5.18d). In both ornaments, the main note is preceded by at least two decorative notes: in the slide, the decorative notes can come from below or above; in the compound appoggiatura, the main note is surrounded by decorative notes from above and below. These can be written as regular-size notes, small notes, or ornament symbols. They are often performed on the beat, but not always.

Figure 5.18.   Appoggiaturas and slides from German sources.

The alto aria "Erbarme dich" from Bach's *St Matthew Passion* is a great example of the different decisions that need to be made regarding the performance of appoggiaturas and slides. Both ornaments appear throughout the aria in both the violin and vocal parts, and they are notated in many different and inconsistent ways.

Figure 5.19.   Bach: "Erbarme dich," a) m. 1; b) mm. 16–17; c) mm. 19–20, from *St Matthew Passion*.

The opening of the solo violin melody includes a slide before the first downbeat and an appoggiatura before the second beat. In some scores you will see the slide notated as an ornament sign, in others you might see it written as small notes. Both these ornaments could be performed stressed and on the beat as recommended by Agricola, but they could also be performed before the beat. In m. 2 of the violin part, a slide-type figure is written in regular-size notes, leading the melody up to the second beat, clearly coming before the beat. When the voice enters with the same melody, no ornaments are indicated in the first measure, yet the written-out slide before the beat occurs in mm. 16 and 17 of the vocal part, as well as in other similar thematic figures. In m. 20, an ornament sign appears before the second beat of the vocal line (some modern scores leave this out), while the violin plays written-out slide figures in regular-size notes that clearly come on beats 1 and 2. So in some of these situations the slide should come before the beat, and in others it should come on the beat. In m. 20, if you want to coordinate with the violin rhythm, you can sing the slide on the beat, but in m. 17, you will both perform the slide before the beat. As we saw with the alteration of French rhythms, you will want to make decisions that seem to work for each situation.

Most of the appoggiaturas in the vocal part come before a dotted quarter note, which gives you plenty of time to sing the dissonant ornamental note stressed and on the beat. However, if you look at the violin part in mm. 16 and 17, you will see the same melodic shape written with both regular-size notes and small, ornamental appoggiaturas. Rather than trying to figure out why the notation is so inconsistent, it is more important to get a feel for the musical gesture itself. If you can use the ornaments to add expressive dissonance to a strong beat, go for it.

In the period instrument performance of this aria included in online example 5-15, note how contralto Delphine Galou varies her vibrato to highlight expressive dissonance, and how the ornaments are performed as decoration but always in service to the meaning of the text. You might also notice that the performers have chosen a faster and more dancelike tempo than some other slower, more legato modern-instrument performances of this aria. ♪

German Trills. If you see a trill notated in late baroque German music, note that it can be performed in a variety of ways: short, long, major, minor, slow, fast, and possibly with a prefix or a suffix. As with everything else, it depends on the situation.

Agricola gave practical advice for how to master a well-executed trill.[10] He recommended practicing with both a whole step and a half step and alternating the notes slowly at first, as if they were slurred and dotted, the lower note slightly longer and the upper note slightly shorter. This helps ensure that the main note is sung louder than the auxiliary note (figure 5.20a). Singers should then gradually increase speed and diminish the dotted quality, all the while making sure that the intonation of the two pitches remains clear and true. If you practice both whole step and half

Figure 5.20.   Agricola: trills from *Anleitung zur Singkunst*.

step trills, you might find that one is easier for you than the other. Eventually, you should start the trill on the upper auxiliary note. If that note happens to be dissonant, don't forget to give it more emphasis and length for added expression. It is also possible to attach an ending or termination (figure 5.20b) or a prefix (figure 5.20f). In a fast, bouncy aria, you may only have time for a short, fast trill. In a slower, melancholy piece, you may choose to do a longer trill with an expressive prefix or a slower conclusion. Trills that come at the end of cadenzas or on final cadences should reflect the dramatic quality of the music and the text. If no trill is indicated, you may certainly add one to final cadences.

Let's look at some examples of these kinds of trills. In Bach's "Et exultavit" (figure 5.3, online example 5-2), the only trill that is marked in most scores is the one at m. 69. This trill is decorating a passing note between G and E on the way to a half cadence. You are already on the upper neighbor note G when you have to start the trill, and there is not much time if you are using a lively tempo, so you can just gently lean on the G and then add one shake between F♯ and G before you sing the termination note E that Bach has written in. While Bach did not notate a trill in m. 50, you can definitely add one for this final cadence of the opening section. You should start the third beat of the measure by returning to the B of beat 1 and lean on it as a dissonant upper neighbor note to the A♯. You have time here for several shakes between A♯ to B. You can conclude the trill with a B that anticipates the downbeat of m. 51 or leave the end of the trill plain, whichever feels better in your voice and seems to enhance the affect and text of the piece. Similarly, in m. 80, no trill is marked, but you should add one to make the final cadence feel complete. Start the "*me*-o" syllable on beat 2 by going back up to the D from beat 1, lean on it a bit, and trill between the D and C♯. Here, Bach has written in the concluding anticipation note.

In the aria "Ei! wie schmeckt der Coffee süsse" from Bach's *Coffee Cantata*, there are three different kinds of trills notated in the score (online example 5-16 includes a score with the audio performance of the aria). ♪ The first one at m. 75 uses a passing note to decorate beat 2 on the way to a full cadence in m. 76. In a lively, dancelike tempo, you might only have time for a gentle emphasis of the passing note D and one shake before the second syllable of "Cof-*fee*" on the third beat. You have more time for the second trill in m. 88. Here you should start the trill by emphasizing the expressive dissonance of the G on the downbeat. Then you can add several shakes between F♯ and G before the next syllable on beat 3. In m. 137, you have even more time, the whole measure, in fact, to decorate the word "süsse" and show just how sweet and wonderful coffee is. Start this trill on the upper note E, which passes between the F♯ of the previous measure and the D on the downbeat. You may add a fancy concluding turn, or not, as you please. In the online performance by Emma Kirkby with the Academy of Ancient Music (online example 5-16), notice how she adds many extra trills in places where they are not notated. This performance also wonderfully demonstrates a dancelike tempo, heavy/light stress, varied use of vibrato and articulation, and the expressive delivery of the text that we have been talking about in this chapter.

NOTES

1. See Robert Toft, *With Passionate Voice: Re-Creative Singing in Sixteenth Century England and Italy* (New York: Oxford University Press, 2014) 43–77.

2. Leopold Mozart, *Versuch einer gründlichen Violinschule* (Augsburg, 1756), translated by Edith Knocker as *A Treatise on the Fundamental Principles of Violin Playing*, Second edition (Oxford: Oxford University Press, 1985), sec. I.ii.7, 33.

3. Johann Quantz, *Versuch einer Anweisung die Flöte traversiere zu spielen* (Berlin, 1752), translated by Edward Reilly as *On Playing the Flute*, Second edition (New York: Schirmer, 1985) sec. XI.10, 122–23.

4. Johann Friedrich Agricola, *Anleitung zur Singkunst* (Berlin, 1757), translated by Julianne Baird as *Introduction to the Art of Singing* (Cambridge: Cambridge University Press, 1995), 152–53.

5. Eric J. Dobson, *English Pronunciation, 1500–1700*, 2 vols. (Oxford: Clarendon Press, 1968); Timothy J. McGee, ed. *Singing Early Music: The Pronunciation of European Languages in the Late Middle Ages and Renaissance* (Bloomington, IN: Indiana University Press, 1996).

6. The most important rules to follow in this situation are avoiding parallel fifths and parallel motion to a unison or an octave. For more detailed information about counterpoint and voice-leading rules, see the *Grove* article on Counterpoint. There are also many easily accessible online tutorials from an online search for "voice leading."

7. Winton Dean, *G. F. Handel: Three Ornamented Arias* (Oxford: Oxford University Press, 1976); See also Robert Toft, *Tune Thy Musicke to Thy Hart:*

The Art of Eloquent Singing in England, 1597–1622 (Toronto: University of Toronto Press, 1993), 94–100; Robert Toft, *With Passionate Voice: Re-Creative Singing in Sixteenth Century England and Italy* (Oxford: Oxford University Press, 2014), 146–63; and Hellmuth Christian Wolff, "Original Vocal Improvisations from the 16th–18th Centuries," *Anthology of Music* 41 (Cologne: A. Volk, 1972), 109–17.

8. From Robert Toft, *Tune Thy Musicke to Thy Hart: The Art of Eloquent Singing in England, 1597–1622* (Toronto: University of Toronto Press, 1993), 102; and Martha Elliott, *Singing in Style: A Guide to Vocal Performance Practices* (New Haven, CT: Yale University Press, 2006), 36.

9. Jean-Baptiste Bérard, *L'art du chant* (1755), translation and commentary by Sydney Murray (New York: Pro Musica Press, 1969); Michel Pignolet de Montéclair, *Principes de musique* (Paris, 1736), translated in *Cantatas for One and Two Voices*, ed. James R. Anthony and Diran Akmajian (Madison, WI: A-R Editions, 1978); David Tunley, *The Eighteenth-Century French Cantata* (Oxford: Clarendon Press, 1997).

10. Johann Friedrich Agricola, *Anleitung zur Singkunst* (Berlin, 1757), translated by Julianne Baird as *Introduction to the Art of Singing* (Cambridge: Cambridge University Press, 1995), 126–50.

RESOURCES

Agricola, Johann Friedrich. 1995. *Anleitung zur Singkunst (Berlin 1757)*. Translated by Julianne Baird. Cambridge: Cambridge University Press.

Arnold, Franck Thomas. 1931. *The Art of Accompaniment from a Thorough-Bass as Practiced in the Seventeenth and Eighteenth Centuries.* London: Oxford University Press. Reprint: New York: Dover, 1965.

Bérard, Jean-Baptiste. 1969. *L'art du chant (Paris, 1755, Second Edition 1756)*. Translated by Sydney Murray. Milwaukee, WI: Pro Musica Press.

Caccini, Giulio. 1970. "Le nuove musiche (Florence, 1602)." In *Recent Researches in the Music of the Baroque Era 9*, edited by H. Wiley Hitchcock. Madison, WI: A-R Editions.

Carter, Stewart, et al. 2001. *Ornaments*. Vol. 18, in *The New Grove Dictionary of Music and Musicians*, edited by Stanley Sadie, 827–67. London: Macmillan.

Dart, Thursten, and John Morehen. 1980. *Tablature*. Vol. 18, in *The New Grove Dictionary of Music and Musicians*, edited by Stanley Sadie, 506–15. London: Macmillan.

Dean, Winton. 1976. *G. F. Handel: Three Ornamented Arias.* Oxford: Oxford University Press.

Dobson, Eric J. 1968. *English Pronunciation, 1500–1799.* 2 vols. Oxford: Clarendon Press.

Laurin, Anna Paradiso. 2012. "Classical Rhetoric in Baroque Music." *Konstnärlig Masterexamen Institution för klassisk musik.* KMH Kungl. Musikhögskolan. Accessed August 13, 2017. http://kmh.diva-portal.org/smash/get/diva2:529778/FULLTEXT01.

Lindley, Mark. 1984. *Lutes, Viols and Temperaments.* Cambridge: Cambridge University Press.

McGee, Timothy J., ed. 1996. *Singing Early Music: The Pronunciation of European Languages in the Late Middle Ages and Renaissance.* Bloomington, IN: Indiana University Press.

Montéclair, Michel Pignolet. 1978. *Principes de musique.* Edited by James R. and Diran Akmajian Anthony. Madison, WI: A-R Editions.

Mozart, Leopold. 1985. *Versuch einer gründlichen Violinschule (Augsburg, 1756).* Second Edition. Translated by Edith Knocker. Oxford: Oxford University Press.

North, Nigel. 1987. *Continuo Playing on the Lute, Archlute and Theorbo.* Bloomington, IN: Indiana University Press.

O'Dette, Paul, and Jack Ashworth. 1997. "Basso Continuo." In *A Performer's Guide to Seventeenth-Century Music,* edited by Stewart Carter. New York: Schirmer.

Poulton, Diana. 1980. *Lute.* Vol. 11, in *The New Grove Dictionary of Music and Musicians,* edited by Stanley Sadie, 342–65. London: Macmillan.

Quantz, Johann. 1985. *Versuch einer Anweisung die Flöte zu spielen (Berlin, 1752).* Translated by Edward Reilly. New York: Schirmer.

Toft, Robert. 1993. *Tune Thy Musicke to Thy Hart: The Art of Eloquent Singing in England 1597–1622.* Toronto: University of Toronto Press.

———. 2014. *With Passionate Voice: Re-Creative Singing in Sixteenth Century England and Italy.* New York: Oxford University Press.

Williams, Peter. 1970. *Figured Bass Accompaniment.* Edinburgh: Edinburgh University Press.

Wolff, Hellmuth Christian. 1972. "Original Vocal Improvisations from the 16th–18th Centuries." *Anthology of Music* 41 (Cologne: A. Volk, 1972): 109–17.

6

IT'S ALL CHAMBER MUSIC

"So shall the lute and harp awake and sprightly voice sweet descant run."

—Handel, *Judas Maccabaeus* (1746)

In this chapter, we will explore how to sing baroque music as chamber music. As we saw in the repertoire overview of chapter 1, seventeenth- and eighteenth-century vocal music might call for one singer and one instrument, or many singers and many instruments. In all forms, it should feel similar to an intimate collaboration between equal partners. In chapter 5, we mentioned the continuo group and figured bass. This chapter will focus on the specific information that singers need to know to communicate and collaborate with their accompanists. We shall also examine how to choose continuo instruments and the options of working with modern or "period" instruments. We will look at the complex issue of pitch and how singing with early instruments at baroque pitch impacts stylistic choices and vocal technique. In the midst of all these technical matters, we'll discuss how singers can be positive and supportive musical colleagues in both small and large ensembles.

THE CONTINUO

Lute Tablature

Most solo vocal music of the early baroque consists of a vocal line and a bass line accompaniment. As we learned in chapter 1, solo songs in the early seventeenth century could be arrangements of polyphonic works, with several lines of counterpoint condensed into an accompaniment for lute or other plucked instrument. Many nobles in the baroque period, and earlier, considered lute playing to be an indispensable social skill. The instrument came in many different sizes and shapes, with names such as the archlute, chitarrone, or theorbo, and it was a popular choice for solo music and song accompaniment. Composers of lute music used a form of notation called tablature to indicate fingerings for the complex contrapuntal texture. There is extensive literature on lute playing, and I include several sources in this chapter's bibliography if you want to learn more about it. To help you recognize this kind of notation, you can find a brief online introduction to reading lute tablature and a score of a John Dowland song for four voices with a lute accompaniment in tablature in online examples 6-1 and 6-2. ♪

Thoroughbass

For the amateur or less experienced player who found complex tablature difficult to manage, a song accompaniment could be simplified into a single bass line with a few added chords. This kind of accompaniment was known as thoroughbass, or basso continuo. John Dowland's 1603 collection of songs is titled *The Third and Last Book of Songs or Aires: Newly Composed to Sing to the Lute, Orpharion or Viols*. Similar to a lute, the orpharion may have been named after the instrument Orpheus was thought to have played. *Violas da gambas*, or viols, are the six- or seven-string predecessors of the violin family. Viols come in many sizes and ranges, are held between the legs, and played with a bow. A viol can sustain a bass line as well as provide a few chords. With the lengthy title of his 1603 publication, Dowland ensured that musicians with a wide variety of abilities and available instruments would be able to enjoy his songs. In online example 6-3, a reproduction of a period publication, you can see the lute tablature accompaniment under the vocal line, with a separate bass line opposite each page. ♪

Figured Bass

As a more simplified bass line became preferable to accompany the less contrapuntal solo songs of the seventeenth century, composers would occasionally write a sharp, flat, or a number above the bass line to indicate the harmony. This was basically a shorthand method for telling the instrumentalists which chords to play. Giulio Caccini explained this practice in the preface of his *Le nuove musiche* (1602): "I have been accustomed in all the pieces that have come from my pen, to indicate with numbers over the bass part the thirds and sixths—major when there is a sharp, minor when a flat—and likewise when sevenths and other dissonances are to be made in the inner voices as an accompaniment."[1] Some composers preferred not to indicate the harmony at all but rather trust in the skill and experience of the instrumentalist to improvise, or realize, an accompaniment to go with the bass line. Baroque musicians were expected to know rules of harmony and counterpoint and intuit the intended harmony from the melody and bass line. As the seventeenth century progressed, music became more complex, and composers added more numbers or "figures" to the bass part, which became known as "figured bass." Just so you don't get too confused, these "figures" that accompany the bass line are not related to the rhetorical figures, or "figures of speech," that we spoke about at the beginning of chapter 5.

The general approach to reading basso continuo or figured bass is not so different from reading guitar chords or lead sheet symbols in Broadway or pop song scores. These symbols are usually printed above the vocal line or below the left hand of the piano part: "G7," for example, specifies the bass note and the chord that goes with it. The player decides how to get from one chord to the next and what rhythm and embellishment to add. Similarly, in early seventeenth-century music, as Caccini described, a sharp or flat, or a number above the bass note, tells you what other pitches to play over that bass note to fill out the harmony. The baroque continuo player decides how to get from one chord to another and what embellishments to add. As the seventeenth century progressed, harmony, and the figures to describe it, became more complex. Continuo players brought considerable skill and artistry to improvising an accompaniment from the figured bass shorthand. While you don't need to be an expert at realizing a figured bass part, it is important for you to know what it is and appreciate what your accompaniment colleagues are doing. It can also help your interpretation and understanding of the text when you know where the juicy harmonies and dissonances lie, thanks to the figures.

Keyboard Skills.   It is always helpful for singers to have some keyboard skills as an aid to learning music. Playing the melody with just the bass line is often enough to get an idea of what the music sounds like. In fact, it is crucial for singers to be thoroughly familiar with baroque bass lines and understand how they interact with the vocal lines. Learning a few simple and common figured bass patterns will make interacting with this repertoire easier and less intimidating. Online example 6-4 provides a general introduction to figured bass notation from a Colby College music course. I'll provide some highlights below. ♪

A bass note without any added figure usually indicates a root position triad. A sharp or flat tells you to raise or lower the third of the chord. A bass note with a 6 above it usually indicates a first inversion chord with the third of the chord in the bass and the root of the chord a sixth above it. A common formula at a cadence is a 4-3 suspension over a dominant harmony that resolves to a root position tonic chord (figure 6.1).

These basic moves are found all through the operas of Monteverdi and other early baroque music. Beyond these basics, if you see a 2, 4,

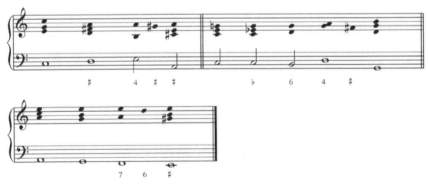

Figure 6.1. Simple figured bass moves.

7, or 9 above the bass note, it indicates an obvious dissonance that you will want to highlight. In general, the more numbers above the bass, the more likely the chord is a dissonant, or at least an interesting one that deserves attention. If you want to learn more about figured bass, I have included some of the many fine books on the subject in the resources of this chapter. Modern scores of baroque repertoire can include a bass line with figures, or a realized accompaniment provided by the editors. We will talk more about evaluating and choosing scores and the advantages and disadvantages to realized accompaniments in chapter 7.

Choosing Accompaniment Instruments

As we have said, baroque musicians had a lot of flexibility as to who played or sang what. John Dowland expected a wide variety of instruments would be used to accompany his songs, either for one or more voices. Plucked instruments, such as lutes or theorbos, came in a variety of sizes, which resulted in instruments with different ranges and tuning systems. Bowed instruments, such as viols, also came in many sizes and ranges, including bass, tenor, alto, and treble. Fretted as the lute, viols were played upright and between the knees, hence the term *viola da gamba*, viol of the legs. Singers could easily accompany themselves on a lute or viol, or have someone else play for them. Organs, with a broad range of designs and capabilities, were used for sacred music.

In the opera house, composers often requested combinations of instruments to provide variety and a richness of texture. In *L'Orfeo* (1607), Monteverdi called for three theorbos, harps, two harpsichords, organ, and a regal, a small portable reed organ. At the Paris Opéra in the 1670s, Lully used a *grand choeur* for the large instrumental sections and a *petit choeur*, including bass viols, theorbos, and a clavichord, to accompany the solo airs.

The harpsichord became popular for vocal music as the seventeenth century progressed, and singers often used it to accompany themselves. Later still, it became popular to combine a sustaining instrument, such as gamba, cello, or bassoon, to double the bass line, with a chordal instrument such as lute, theorbo, harpsichord, or organ to fill out the harmony. This kind of continuo team is commonly used for later baroque repertoire.

Harpsichords and Organs. For modern performances of baroque music, you also have a wide variety of possible choices for accompanying instruments. Usually, a harpsichord features prominently in the continuo complement. Today, harpsichords are fairly common and surprisingly easy to borrow or rent. They are more portable than you might think and many players transport them in their cars or vans, though harpsichords always need tender loving care when moved. Pianists can accompany on a harpsichord, but since the plucked action feels very different from that of a piano, a trained harpsichordist will bring more knowledge and experience to the collaboration. Similarly, most keyboard players can probably find their way around an organ, but a trained organist is usually preferable for sacred repertoire. If you are performing in a church, an organ and organist may be readily available. It is also possible to rent a small portable organ for a concert venue. If you want to sing lute songs, it is a delight to work with an experienced lutenist or theorbo player, though transcriptions of lute music also exist for guitar as well as keyboard.

Bass Line Instruments. The most common continuo team for modern performances of baroque music is a cellist playing the bass line and a harpsichordist filling in the chords. You can also use a viola da gamba instead of a cello if you know a knowledgeable player. Some modern cellists also play baroque cello and/or gamba, while other players specialize in viola da gamba exclusively. Choosing a bassoon for the bass line adds a different sound quality and type of articulation to the mix. Bassoon and harpsichord create one kind of character, while bassoon and organ create something very different. Hopefully, you can take into consideration the mood and dramatic context of the piece and, of course, the meaning of the text when you choose accompaniment instruments. Or you may have to use whoever is available, just as musicians in the seventeenth and eighteenth centuries did.

Different Kinds of Bands. Two online videos of *Zefiro torna e di soavi accenti* by Monteverdi show some of the possible choices available for early seventeenth-century music. Composed in 1632 and then included in *Madrigals Book 9* from 1651, Monteverdi's score shows a bass line and two vocal parts written in tenor clef. In online example 6-5, we see two medium to high male voices accompanied by a harpsichord, small organ, cello, and baroque guitar. The continuo group plays the bass line and some chords while the two singers sing the lines with text. ♪

In online example 6-6, we see a much bigger band made up of theorbo, archlute, bass viol, and percussion, accompanying two treble voices, a male countertenor and a female soprano. Two treble instruments, a violin, and a cornetto, join the band to insert instrumental versions of the vocal parts between the sung sections.[2] ♪

When my students performed this piece for a Monteverdi class I taught a few years ago, each soprano was also an experienced instrumentalist. One played violin, the other flute, and they both knew jazz improvisation as well. My teaching colleague played harpsichord while I played percussion to complete the band. In the performance, each soprano sang her vocal part, and then improvised instrumental breaks, both separately and together. It was a tour de force display that was great fun for performers and audience alike and totally in keeping with the flexible nature and varied possibilities for baroque performances.

OBBLIGATO INSTRUMENTS

As previously mentioned, baroque vocal music often includes parts for treble instruments providing melody lines that either double the vocal parts or provide a complementary solo or counterpoint line. Sometimes an instrument is specified, but often, the line can be played by a variety of instruments. A recorder can substitute for a flute, a flute for a violin, and a violin for an oboe, provided the music fits the range and character of the instrument. As we saw in *Zefiro torna*, instrumental lines can be added. Composers might also write solo lines for medium range instruments, such as an oboe d'amore, or bass instruments in addition to the continuo line. In later baroque music, it was more common for composers to write for specific instruments with distinctive sound and articulation qualities. In these cases, it is best not to substitute another instrument.

Counterpoint Texture

Obbligato instrumental lines are an equally important part of the musical texture. Just as singers need to understand how their vocal part interacts with the bass line, they also need to explore how their melody interacts with the other melody lines. Often there will be a give and take or a call and response. Other times the lines will be intricately intertwined in an intimate sharing of the melody. In many Bach arias, the voice sings an inner counter melody while the solo instrument has the main tune. Singers can always learn something about phrasing and articulation from their instrumental colleagues. Singing with a flute feels very different from singing with a violin or oboe. Phrasing and articulation will change with each new instrument. Instrumentalists must also study the meaning and phrasing of the text and listen to a singer's diction and breaths to decide on their own phrasing and articulation. Even with a larger ensemble, it is important for singers and instrumentalists to know how their individual lines fit together and interact with the text and the continuo. It is a wonderfully collaborative process, and every member of an ensemble, whether small or large, has something important and valuable to contribute.

PITCH AND TUNING SYSTEMS

Pitch was not consistent or standardized in the seventeenth and eighteenth centuries, and contemporary scholars have struggled to piece together the complexity of tuning in the baroque era. Organs in different churches and towns were tuned to varying pitches depending on their individual construction and pipe configuration. Organs varied in pitch as much as a fourth depending on which country they resided in. The temperature inside a church and its organ pipes could also affect the pitch, which might change as much as a whole tone depending on the weather. Lutes and viols came in all sizes, each with its own range and tuning system. Wind and brass instruments that survive from the period reveal still more evidence of widely varying pitch standards in different places. When instruments with different tuning systems and pitches tried to play together, they needed complex systems of transposition and extra crooks and valves to provide some common ground. Even though typical vocal ranges were much more standard and predictable than those of early instruments, singers had to adjust to the tuning systems of different instruments in different locations. Singers were encouraged, however, to choose songs and transpositions that would show off their voices in a comfortable range.

The standard modern pitch of A440 was established in 1939 at an international conference in London, but the tradition of using A415 as a standard for baroque instruments came into practice much more recently. In the 1980s, with the explosion of interest in early music and historical performance practice, players and instrument makers settled on 415, which is about a half step lower than 440, mostly as a convenient solution to the complex problems of establishing historical pitch levels. Some modern performers of baroque music choose even lower or higher pitch levels for various reasons, some historical, some practical. You should know that these conventions exist, and the choice of pitch for your performance of baroque repertoire will have a significant impact on the way your voice feels when singing the music.

WORKING WITH PERIOD INSTRUMENTS

Instrumental Construction and Sound

When performing baroque music, you may have a choice about what kinds of instruments you sing with as well as the pitch level. Many combinations exist for modern performances of baroque repertoire. If you work with period instruments (restored original instruments or new reproductions of early instruments) you are in for a treat. Due to their different construction and materials, these instruments often possess a softer, gentler, and mellower sound than their modern counterparts. Thanks to the complexities of early tuning systems, many early instruments can create an interesting variety of tone colors and intonation, depending on what key they are playing in. Players who are skilled and knowledgeable about the techniques of these early instruments can demonstrate characteristic instrumental gestures such as crisp, detached articulation or the gentle rising and falling of bow pressure described in instrumental treatises. Singers can emulate the sound quality, color variety, and articulation of their instrumental colleagues. Early instruments tend to have a less brilliant and consistent tone than modern instruments, and because the total amount of volume from an ensemble of period instruments is much softer than a comparable group of modern instruments, you can sing with the gentle, unforced production recommended by early treatises on singing.

Baroque vs. Modern Pitch

Singing at 415 pitch will make a tremendous difference in the expressive and technical qualities of your voice. Singing a half step lower may afford you a more relaxed vocal production and sound and may allow you to sing with less vibrato and use more variety in articulation and color. The lower pitch may make certain ornaments easier to execute. It may also solve certain range issues, particularly for tenors singing French haute-contre repertoire, or countertenors singing English music. The opposite is also true. Sopranos and mezzos may find that some music sits too low or the passaggio notes are in an unfamiliar place. Learning music with a modern piano at 440 and then rehearsing with a harpsichord at 415 will undoubtedly prove frustrating for both ear and vocal tract, and I don't recommend it. If you know you will be performing a work at 415, plan to learn and practice it at the lower pitch.

Harpsichords and Pianos

Harpsichords are frequently tuned to 440 as well, and some are transposable between 440 and 415, so make sure you know what pitch will be used before you start to practice. Occasionally, you may have to sing a performance of *Messiah* at 415 one weekend and 440 the next. This can cause utter confusion for your breath support and placement, but it might be unavoidable. In this case, practice both "versions" of the music: one high and the other a half step lower. Some of my students were preparing for a performance of *Messiah* using period instruments at 415. They had an opportunity to sing for a guest teacher the day before the performance. Unfortunately, the only space available for the masterclass had a piano tuned to 440. While not an ideal situation, the singers coped bravely and learned a lot about the subtle differences of singing with period instruments and modern ones.

Some modern performances of baroque repertoire use a combination or hybrid approach. Modern string instruments using gut strings and baroque bows can achieve some of the articulation and sound quality of early instruments but at modern pitch. In this case you will want to match the articulation style of the instruments you are working with but at the higher pitch level. All of these scenarios are possible and workable if you are ready for them.

PERFORMANCE SPACES

The space you perform in also impacts the choices you make about articulation, phrasing, vibrato, and volume. Much of the music of the period was intended for intimate spaces. Opera houses of the day were typically smaller than modern theaters. Performers in courts and stately homes often entertained small gatherings. In contrast, some court festivities called for extravagant productions of lavish entertainments with large forces, sometimes performing outside. While some baroque churches may have been large, composers knew how to take advantage of the acoustics, and singers knew how to fill the space without forcing.

Modern performances of baroque music can take place in a wide variety of spaces, including churches large and small, concert halls, opera houses, or recital spaces, private homes, or other small venues. Depending on the acoustics of the space, you may be able to sing with a soft and gentle approach, or you may have to project with a more full-bodied sound. If the acoustic is very live, as in a church, sing with less vibrato, which will clarify intonation and ornaments. You may also need to sing with a more detached articulation to make rhythm and phrasing clear. If the space is large and dry, you may be able to get away with more legato phrasing and slightly more vibrato, while still including the style elements we talked about in chapter 5.

LARGE AND SMALL COMBINATIONS

The combination of performance space and accompanying instruments provides still more possible approaches. If you are singing in a small space, accompanied by two or three instrumentalists playing period instruments, you can most likely sing with less sound and more of the style elements we talked about earlier. If you take part in a production of a Handel opera, presented in a large opera house, accompanied by a modern orchestra at modern pitch, you may want to bring a more modern operatic vocal production to the project. However, modern opera companies are becoming more knowledgeable about baroque opera, and if you sing with an appropriate stylistic approach, your colleagues will most likely appreciate it. Performances of *Messiah* and the Bach *Passions* come in all sizes and approaches as well: large choruses and orchestras with opera singer soloists in large concert halls; chamber choirs and period instruments with soloists from the choir performing in small churches; and everything in between. Keep in mind that you can adapt your vocal approach to the acoustic and performance space, while still incorporating elements of baroque style.

Leading and Following

The size of the ensemble has an impact on other elements as well. If you are singing lute songs with one other player, this is the most intimate kind of music-making and, hopefully, you will share in the decision-making and leadership roles. If you and your accompanist get used to working together, you may get to the point where you can make musical and expressive choices without even talking about them. In a small chamber ensemble, it is a wonderful feeling when everyone can contribute equally to decisions about repertoire, musicality, and style. Sometimes, the keyboard player or first violinist may act as a leader of the group. Often, the founder of the ensemble, or the concert organizer, will take more responsibility. Whatever the situation, I recommend that you be open and flexible about who is in charge of the ensemble.

A larger ensemble will likely have a conductor who will either lead from a podium, as modern conductors do, or from the keyboard or other instrument. Conductors may make decisions about tempo and ornamentation, or they may ask for your input and expect you to come with your own ornaments already worked out. Instrumental leaders may want to make decisions about repertoire and instrumentation. If they know more about historical performance practice than you do, it is a great opportunity to learn from their experience. You should always bring your own ideas to the rehearsal process and be ready to collaborate, compromise, or acquiesce depending on the chemistry of the group.

Chamber Music

As the title of this chapter states, most of the vocal repertoire of the baroque era is chamber music. Even in large-scale works, individual arias often call for small forces of continuo and one or two other obbligato instruments. You should approach each opportunity to sing baroque repertoire as if it is chamber music. In this kind of music, everyone must be aware of what their own part and the other parts are contributing to the whole; sometimes you are leading, and sometimes you are following; sometimes you are the prominent line, and sometimes you are an accompanying line; there should always be give-and-take. It can be a very intimate and supportive environment in which to make music.

BEING A GOOD COLLEAGUE AND OTHER PRACTICAL MATTERS

With any kind of music-making, it is always important to be a good colleague. This will surely include being a good listener, letting each member of the group express their thoughts, opinions, and musical needs without interrupting, and then contributing your own input. As a solo singer, you can often show the group what you need just by the way you sing without having to get into any discussion at all. In other instances, you can ask for more time to breath here or a faster tempo there. You can help the instrumentalists by translating the text for them and explaining the dramatic character of the piece. You should also warn instrumentalists about any ornaments and cadenzas you will do and practice getting in and out of places where you want to pause for vocal showmanship. However, remember that even if your vocal display is soloistic and showy, you are still part of an ensemble in which everyone contributes something important.

With most ensembles, I like to come on and off stage with the instrumentalists, bow together before and after the music, and wait patiently while they tune. This might take longer with period instruments than with modern ones, as the instruments and strings are more sensitive. In a larger ensemble or an opera production, the singers and conductor may come on and off separately from the orchestra. In these cases, you should defer to the conductor or director.

I usually hold music in a folder or use a music stand for chamber music, though you could certainly have your music memorized. For concerts of opera arias with orchestra, it seems to be more appropriate not to use music. And even though most *Messiah* soloists know those arias cold, it is traditional to hold a score, even if you never look at it! For Bach's *Passions* and other church cantatas and oratorios, it is common to hold music as well.

STAGE STUFF

Since its beginnings in the early seventeenth century, opera has held a central place in baroque repertory. Dramatic productions could be lavish and extravagant or small and modest. Chamber cantatas and sacred oratorios could also include dramatic elements. Many baroque operas also included dance. Modern productions of baroque dramatic works come in all shapes and sizes. Some productions of baroque opera include lavish period costumes and traditional stage effects—gods and goddesses descending from the heavens or furies and demons rising up from the underworld. As baroque opera has become more mainstream, however, productions with modern settings are increasingly popular, so be ready for anything! Your production may include a dance element. If there is a baroque dance specialist as part of the production team, you may get a chance to learn some of the basic steps and postures that laid the foundation for modern ballet. Or you may get the pleasure of watching experienced dancers work their magic. Modern productions may include dance that is in a modern style as well, or the dance pieces may be staged in a different way entirely. Again, be ready for anything.

Opera productions may be more modest, semi-staged, or even concert versions with singers and instrumentalists on stage together. Directors may also choose to stage secular cantatas or sacred works, such as the Bach's *Passions*, and transform them into dramatic settings or even ballets. Singers can be on stage as part of the action or even in the pit. Traditional or modern dramatic choices can be combined with period or modern instrument choices using baroque or modern pitch to produce still more possibilities. These days, anything and everything goes. Directors and conductors can choose to cast the roles that were originally intended for castrati with male countertenors, female mezzo-sopranos, or even tenors singing an octave lower. Once again, be ready for any and all possibilities. Moreover, even if you are onstage and the accompanying instruments are in a pit, or you are in a pit with dancers onstage, the music can still feel similar to chamber music if you approach it that way.

The remaining online examples for this chapter on the companion website include a wide variety of videos of baroque stage productions including traditional staging with period instruments, traditional staging with modern instruments, modern productions with period instruments, modern productions with modern instruments and period style, semi-staged operas, cantatas and oratorios, and fully staged oratorios. Please enjoy these and explore the many other videos and recordings available. ♪

NOTES

1. Giulio Caccini, *Le nuove musiche* (Florence, 1602), translated and edited by H. Wiley Hitchcock, *Recent Researches in the Music of the Baroque Era*, Vol. 9 (Madison, WI: A-R Editions, 1970), 56.

2. Monteverdi: Teatro D'Amore; L'Arpeggiata, Christina Pluhar, Virgin Classics.

RESOURCES

Arnold, Franck Thomas. 1931. *The Art of Accompaniment from a Thorough-Bass as Practiced in the Seventeenth and Eighteenth Centuries.* London: Oxford University Press. Reprint: New York: Dover, 1965.

Caccini, Giulio. 1970. "Le nuove musiche (Florence, 1602)." In *Recent Researches in the Music of the Baroque Era 9*, edited by H. Wiley Hitchcock. Madison, WI: A-R Editions.

Dart, Thursten, and John Morehen. 1980. *Tablature*. Vol. 18, in *The New Grove Dictionary of Music and Musicians*, edited by Stanley Sadie, 506–15. London: Macmillan.

Lindley, Mark. 1984. *Lutes, Viols and Temperaments*. Cambridge: Cambridge University Press.

North, Nigel. 1987. *Continuo Playing on the Lute, Archlute and Theorbo*. Bloomington, IN: Indiana University Press.

O'Dette, Paul and Jack Ashworth. 1997. "Basso Continuo." In *A Performer's Guide to Seventeenth-Century Music*, edited by Stewart Carter. New York: Schirmer.

Poulton, Diana. 1980. *Lute*. Vol. 11, in *The New Grove Dictionary of Music and Musicians*, edited by Stanley Sadie, 342–65. London: Macmillan.

Williams, Peter. 1970. *Figured Bass Accompaniment*. Edinburgh: Edinburgh University Press.

7

KNOW THE SCORE

"We write differently than we play."

—François Couperin, *L'art de toucher le clavecin* (Paris, 1717)

In this chapter, we will investigate how to find, evaluate, and choose musical materials for baroque repertoire, which takes more care and attention than you might think. As modern classical singers, we have come to rely on the infallible authority of the printed score. We have been taught to follow and execute what is on the page faithfully. However, as you have learned in the previous chapters, a score of baroque music is just a starting place and not a complete set of performing instructions. Performers are expected to add many elements that are not notated. Over the years, scholars and editors have attempted to supply this missing information as well as fix inconsistencies, decipher hard to read manuscripts, and make decisions about problematic issues. What we are left with today are many different interpretations of the original intentions of baroque composers, reflecting changing fashions in scholarship and performance practice. When you pick up a score of baroque music, you need to have a knowledgeable and critical eye.

Some of the questions you need to ask and choices you need to make are: do you want to work with an original manuscript, a published score from the period, a scholarly edition from the nineteenth century, or a more recent performing edition? Do you want to see an open score or a piano reduction? Do you need instrumental parts? Do you want a realized accompaniment or just the figured bass? Do you want to use someone else's ornaments or create your own? Can you recognize the additions made by editors so you can choose to take their advice or not? We will address all these questions as we look at the possible materials you can find in libraries and online. Toward the end of this chapter, we will compare different scores of works by a number of composers so you can get an idea of the process.

USE THE LIBRARY

When I ask my students to bring in a Handel aria or a song by Purcell or Dowland, they usually go directly to the computer and check online. While we will devote a whole section below to the resources available online, I'd like to recommend that the first place to look for scores of baroque music is in a library. The library will also have many other useful resources, including reference books, facsimiles of manuscripts, and scholarly editions. Please don't hesitate to ask a librarian for help using the catalog and finding reference materials.

Complete Works Editions

Research libraries in universities and music schools usually have complete works editions for major composers, intended for use by both scholars and performers. They are also sometimes called "critical editions." In chapter 1, I mentioned many of these collections in discussing individual composers.[1] Since scholarship has changed over the years, you will find that some composers merit both an "old" critical edition from the nineteenth century and a newer, more recent complete edition. As the title suggests, these complete editions, usually prepared by a team of scholars and editors, contain all the compositions by a single composer, presented with the most up-to-date scholarly information at the time of the publication. In many cases, these collections are noncirculating to the public and only available for reference. Often, however, they might also include circulating performing scores of specific pieces based on the complete edition. The Bärenreiter piano-vocal scores of the Bach's *Passions*, for example, are based on the *Neue Bach-Ausgabe* (NBA), the most recent scholarly edition of Bach.

Grove

If you are not a musicologist and aren't familiar with editions off the top of your head, the best place to find information about publications and editions for different composers is in the *Grove Dictionary of Music and Musicians*. This multi-volume encyclopedia can usually be found in the library, as well as online. Published by Oxford University Press, Grove Music Online is accessible through www.oxfordmusiconline.com where you will also find the *Oxford Dictionary of Music* and the *Oxford Companion to Music*. Your school's library will probably have a subscription to these online resources, or you can subscribe yourself for access. You might also want to check musical organizations—a benefit of becoming a member of the community Early Music America is access to Grove Music Online. We will talk more about these kinds of resources in chapter 8. Hard copies of all of these volumes can usually be found in a library. At the end of the Grove article for each composer, you will find a list of works, which details publications, and location in the collected editions for each composition.

So here is a bit of sleuthing you can do: look up the work you are interested in via the works list of the composer article in Grove; find the volume and page number for that piece in a collected works edition; then find that volume in the reference section of the library and look at the score. You may be able to make a copy of it if you decide you want to perform from this edition or use it as a reference to compare it to other editions you have found. You may want to check a particular pitch, rhythm, slur, or other articulation mark, or an ornament indication or text underlay. What you find may not necessarily be the last word on that issue, but you can trust that the scholars and editors who made that particular choice have brought considerable experience and knowledge to their decision.

Digital Catalogs

Libraries also house scores of specific works in a variety of publication formats. Unfortunately, you may need different sleuthing skills to find individual scores. Most library catalogs are completely digital, with search engines designed to search for books rather than music. This can make it difficult to find a score that is sitting on the shelf unless you request it in just the right way. Librarians are likely to know creative ways to use the advanced search features for their catalogs, so don't hesitate to ask a librarian for help. I recommend requesting general fields such as "Purcell/songs" or "Rameau/cantatas." While you may have to sort through too many results, it is better than asking for something very specific and missing it because of a misspelling or incorrect title. Library staff can also help you understand the information in a catalog entry for a specific piece to see if it is what you are looking for, such as a full score, piano reduction, or complete parts.

Evaluating What You Find

Once you have a paper score in hand, you will need to evaluate it to see if it contains the elements you want. Check if there is any scholarly commentary or explanation of the editorial process. Detailed notes may indicate a more knowledgeable presentation of the music. You can always look up the editor in an online search to learn about their background and credentials. The date of the score may also shed some light on the editorial context in which it was created. Scores from the nineteenth or early to mid-twentieth centuries reflect a different approach to scholarship and performance style than those created since the explosion of interest in historically informed performance practice in the 1980s. In general, the plainer the score, the closer it probably is to what the composer originally wrote. Tempo and metronome indications, dynamics, phrasing and expression marks, and elaborate accompaniments were probably added by an editor. While these may be helpful guides to shaping your performance, they were most likely not written by the composer, and it is totally up to you if you follow them or not.

Scores and Parts

Different kinds of scores may be useful in different kinds of performing situations. If you are working with a chamber ensemble, you will need separate parts for the instrumentalists. Many pieces you find in libraries happily include individual parts for the bass line, keyboard player, and obbligato instruments as well as a score. If you locate a score of a piece you want to perform with a chamber ensemble that doesn't include parts, you can always make your own. You will need to copy the full score and then "cut and paste" the individual lines into separate performing parts for each player. This is a bit time-consuming, and you have to be very careful not to mix up the different lines of music, but it is well worth it and necessary if you want to perform that piece. There are online tools available as well, which will be discussed shortly.

Some full, or open, scores use clefs to notate special ranges. In addition to the treble and bass clefs we are familiar with in most piano-vocal scores, orchestra scores use alto clef for the viola part and tenor clef for a high cello part or another middle-range instrument. These "C clefs" point to the line on the staff that represents middle C for that instrument. Vocal lines may also be notated with the C clef corresponding to their ranges: soprano clef with middle C on the bottom line of the staff for a soprano part; alto clef with middle C on the third line of the staff for an alto part; tenor clef with middle C on the fourth line of the staff for a tenor part; and so on. Some early scores also use movable G and F clefs, including French violin clef and baritone clef (See figure 7.1). Some scores may transcribe the line into treble or bass clef, indicating the original clef in the margin. Reading soprano or alto clef is actually not that difficult, but it does take some getting used to.

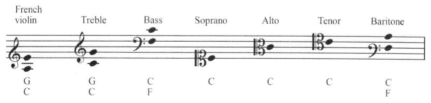

Figure 7.1.   Clefs.

Full Scores and Piano Reductions

While you may not need to provide the performing materials for the ensemble or orchestra with whom you will be singing, you should plan to study a full score of the piece so you can see each individual line of counterpoint. As we said in the previous chapter, it is important to understand how your vocal line interacts with the bass line and obbligato melody lines. If you are looking at a piano reduction of the whole texture into two staves, you might not be able to tell the difference between added harmony for the continuo and an obbligato melody line, or when your line moves in parallel or contrary motion to an instrumental line. If your accompanist is an experienced continuo player, they will probably prefer a plainer accompaniment so that they don't have to "un-read" the piano reduction. On the other hand, if you are singing a Handel aria as part of an audition or competition, your accompanist will most likely appreciate playing from a realized piano part rather than a full orchestra score or just a bass line with figures.

The same applies if you are singing Purcell songs on a recital with a pianist who doesn't know how to read figured bass. You might even consider using the realized accompaniments composed by Benjamin Britten. In the spirit of improvising an accompaniment from the figured bass, Britten created his own realizations for the Purcell songs he and Peter Pears included on their recitals. Dating from the 1930s and 1940s, a time when Purcell songs were surprisingly unknown and unavailable in England, the Britten realizations reflect a fascinating early twentieth-century approach to baroque repertoire. They should be understood and presented as compositions by Benjamin Britten, intended for modern piano, and not mistaken for just any Purcell figured bass realization.

Some Standard Editions

I am grateful for my colleagues' recommendations of standard baroque vocal music publications.[2] Bärenreiter scores are generally considered very high quality. Most are "Urtext" or scholarly editions based on original sources. However, even original sources can contain mistakes that may make their way into modern editions. Bärenreiter produces piano vocal scores as well as performing editions with parts based on the complete Urtext editions, including many works by Bach and Handel. I have a wonderful performing edition of Handel's *Nine German Arias* that includes an open score with vocal and instrumental lines on separate staves and a bass line with suggested realization. It also includes separate parts for the obbligato instruments and continuo bass part. Bärenreiter also features full opera scores by Handel, Monteverdi, and Cavalli, cantatas by Telemann, and much more. You can borrow these editions from a library or purchase them for your own collection.

Scores by Universal, Boosey & Hawkes, Breitkopf & Härtel, and Novello & Co. are also usually trustworthy, while those of G. Schirmer, Inc and Edwin F. Kalmus & Co. tend to have more mistakes. I have Bach arias in a Kalmus edition that is based on the first complete Bach edition. It includes separate parts for the continuo and obbligato instruments. I also have a Kalmus miniature score of various Handel cantatas based on the complete Handel edition from the nineteenth century. These inexpensive scores are handy to have but worth comparing to a newer edition. The collections of Handel arias and Purcell songs edited by Sergius Kagen and published by International are also useful in that they present many pieces in one convenient place with good piano accompaniments in both high and low keys. It is always wise, however, to compare these scores to a scholarly source to check for inaccuracies and mistakes.

The same advice applies to the volumes in the Hal Leonard Vocal Library series, including pieces in the *Oratorio Anthology* and *English Songs: Renaissance to Baroque*. These volumes present many well-known pieces in one place, but they are intended for accompaniment by modern piano and don't contain much scholarly commentary. However, the Hal Leonard edition of *26 Italian Songs and Arias* presents restored versions of the favorite songs included in the nineteenth-century collection of *24 Italian Songs and Arias*, which is still published by Schirmer. This valuable alternative collection, edited by John Glen Paton, includes reproductions of some original manuscripts as well as word-for-word translations, pronunciation guides, historical information on the sources, and suggested ornaments. It is fascinating to compare the same songs in each of these two editions.

Dover's vocal catalog includes many useful volumes of early music. Most are inexpensive reprints of nineteenth- and twentieth-century editions that also include explanations of the sources and other supplemental

material. *An English Medieval and Renaissance Song Book* has newly
edited and arranged works for one to six voices by a mid-twentieth-
century pioneer of the early music movement, Noah Greenberg.
(Noah Greenberg has also edited a wonderful collection of lute songs
published by Doubleday.) The two volumes of *Lute Songs of John
Dowland* include original editions of the four books of songs with original lute tablature as well as new transcriptions for voice and guitar.
Two volumes of *Monteverdi Madrigals* and a collection of *Palestrina
Masses and Motets* reproduce the plates from the nineteenth-century
collected works editions. Purcell's *Fairy Queen*, a reproduction of the
1903 Purcell Society score published by Novello, includes the bass line
with figures as well as a keyboard realization. The soprano songs are in
treble clef, but the alto and tenor songs use C clefs. Dover also offers
a full score of Purcell's *Dido and Aeneas* from the same Purcell Society collection. A full score of Handel's *Giulio Cesare* reproduces the
authoritative nineteenth-century Händel-Gesellschaft edition. Dover
also has reprinted a number of Bach full scores from the nineteenth-
century Bach-Gesellschaft critical edition. These are all convenient to
use and easy to find. However, remember to compare them to a more
recent scholarly source whenever possible.

Some Scholarly Editions

As mentioned above, Bärenreiter scores present the latest scholarly
research for a wide range of composers. Another fantastic scholarly
resource is the series *Recent Researches in the Music of the Baroque
Era*, published by A-R Editions. (There is also a similar series of *Recent
Researches in the Music of the Renaissance*.) Comprising almost 200
volumes, this series includes *Le nuove musiche* by Caccini in vol. 9, cantatas by Vivaldi in vol. 32–33, Montéclaire in vol. 29–30, Clérambault in
vol. 27, songs and arias by Barbara Strozzi in vol. 83, chamber duets by
Steffani in vol. 53, songs by William Lawes in vol. 120–123, and much,
much more. Residing mostly in libraries, these volumes may be noncirculating, reference only, but you can possibly scan them, make copies, or compare them to other sources. Keep in mind that some recent
scholarly editions are still under copyright and not in the public domain.

Novello offers full scores to Monteverdi's *Poppea* and *Ulysses*, edited by Alan Curtis, who is a musicologist, harpsichordist, and opera conductor. These are authoritative and easy to read. Beware that the bass lines contain figures but have no keyboard realization. A full score of Purcell's *Dido and Aeneas*, edited by scholar Ellen Harris, published by Oxford in 1987, also includes just the bass line.

Manuscripts and Facsimiles

Libraries also contain reproductions of original manuscripts or early published scores. These are sometimes called facsimiles. A great example is the seventeen-volume set of *Eighteenth Century French Cantatas* edited by David Tunley, published in 1990 by Garland. Bärenreiter has printed facsimile editions of Bach's *Mass in B minor* and the *St Matthew Passion*. Your library may have these in the reference section. Many facsimiles are available online as well. It can be fascinating and inspiring to look at handwritten scores and parts by the composers themselves or their copyists. Seeing the original penmanship or typesetting from a first publication can give an ineffable flavor of the period as well as the context in which a piece was originally heard. Facsimiles can also be difficult to read, confusing, and intimidating, but don't be discouraged. Scholars spend years learning to decipher early manuscripts, but it is easier than you might think and well worth a try.

Depending on the score, it may even be possible to perform from a manuscript facsimile once you get used to the idiosyncrasies of the penmanship. Clefs, rests, note heads, and flags may look different than what you are used to. Text may use printed or script letters that you don't recognize or old ways of spelling that are unfamiliar. Bar lines and spacing within a measure may be inconsistent and uneven. The more time you spend with the score, however, the more you will get accustomed to the unfamiliar notation. Adding your own pencil marks to clarify rhythms and text is, of course, invaluable. Comparing the facsimile to a more recent edition is also extremely helpful. You might even decide you prefer performing from the original. We'll look at some facsimiles when we compare scores shortly.

ONLINE RESOURCES

When you search online for baroque (or earlier) vocal repertoire, you must bring a critical and knowledgeable eye to what you find. The first thing that comes up may not be the best source, and it could very well be a terrible one, so you need to be very careful and discerning. Be particularly wary of scores from free sites such as MusicNotes, MuseScore, or SheetMusicPlus, and please take the audio accompaniment tracks that appear on these sites with a truckload of salt. Tempos, articulation, and ornament executions found here are not the best models. It can be helpful to hear the music rendered by a MIDI file, but it in no way represents how you would want to perform the piece. The site that comes up most frequently in an online search is the International Music Score Library Project (IMSLP), and you should certainly start there.

IMSLP

The International Music Score Library Project, also known as the Petrucci Music Library, named after the pioneering sixteenth-century Italian music publisher Ottaviano Petrucci, is a virtual library of musical scores in the public domain. Launched in 2006, it started out with scans of old editions no longer under copyright. It now contains over 370,000 scores from over 14,000 composers, including new compositions as well as new editions of older works. An invaluable resource, it is maintained as a subscription-based project. If you use it even a few times, you should subscribe and support the work it does so we can continue to benefit from this rich cooperative repository (see online example 7-1). ♪

When you search for seventeenth- or eighteenth-century music on IMSLP, you are never sure what you will get. You might see a complete works edition from the nineteenth century or perhaps a first edition or even a manuscript. Some works include both full scores and piano-vocal scores, as well as instrumental parts, transcriptions, or transpositions and even sound files. Tabs at the top of the search page for the work take you to listings for each kind of resource. You might also find a Creative Commons Attribution score, a newly made edition contributed to the site by an individual. As with contributions to Wikipedia, these scores are not subject to scholarly peer review or editorial oversight, but they might be helpful and useable transcriptions of earlier editions. You must bring the same critical eye to these sources as you would bring to a score you found in the library. The cleaner the score, the closer it probably is to what the composer wrote. You can also search for the editor online and learn about their background.

You may search for a specific cantata and find it published in a collection or search for a particular aria and find a full score of the complete opera or oratorio. Sometimes individual arias or songs are posted separately, but you may need to download the larger work and then scroll through it to find the selection you want. Sometimes you need to be creative in your search criteria to find the specific piece you are looking for. If you find a manuscript or an early edition, go ahead and download it. You can compare it to a modern edition you find on IMSLP or elsewhere, or you may decide you want to perform from it. If you don't find a modern transcription of the original manuscript, make your own! If you come across an edition that is still under copyright (some things from the *Neue Bach-Ausgabe* will show up on IMSLP with a warning in red), please do not download it. This is stealing, and it undermines the integrity of the scholarly work currently being done.

Occasionally, a work on IMSLP will be available only in score form, but you can make parts relatively easily using the automated tool known as Partifi (see online example 7-2). It may take a little getting used to, but it is quite straightforward once you get the hang of it, and you can either use a PDF of a score or import one directly from IMSLP. It's a whole lot easier and quicker than manually cutting and pasting lines from a score, and the end result is quite readable. ♪

WorldCat.org

WorldCat is a database of library collections around the world. You can search for a particular piece and see which libraries have it. You can also see if and where it is published if you want to buy a hard copy for yourself. Listings also indicate downloadable online scores with links to the sources (see online example 7-3). As with other digital library records, you will have to look carefully to see if the source is what you want. ♪

CPDL

ChoralWiki is home to the Choral Public Domain Library (CPDL), which is a free database of choral and vocal music in the public domain. Similar to IMSLP, it features vocal ensemble repertoire and includes compositions from the medieval period to the present. You can search repertoire by period, genre, composer, language, or specific piece. Digital scores are available to download in a variety of formats with explanatory information (see online example 7-4). ♪

SSCM

The Society for Seventeenth-Century Music (SSCM) produces a scholarly journal, a newsletter for members, and offers a free "Web Library of Seventeenth-Century Music" to the general public. Its growing digital collection features modern peer-reviewed editions of seventeenth-century music for scholars, performers, and students. You can browse the catalog by composer or search for something specific. The collection tends to feature more off-the-beaten-path things, but you can find downloadable cantatas by Scarlatti, Cesti, and others, and new works are constantly being added (see online example 7-5). ♪

Bach Digital

Bach Digital is a huge online database of research and source materials relating to Johann Sebastian Bach and his family members. Here you can find high-resolution scans of handwritten manuscripts by Bach and his copyists, as well as scans of parts and various editions of his works. There is so much material here that it is a bit overwhelming, but there are plenty of helpful instructions as you peruse the site. I recommend navigating in English instead of German by clicking the language choice at the top of the welcome page and searching for individual works by BWV number. This is the *Bach-Werke-Verzeichnis* catalog system created by Wolfgang Schmieder in the mid-twentieth century: the *Coffee Cantata* is BWV 211, the *St Matthew Passion* is BWV 244, and so on. Once you get to a page with a list of sources relating to that work, click on the blue links with an eye icon to take you to the manuscript pages.

Some sources are in other libraries, and you may be directed to click on an external-link button (see online example 7-6). ♪

The Virtual Messiah

The British Library offers a wonderful interactive presentation of Handel's original manuscript for *Messiah*. You can click on the high-resolution photo of the folio to turn the pages of the manuscript. Explanatory notes that appear in the corner elucidate each page (see online example 7-7). ♪

A-R Editions

The A-R Editions website features their complete publications, and it is searchable by composer, genre, or period in an easy-to-use format. You can see all the volumes of the different *Recent Researches in Music* series and purchase them online. Some individual items are download-able (see online example 7-8). ♪

Bärenreiter-Verlag

The Bärenreiter site is also very welcoming and easy to use. You can search composers, genres, or collections. You can find specific pieces in the complete works editions or search performance editions listed in the shop composers section. Most works are available for purchase, while some are only available for rental (see online example 7-9). ♪

The Early Music Shop

The Early Music Shop of London boasts that it has the largest collection of medieval, Renaissance, and baroque instruments and sheet music online. The site makes it easy to browse or search for music to purchase that might not be available anywhere else (see online example 7-10). ♪

Clifford Bartlett

The British editor Clifford Bartlett has prepared editions of various works for discerning performers upon request. His company, called

King's Music, now offers his editions for hire or purchase (see online example 7-11). He will also make an edition of something for you if you contact him. ♪

It's a Small World

The early music world is relatively small and quite welcoming. One of my colleagues suggested that you should not hesitate to contact the performers of a work that interests you and ask them where they got their performing materials. They may be happy to share a contact with you or let you rent, buy, or borrow their scores and parts.

COMPARING SCORES

In this section, we will look at many pieces and compare different scores, including manuscript facsimiles as well as old and newly published editions. I'll give you a tour through each score and point out interesting issues to consider as you build your critical eye and evaluating skills. In the companion website, I'll include examples of scores in the public domain and available online. I'll also mention copyrighted scores and let you find and compare them on your own. The examples cover a number of composers and works and go into a lot of detail, so feel free to choose the ones you find most useful.

Caccini: "Amarilli, mia bella"

We talked about this most famous song from *Le nuove musiche* in chapter 5. You saw the nineteenth-century edited version of the piece as it is included in the Schirmer publication *24 Italian Songs and Arias* (see online example 5-4), as well as a bare-bones score that accompanied an audio performance (see online example 5-5). Let's compare those two renditions of the piece to a facsimile of the first publication of *Le nuove musiche* from 1602 (see online example 7-12) ♪

The manuscript is in G minor and uses treble clef for the vocal line and baritone clef for the bass line. This means that F is located on the middle line, between the two dots of the F clef. We only see B♭ indicated in the key signature, and the time signature shows cut time or two large beats (whole notes) per measure. The first letter of the text is a beautifully decorative "A" to the left of the staff. You can see what looks like an "x" in front of the second half note in the bass part, which indicates F♯, as well as a small "6" above that note, a figure which suggests the harmony. You can also see an F♯ indicated in the vocal part, on the second quarter note of that first large measure. The pitches, with square-shaped note heads, are clearly legible, and the alignment is also quite good. When you get to "dolce desio, desser tu" in the text, you will see something that looks like an "f" to indicate the "s" in those words.

On the first page of this song, printed in the A-R modern scholarly edition of *Le nuove musiche* (see online example 7-13, scroll down to get to the first page of music), you will see a simple but faithful transcription of the manuscript. (A-R offers the first page as a sample, but the whole score is under copyright and not available to us here.) ♪ The editors have put the bass part in bass clef, which is much more user-friendly, but they have indicated the original clefs to the left of the staff. They have added bar lines to make counting easier with two half notes per measure. They have also indicated some possible vocal ornaments in brackets; an *esclamazione* above the first D and above the downbeat of m. 11 at "Credilo pur," as well as a *trillo* on "mio" in m. 10, in accordance with Caccini's instructions in the introduction of the collection of songs. The brackets indicate editorial additions not originally included in the manuscript.

Terence Charlston's transcription that accompanies Fernando Guimarães's performance in online example 5-5 also uses bass clef for the bass part and adds bar lines. He includes the missing E♭ in the key signature and the figures in the bass part but no suggested ornamentation. Guimarães adds his own. ♪

Now look at the nineteenth-century score again (see online example 5-4). The pitches and rhythms of the vocal line are actually quite faithful to the original manuscript, but the editors have added dynamics, articulation, and phrasing markings, tempo and metronome indications, breathing suggestions, and a realized accompaniment. They have also smoothed out the rhythms in some of the more characteristic ornamental gestures of mm. 21 and 23. In the manuscript, Caccini gives each note head its own flag, so the dotted sixteenth followed by a thirty-second note and eighth note on "Amarilli" is very clear. ♪

Figure 7.2. Caccini: "Amarilli, mia bella" a) mm. 21–24, 1602 version; b) mm. 47–50, 1602 version; c) mm. 21–24, nineteenth-century version; d) mm. 47–50, nineteenth-century version.

Terence Charlston and A-R have kept that interesting rhythm intact but added a beam for visual clarity. The nineteenth-century editors made the whole gesture into two sixteenth notes and an eighth, and then they added a romantic-style trill before the repetition for intensification. They also smoothed out the rhythm of the final cadential flourish on the penultimate syllable. In the Alfred edition of *26 Italian Songs and Arias* (which you can find on your own), John Glen Paton has preserved the original ornamental rhythms in the vocal line while suggesting possible additional ornaments, dynamics, and phrasing. He has also provided a realized accompaniment and a reproduced page of the manuscript. Figure 7.2 shows a comparison of the different versions of mm. 21–24 and the final flourish in mm. 47–50.

Dowland: "Weep You No More Sad Fountains"

The next song we will look at is from John Dowland's *Third and Last Book of Songs*, published in 1603. The first score (see online example

7-14) is a facsimile of the first publication. It shows the soprano vocal line with lute tablature under it on the left, while parts for alto, tenor, and bass are on the right, arranged so everyone can sit around a small table and see their line from a different direction. The soprano part is in treble clef, the bass part in bass clef, the alto part uses soprano clef, and the tenor part uses alto clef. The letter "s" in the text looks like that "f" we saw in "Amarilli." As mentioned in chapter 6, Dowland's songs could be performed by a single singer accompanied by a plucked instrument, perhaps a lute or an orpharion. A solo singer could also be accompanied by a bowed viol playing the bass part on the right page, joined by other singers, or any combination. When you see the score laid out this way, you can imagine such a gathering. ♪

Online example 7-15 shows a clear transcription of all four vocal parts in the more familiar vertical arrangement as well as the lute tablature. Interestingly, this editor has chosen to put the alto part in treble clef and keep the tenor part in alto clef. They have also added bar lines to make reading the rhythms easier. ♪

In the Dover publication of this song, David Nadal has put the soprano vocal line into treble clef and added bar lines to clarify the rhythm. He has also provided a transcription for modern guitar while preserving the original lute tablature with original bar lines below it. While this specific song is not available for viewing, you can get a sense of the layout by clicking on the "look inside" icon for the volume below, as there are three other Dowland song examples (see online example 7-16). ♪

Noah Greenberg, for his *An Anthology of Elizabethan Lute Songs, Madrigals and Rounds*, has provided a keyboard accompaniment that preserves the original bar lines and adds additional dotted bar lines for rhythmic clarity. Online example 7-17 from ChoralWiki shows a similar piano transcription, without the added bar lines, and transposed to E minor. ♪

Monteverdi: "Possente spirito" from *L'Orfeo* 1607

At the beginning of Act 3 of his opera *L'Orfeo*, Monteverdi wrote a tour de force aria for his leading tenor that included two possible vocal lines. One is very plain, while the other, notated just below, is highly ornamented. Was the ornamented version preferable, or optional, or merely a suggestion of the types of ornaments the singer should improvise on his own? We will never know the definitive answer to this question, but Monteverdi's score provides a fascinating look at the kinds of ornaments that were stylistic at the time. Online example 7-18 shows a few pages from a printed score from 1607. ♪

Orfeo's lines are written in tenor clef while the violin parts are notated in soprano clef and the continuo line is in bass clef. As you become more familiar with earlier notation and typesetting, you will notice how surprisingly easy it is to read the clefs and separate flags for every note head. Online example 7-19 shows a clean and readable modern transcription. ♪

In this contemporary edition transcribed by Damian H. Zanette, clefs are adjusted to treble and bass, long melismas are beamed using modern conventions to make the rhythm easier to see, and the original layout is preserved to show all the separate instrumental lines as well as the two vocal lines. The Bärenreiter piano-vocal score is another modern edition that also preserves both simple and ornamented vocal lines but incorporates the instrumental ritornelli lines into a keyboard realization.

Monteverdi: "Lamento d'Arianna"

In 1608, the year after *L'Orfeo*, Monteverdi composed an opera entitled *L'Arianna*. All that remains of the now lost opera is a single aria for the title character known as "Lamento d'Arianna." This was popular in its day and published in a variety of forms, including a setting for five voices in 1614 and a solo version in 1623. The opening section of the aria, "Lasciatemi morire," appeared in the nineteenth-century collection of *24 Italian Songs and Arias*. Due to the multiple sources, it is challenging to come up with a definitive version of the aria.

Online example 7-20 shows the version you may know based on the 1894 Schirmer edition. Notice the tempo and dynamic markings so typical of editors of this period. ♪

Now look at online example 7-21, which is a facsimile of the 1623 solo version of the aria. (Scroll past the title page to see the opening "Lasciatemi morire" section.) The D minor vocal part is written in soprano clef, with the bass part in bass clef. The bass line includes accidentals in front of certain notes to indicate the raised or lowered thirds in the harmony. ♪

Most interesting are the pitches in the last measure of the first line of the vocal part. Here the second statement of "lasciatemi" is clearly B, C♯, and D, instead of the more chromatic B, C♮, C♯, and D of the other version. (Figure 7.3 shows the contrasting versions of this measure.) The rhythm is slightly different as well. It is possible that this was a mistake in the printing that Monteverdi did not see or catch. You can see another mistake at the bottom of the first page in the restatement of "lasciatemi morire," which shows F on the last two syllables of "morire" instead of E. The final statement of "lasciatemi morire" is again B, C♯, D. Interestingly, it is this less chromatic version of the opening melody that made its way into the old complete works edition from 1913 in both mm. 4 and 17 (figure 7.3a). The editors did correct the mistaken F in m. 15 at the bottom of the page, however. You can see plates from this edition in online example 7-22. ♪

The newest scholarly edition of Monteverdi chooses the more chromatic version, based on a handwritten manuscript from the period in the British Library that clearly shows the more chromatic melody line with C, C♯, and D (figure 7.3b). You can see the facsimile and the transcription in volume 8 of the new critical Monteverdi edition. In this particular instance, the critical edition agrees with the choice the nineteenth-century editors made for the Schirmer collection, but many other choices about word underlay, rhythm, and harmony do not. John Glenn Paton includes the 1623 facsimile along with his edited version of the opening of the aria in the Alfred publication *26 Italian Songs and Arias*. He chooses the more chromatic melody for the opening and corrected rhythms and word underlay in line with the scholarly edition. The YouTube clip of Anne Sofie von Otter with a score in online example 7-23 uses the less chromatic version from the old complete works edition. ♪

Figure 7.3. Monteverdi: "Lamento d'Arianna" mm. 4–5; a) 1913 complete works; b) nineteenth-century Schirmer edition.

Purcell: "Music for a While"

Purcell's song "Music for a While," one of his most well-known and beloved, was originally composed as incidental music for a theatrical production of *Oedipus* in 1692. It was also included in the posthumous collection of Purcell's songs *Orpheus Britannicus*, published in two volumes in 1698 and 1702. As with "Lasciatemi moririe," there are a number of different versions of the song to choose from, and details vary within them.

To begin with, how you search online for the song will yield different results: asking for "Music for a While" will get you one set of results, while searching for *Oedipus* will get you another, and a search for *Orpheus Britannicus* yields still a third set. Also, be aware that there were various eighteenth-century printings of *Orpheus Britannicus* and that song appears in the second volume, so you may search through a volume called *Orpheus Britannicus* and be frustrated not to find the song!

First, let's look at a facsimile and transcription of the song as it appeared in the second volume of *Orpheus Britannicus* published by John Playford in 1702. You can find this on IMSLP. (I found paper copies of *Orpheus Britannicus* in my library reprinted in 1721 with the same plates.) Online music example 7-24 is the facsimile, and online example 7-25 is a clean transcription, edited by R. D. Tennent. ♪

Here the song is in C minor, though only two flats are included in the key signature. The bass line is notated in bass clef, and the vocal line is in treble clef. An important detail can be seen in the very first measure of the bass line. The third pitch in the repeating ground bass sequence has a flat sign in front of it. When the next A appears on the sixth eighth note of the first measure, no flat sign is given. This then creates a question for performers and editors: should that note be A♭ or A♮? (See figure 7.4a.) Does the accidental sign apply for the whole measure or just for the note on which it is written? While nowadays we assume accidentals are good for complete measures, that was not the case in the baroque. Different editors have made different choices. Most performances you hear, in whatever key the song is transposed to, choose a half step higher for the second note, making a rising chromatic sequence that is heard in many other places throughout the piece. Many scores choose this solution as well. You will see scores, however, that make the second pitch match the first. Benjamin Britten chose this solution in his realization of the accompaniment.

The next detail to notice is on the third beat of m. 8. In the facsimile, the quarter note on "all" is a minor third down from the eighth note "shall" preceding it. Some scores, including the international edition edited by Sergius Kagen, lower the "all" by a half step, making this interval into a major third. Another point of difference comes in mm. 9–10 on "cares beguile." Here the melody moves down from E♭ to C, arriving on C on the downbeat of m. 10. Some scores repeat the dotted rhythm and melodic pattern from mm. 6–7 for the cadence in mm. 9–10 (see figure 7.4b). The next contrasting detail is the rhythm of "wond'ring" in mm. 10–11. In the facsimile, we see a dotted eighth and sixteenth starting right on the third beat of each measure. Some scores have this rhythm as a dotted sixteenth and thirty-second note starting on the second eighth note of the third beat (see figure 7.4c). One more interesting spot is on the word "eternal" in m. 19. The facsimile shows a whole step melisma from B♭ to C. Some scores lower the upper note, making this into a half-step oscillation.

So where do all these differences come from, and which ones are right? If you check the Purcell Society scholarly edition from 1961, you'll see the song included in the incidental music for *Oedipus* in volume 21. It is notated in treble clef and listed for countertenor in C minor. The bass line in m. 1 has A♭ then A♮, and m. 8 has A♮ on beat 3 for a

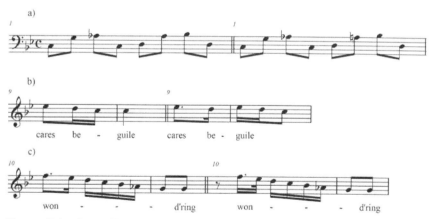

Figure 7.4.   Purcell: "Music for a While" variants: a) m. 1; b) mm. 9–10; c) mm. 10–11.

minor third "shall all." The cadence in mm. 9–10 matches the facsimile, as does the rhythm on "wond'ring" in mm. 10–11, and the whole step melisma on "eternal" in m. 19. However, if you look at the earlier Purcell Society complete edition from 1917, you'll see the details are quite changed. While the song is still in volume 21 with music for *Oedipus*, it is now written in alto clef and listed as an alto solo. As in the 1961 edition, the first measure chooses A♭, then A♮ for the bass line, and a minor third "shall all" in m. 8, but you will see the alternate rhythms for "cares beguiles" and "wond'ring," and a half step melisma for "eternal."

Perhaps the scholars at the beginning of the twentieth century consulted other sources that the later scholars disregarded. (The earlier edition lists at least four other manuscript sources in addition to the published version in *Orpheus Britannicus*.) We may never know for sure, but what this fascinating bit of detective work shows is that you should be ready for questions like this. As you look through the numerous free versions of this song that come up in an online search, you will no doubt find all different combinations of these details, as well as better and worse suggested realizations. Ultimately, you need to make an informed choice about which score with which details you want to use. Here are two more online scores in different keys, which use various combinations of these details (see online examples 7-26 and 7-27). ♪

French Cantatas

Campra: Arion, "L'Onde et les Zephirs." Not long after *Orpheus Britannicus* was published in London, André Campra published his *First Book of Cantatas* in Paris in 1708. Online example 7-28 shows a facsimile of two pages of the *ariette* "L'Onde et les Zephirs" from the cantata *Arion* in the 1708 publication. (If you search for an online score to *Arion* by Campra, you will get the IMSLP search page for *Cantates françoises*. Select the full score for Livre I, download the whole thing, and then scroll to part 90 to see the complete cantata.) ♪

The flute part, which is specified at the beginning of the cantata, is notated in French violin clef, with the circle of a G clef centered on the first line of the staff (see figure 7.1). The vocal part is notated in soprano clef, indicated by the usual C clef on the first line. The bass part has some figures both above and below the notes, with sharps notated by star-shaped crosses. The printed text includes the old f-shaped "s" and aligns only approximately with the notes of the vocal part. The alignment of the vocal part with the instrumental lines is also fudged to fit in as best as possible. In chapter 5, we used this *ariette* to discuss rhythmic alteration and the tradition of adjusting the contrasting dotted and triplet rhythms to agree. When you see these different rhythms printed in a modern transcription, as in figure 5.4, you may be tempted to make them clearly contrasting. When you view them in the original edition, you can understand how performers likely adjusted the rhythms to fit together and meet at the next downbeat. Ornaments are indicated by small notes in very light printing as well as tiny crosses for trills that are easy to miss.

Rameau: Orphée and Le berger fidèle. If you search for Jean-Philippe Rameau's 1721 cantata *Orphée* online, you will find it on IMSLP, in the old complete works edition supervised by Camille Saint-Saëns and published in 1897 (see online example 7-29). The score is easy to read in modern clefs with both a bass part with figures for the continuo and a piano reduction of all the instrumental parts. Unfortunately, IMSLP does not include separate instrumental parts so you would have to make your own from the full score. Ornaments are indicated with small notes for *port de voix* and mordent signs for trills. There are minimally added markings for tempo or articulation. ♪

Online example 7-30 shows the first three pages from a 1721 handwritten score by one of Rameau's copyists. The pitches and rhythms are fairly clear in treble and bass clef, and the alignment is not bad, but the text is difficult to decipher. It is interesting to see the various ways this copyist notates sixteenth notes: with a double flag, with a squiggly flag, or beamed together with a double line. You might not want to perform from this facsimile, but it is useful to compare to the Saint-Saëns edition or the new critical edition, *Opera omnia*, edited by the Societé Jean-Philippe Rameau, available from Bärenreiter and in your library. ♪

A search for *Orphée* by Rameau on worldcat.org doesn't yield many results, while a search for another Rameau cantata, *Le berger fidèle*, shows that my library has a facsimile of the score, and when you click the link, it takes you right to the catalog entry and the call number. It turns out this facsimile collection also includes *Orphée* (shown above). IMSLP has a very readable edition of *Le berger fidèle* from 1728 as well as the Saint-Saëns complete works edition from 1897. Online example 7-31 shows the search page for the volume of *French Cantatas* that includes *Le berger fidèle*. In the edition from 1728, it is the first cantata in the volume. In the edition from 1897, it is third. ♪

Montéclair: Ariane et Bachus, "Plus cruels que le Mino-taure." Michel Pignolet de Montéclair's *Third Book of Cantatas* for one and two voices was also published in 1728. Online example 7-32 shows a page of the first aria from the cantata *Ariane et Bachus* that we discussed in chapter 5. The penmanship is remarkably readable, with plenty of well-notated figures for the continuo and extremely clear French text and syllable underlay. Montéclair indicates a triple meter and even gives a tempo marking of Lent. The flue part is notated in French violin clef using a G clef with the circle centered on the first line of the staff. The vocal part is in soprano clef, with the usual C clef on the first line. Ornaments in both parts are notated using both small notes for *port de voix* and crosses for trills. You could easily perform from this facsimile. Compare this to Fig 5.17, and you will see a very clean transcription from the A-R edition. ♪

Bach

St Matthew Passion, "Erbarme dich." There are many scores available of the major works and cantatas of J. S. Bach. Scores based on the first complete works edition, the *Bach-Gesellschaft-Ausgabe*, are generally reliable. As mentioned earlier, vocal scores by Bärenreiter are based on the new critical edition, the *Neue Bach-Ausgabe*. Piano-vocal scores usually reduce all the instrumental parts into two staves, which may be convenient for some performing situations. Ornaments are indicated by smaller notes or signs for trills and slides (see figure 5.19 for examples of both). The IMSLP home page for *St Matthew Passion* (online example 7-33) has a wide variety of materials, including performance recordings and accompaniment tracks. ♪

Scroll down to see the sheet music offerings, which include full scores, facsimiles, and vocal scores both old and new. Click on the tabs at the top of the sheet music listings to see full scores, parts, vocal scores, or arrangements. Look carefully to see the publisher, date, and copyright information before you select the one you want. If the edition is in the public domain, you may download it. If there is a note in red that says Non-PD US, do not download it. A few selected arias are listed separately. For the alto aria "Erbarme dich," which is number 39 in Part II, you would have to download a complete score and scroll through to get to the right page.

Online example 7-34 shows a page of the full score manuscript facsimile from Bach Digital. The top line shows the solo violin part starting on the fourth beat of m. 6. The voice enters in the last bar of the top system. While it is difficult to make out the script of the German text, the notes and rhythms are quite legible. ♪

Online example 7-35 shows a clean transcription of the full score from ChoralWiki. There are a few details, including some ornaments and dynamics, which were not present in the autograph manuscript but were added to the individual parts by Bach's chief copyist.[3] We rely on the scholars to give us a complete picture of the composers' intentions. ♪

Online example 7-36 shows a free score from 8notes.com. At first glance, it looks like a serviceable piano reduction, but there are a number of mistakes and wrong notes, including the C♯ in m. 3, which should be a C♮, and a missing ornament before beat 2 in the vocal part of m. 20. The execution of the ornaments in the MIDI audio file is also not stylistic at all. I much prefer the audio accompaniment file on the IMSLP site. ♪

The version of the aria included in the *Vocal Library Oratorio Anthology* is quite good. It includes a minimal piano reduction with the violin part written in smaller type in the right hand so you can see it clearly. The keyboardist could play it if you didn't have a solo violin or easily leave it out if you did. The collection also includes a separate violin part.

Coffee Cantata. You can find a similar range of scores for Bach's secular cantata, *Schweigt stille, plaudert nicht*, BWV 211, better known as the *Coffee Cantata*. The IMSLP search page (online example 7-37) offers suggested recordings and a MIDI realization of the aria "Ei! Wie schmeckt der Coffee süsse." If you scroll down the page, you can choose from several full scores of the complete cantata from the nineteenth and early twentieth centuries. You can also see the composer's manuscript from 1734. The site also includes a nineteenth-century piano-vocal score of the whole work as well as a clean transcription of the soprano aria mentioned previously, in an open score that does not include a keyboard realization but does include instrumental parts. Remember to click on the tabs at the top of the sheet music listings to move from full scores to vocal scores, parts, and other materials. ♪

We also saw a clean transcription of the soprano aria in the YouTube clip in online example 5-16. ♪

You can also find free versions of the soprano aria online on muse-score.org and www.scoreexchange.com, but if you look closely, you will find that they are transcriptions for oboe and violin and thus don't include the text for the vocal part.

The composer's manuscript for this cantata is also available on Bach Digital (online example 7-38). Online example 7-39 shows the soprano aria by another copyist. ♪

There is a characteristic triplet rhythm that appears in the flute part on the second beat of the first measure. In both facsimile examples, when the voice enters in m. 22, the rhythm is notated as two sixteenth notes instead of a triplet. The accompanying commentary in both the old and new Bach critical editions explains that this very rhythm is a triplet in the separate vocal part, and it is the preferred reading. Consequently, it appears as a triplet throughout the aria in every score you see. Online example 7-40 is a link to the archive in Vienna where you can see the original part. (Once you get to the page, click the manuscript to the right and go to page 27 to see the triplet rhythm in the vocal part.) ♪

Here again, it is best to rely on the professional scholars to put all the pieces together and make choices about difficult and subtle issues. Conductor and Bach specialist Joshua Rifkin advised that Bach's parts "virtually always take precedence: the score, in most instances (and definitely with BWV 211), is where he works out his ideas; but it's only when copying or revising the parts that he'll finalize things (after all, it's what singers sing and players play that counts!)."[4]

Handel

Operas and Cantatas. Scores of Handel operas are readily available to borrow from libraries or buy online. If you search for a specific aria on IMSLP, you may well find a full or piano-vocal score to the complete opera, which you can then look through to find the particular aria you want. Some operas may list certain arias separately, as we saw with the larger works by Bach. Let's say you want to sing "Ombra mai fu," an aria from the opera *Serse*. Online example 7-41 shows the search page on IMSLP for the complete opera. You will see recommended recordings and synthesized MIDI files. Scroll down and you can choose a full score from the old complete works edition entitled *Georg Friedrich Händels Werke*, which was edited by Friedrich Chrysander and is very reliable. IMSLP also has several full piano-vocal scores from the nineteenth and twentieth centuries, including the new critical edition *Hallische Händel-Ausgabe*. The site also offers separate full and piano scores for "Ombra mai fu" in various transpositions. I would trust these sources more than versions you might find on the free sites. ♪

Scores of sacred and secular cantatas and oratorios are also available to buy, to borrow from libraries, and to download online. If you want to sing an aria from an oratorio or cantata, as with the operas, it is best to search for the complete work by title and then find the specific aria you are interested in.

Messiah.   As we said in chapter 1, most singers reading this book will probably have some experience with Handel's most famous oratorio, *Messiah*. The piece has a long and rich history, having been performed in one form or another every year since its first performance in 1742. Each production in Handel's lifetime used somewhat different performing forces depending on the location and the available personnel. Handel made abundant changes to the score, rearranging and rewriting many passages and redistributing arias to different singers. It is difficult to determine what changes were made for purely practical purposes and what revisions represented Handel's changing preferences. By the time Handel died in 1659, a slightly more standard version had evolved, incorporating changes the composer made in 1750 for the famous Italian castrati Guadagni, who sang some of the arias formerly performed by English female altos. A full score, published in 1767, further standardized the work, making it available to the general public. Mozart contributed an orchestration for performances in his lifetime that remained popular for generations. As the nineteenth century progressed, it became fashionable to perform the work with larger and larger forces. By the mid-twentieth century, new scholarship and an interest in authentic performance practice turned the tide back toward performances with more modest forces. Today, many different approaches are possible.

A search on Amazon will show you the variety of scores available for purchase, and you may want to own more than one edition of the work. The Schirmer piano-vocal score from 1912, based on the most up-to-date scholarship of the time, includes lengthy explanatory notes. It also reflects late nineteenth-century performance tradition and the standardized version of the score that was popular after Handel's death. J. M. Coopersmith's score, published by Carl Fischer in 1946, includes more commentary and revisions, as well as some alternative versions of arias based on original sources. The Watkins Shaw edition, published in 1958, the result of an exhaustive study of all the eighteenth-century sources, includes aria variants, suggested ornaments, and a minimal piano reduction with figures. This edition, with an accompanying volume of commentary by librarian and scholar Harold Watkins Shaw, changed the face of *Messiah* scholarship and performance practice to follow. John Tobin's critical edition from 1965 for the *Hallische Händel-Ausgabe* also considers the eighteenth-century sources but does not necessarily improve upon the work of Watkins Shaw.[5] Tobin's edition is available from Bärenreiter in both full and piano-vocal formats. Alfred Mann's full score from 1961 also considers sources from Handel's lifetime. Published by Dover in 1989, it is an affordable and up-to-date presentation of recent scholarship.

IMSLP has a wide variety of *Messiah* scores available online (see online example 7-42), including a facsimile of Handel's manuscript, the nineteenth-century complete works edition by Friedrich Chrysander, and the John Tobin Urtext edition, with a Non-PD US warning. ♪

I was particularly interested to see a Creative Commons Attribution score of Part III by Nicholas McGegan, conductor of the San Francisco Bay area's Philharmonia Baroque period instrument orchestra. You can also find a variety of complete piano-vocal scores, individual arias, and tracks of synthesized MIDI and piano accompaniments. The individual *Messiah* arias that appear in the *Vocal Library Oratorio Anthology* have piano-based accompaniments in the style of the nineteenth-century scores, rather than a realization of the figured bass.

Here are only a few of the noticeable differences between the old and new presentations of the score: the old scores include a version of "Thou Art Gone up on High" for bass. The newer scores have a version of this aria for alto. In "I know That My Redeemer Liveth," some syllable distribution and word underlay are different, particularly the setting of the final "first fruits of them that sleep." Many more details vary from edition to edition. For a more in-depth history of the work and its performance traditions, read the *Grove* article on Handel or several comprehensive studies by Jens Peter Larsen, Donald Burrows, and Watkins Shaw listed in the resources at the end of this chapter.

NOTES

1. The resources section at the end of this chapter lists complete works editions by the major composers mentioned in this chapter, as well as other scores mentioned in the text.

2. I am grateful to the following colleagues for their input on finding and evaluating scores: Wendy Heller is currently the chairman of the Music Department at Princeton University. A brilliant scholar and specialist in seventeenth-century Italian opera, she is the author of the Norton text *Music in the Baroque*. Gabriel Crouch, conductor and singer, is the director of choral activities at Princeton University, and he has contributed an appendix on consort singing. Sarah Hagenbuch, founder of Shoe Box Baroque Opera Company in Berkeley, is currently on the library staff in the Mendel Music Library at Princeton. Wendy Young, harpsichordist, is on the performance faculty at Princeton. Nancy Wilson, baroque violinist, is also on the performance faculty at Princeton as well as at the Mannes School of Music in New York City. Sarah Freiberg, baroque cellist, is on the faculty of the Boston University School of Music.

3. Frederick Neumann, *Ornamentation in Baroque and Post-Baroque Music, with Special Emphasis on J. S. Bach* (Princeton, NJ: Princeton University Press, 1978), 145–46.

4. Joshua Rifkin, email correspondence, February 2, 2018.

5. Donald Burrows, *Handel: Messiah* (Cambridge: Cambridge University Press, 1991), 53.

RESOURCES

Bach, J. S. 1949. *Arias from Church Cantatas for Soprano, with an obligato instrument and Piano or Organ*. New York: Kalmus.

———. 1954. *Neue Ausgabe sämtliche Werke (Neue Bach-Ausgabe)*, edited by Johann-Sebastian-Bach-Institute, Göttigen and Bach-Archiv, Leipzig Kassel: Bärenreiter.

———. 1974. *St Matthew Passion*. Kassel: Bärenreiter.

———. 1851–99. *Werke*. Leipzig: Bach-Gesellschaft.

Burrows, Donald. 1991. *Handel: Messiah*. Cambridge: Cambridge University Press.

Caccini, Giulio. 1970. *Le nuove musiche/Giulio Caccini*; edited by H. Wiley Hitchcock. Madison, WI: A-R Editions.

Campra, André. 1974. *Cantates Françaises: Arion*. Paris: Heugel & Co.

Cavalli, Francesco. 2012. *Opere*. Kassel: Bärenreiter.

Dowland, John. 2002. *John Dowland's Lute Songs, third and fourth books*. Mineola, NY: Dover.

Greenberg, Noah. 1955. *An Anthology of Elizabethan Lute Songs, Madrigals and Rounds*. New York: Norton.

Greenberg, Noah, ed. 2000. *An English Medieval and Renaissance Song Book*. Mineola, NY: Dover.

Handel, G. F. 1989. *Messiah: in Full Score*, edited by Alfred Mann. Mineola, NY: Dover.

———. 1959. *45 Arias from Operas and Oratorios*, selected and edited by Sergius Kagen. New York: International.

———. 1946. *Messiah: An Oratorio*, edited by J. M. Coopersmith. New York: Carl Fischer.

———. 1966. *Messiah*, edited by Watkins Shaw. Kent: Novello.

———. 1912. *The Messiah*. New York: Schirmer.

———. 1858–94. *Georg Friedrich Händels Werke*, edited by F. W. Chrysander. Leipzig: Ausgabe der Deutschen Händelgesellschaft.

———. 1955. *Hallische Händel-Ausgabe*, edited by Georg Friedrich Händel-Gesellschaft. Kassel: Bärenreiter.

———. 1981. *Neun deutsche Arien*. Kassel: Bärenreiter.

Larsen, Jens Peter. 1990. *Handel's Messiah: Origins, Composition, Sources*. Westport, CT: Greenwood Press.

Montéclair, Michel Pignolet de. 1978. *Cantatas for One and Two Voices*, edited by James R. Anthony and Diran Akmajian. Madison, WI: A-R Editions.

Monteverdi, Claudio. 2002. *Il ritorno d'Ulisse in patria*, edited by Alan Curtis. London: Novello.

———. 1989. *L'Incoronazione di Poppea*, edited by Alan Curtis. London: Novello.

———. 2012. *L'Orfeo*. Basel, Switzerland: Bärenreiter.

———. 1991. *Madrigals, book VIII*. Mineola, NY: Dover.

———. 1986. *Madrigals, books IV and V*. Mineola, NY: Dover.

———. 1970. *Opera omnia*. Cremona, Italy: Fondazione Claudio Monteverdi.

———. 1926–42; 1954–68. *Tutte le opere*. Asolo, Italy: G. F. Malipiero.

Neumann, Frederick. 1978. *Ornamentation in Baroque and Post Baroque Music with Special Emphasis on J. S. Bach.* Princeton, NJ: Princeton University Press.

Palestrina, Giovanni Pierluigi. 1993. *Masses and Motets.* Mineola, NY: Dover.

Purcell, Henry. 1958. *40 Songs for Voice and Piano*, realization of the figured bass and editing by Sergius Kagen. New York: International.

———. 2009. *12 Selected Songs*, realized by Benjamin Britten. Milwaukee, WI: Hal Leonard.

———. 1987. *Dido and Aeneas*, edited by Ellen Harris. New York: Oxford.

———. 1947. *Seven Songs: Orpheus Britannicus/Henry Purcell*; the figured bass realized by Benjamin Britten; the vocal parts edited by Peter Pears. New York: Boosey & Hawkes.

———. 2000. *The Fairy Queen, in Full Score.* Mineola, NY: Dover.

———. 1878–1965. *The Works of Henry Purcell: The Purcell Society.* London: Novello.

———. 1961. *The Works of Henry Purcell: The Purcell Society*, newly edited and revised. London: Stainer & Bell.

Rameau, Jean-Philippe. 1995. *Cantates Françaises: copies manuscrites.* Courlay, France: Edition J. M. Fuzeau.

———. 1895–1924. *Oeuvres complètes*, edited by C. Saint-Saëns. Paris: Durand.

———. 1964. *Recent Researches in Music of the Baroque Era.* Madison, WI: A-R Editions.

Shaw, Watkins. 1965. *A Textual and Historical Companion to Handel's "Messiah."* London: Novello.

Tarling, Judy. 2014. *Handel's Messiah: A Rhetorical Guide.* St. Albans, UK: Corda Music Publications.

Telemann, Georg Philipp. 1950. *Musikalische Werke.* Kassel: Bärenreiter and Gesellschaft für Musikforschung.

Tunley, David, ed. 1990. *Eighteenth Century French Cantatas.* New York: Garland.

8

USING ALL THE TOOLS

"Where 'ere you walk, cool gales shall fan the glade."

—Handel, *Semele* (1744)

Now that you have learned about early music repertoire and some of the stylistic and research tools you need to sing it, you will need to decide when and where to put this information into practice. There are many opportunities to sing early music whether you are a student, an amateur or a professional, a soloist or an ensemble member, in sacred or secular settings. This chapter will provide a map of sorts with suggestions about where you might go to learn more and get involved in performing early music. In previous chapters, we focused mostly on the solo singer in the repertoire of the baroque. In this chapter, we broaden the view and include opportunities to perform the wide range of earlier and later repertoire presented in chapter 1, including college and university programs, summer festivals and workshops, competitions, and other helpful resources in the United States and beyond. In most cases, information about an organization is taken from its website, which is listed on the companion website for this book. Please explore these sites for more details.

FOR EVERYONE

Early Music America

   The first place you should look for information about getting involved in early music is Early Music America (EMA). This non-profit
service organization aims to increase awareness about the music of the
medieval, Renaissance, baroque, and classical periods, and it provides
valuable information and services to its members. Membership benefits
include a subscription to their magazine, which features in-depth articles by scholars and performers, as well as advertisements for products
and services. Members also enjoy a weekly e-newsletter, access to Grove
Music Online and the Naxos Music Library, eligibility for competitions
and festivals, discounts for various other publications, and inclusion in
a community of like-minded musicians and early music enthusiasts. A
membership directory, classified listings, recording archive, and online
score source add to the resources and networking possibilities for members. EMA provides scholarships and grants for early music educational
opportunities, and their website includes a database of university and
college degree programs and ensembles, complete with contact information and web links. You can limit the search criteria by location,
ensemble, or degree offerings. You will also find calendars with listings
of concerts, festivals, and workshops all over North America with links
to each organization. You can search specifically for baroque offerings or
vocal programs or look through listings for all periods, instruments, and
voices. EMA also sponsors an emerging artist showcase and offers travel
grants for young performers to participate in workshops and competitions. Be sure to take advantage of the wealth of great information the
EMA website has to offer. ♪

FOR STUDENTS

Academic Programs

   More and more schools are offering early music instruction as part
of a college, university, or conservatory program. Some undergraduate
music departments have an early music performing ensemble, while

others offer a special degree program. Some have a special vocal program for early music singers. Some degree programs are just for instrumentalists while others include singers from the regular vocal or opera department. Some degree programs are just for graduate students or musicologists. Some schools, such as mine, may not even be listed in the EMA database but still offer many opportunities to sing early music in large and small ensembles, as a soloist or chorus member, and in chamber music and opera. If you start searching, you may be surprised by what you find or can create yourself. What follows are some of the larger and more well-known academic early music programs. Be sure to visit each specific website for more detailed information.

Indiana University.   The Jacobs School of Music at Indiana University Bloomington has a special Historical Performance Institute (HPI) that includes undergraduate and graduate degree programs in early music with a vocal emphasis. Students take lessons with members of the early music department voice faculty and participate in department performance ensembles. They also take academic courses in performance practice and research, as well as courses in history, literature, and languages. Indiana has a separate vocal and opera department with its own voice faculty and coaching staff. Students from the modern vocal department are welcome to audition for smaller concerts and larger productions in the HPI as are HPI singers invited to audition for the modern opera productions. ♪

McGill University.   The Schulich School of Music at McGill University in Montreal offers undergraduate and graduate degree programs in early music with a voice emphasis. The program includes private study with one of the early music voice faculty, participation in small and large ensembles, and coursework in historical performance practice, as well as master classes, workshops, and research projects. McGill owns a large and important collection of early instruments and boasts a yearly production of a fully staged baroque opera. It also has a separate vocal and opera department. I don't know how much interaction takes place between the early music singers and the other vocal students. ♪

Peabody Institute.   The Peabody Institute at Johns Hopkins University has a Historical Performance Department that trains singers and instrumentalists in undergraduate and graduate degree programs. Singers can be voice majors in the regular vocal department with an

Early Music Concentration that includes private lessons with one of the Historical Performance Department voice faculty, courses in baroque ornamentation and early vocal literature, as well as participation in opera productions and small and large ensembles. ♪

Yale University Institute of Sacred Music. The Institute of Sacred Music at Yale has a graduate vocal program in early music, oratorio, and chamber music. It is jointly sponsored by the Institute of Sacred Music and the Yale School of Music. The program includes private lessons with members of the early music voice faculty, coachings in oratorio repertoire, participation in small and large vocal ensembles, including the famed Schola Cantorum, and courses in historical performance practice. In addition to early music, the program includes the study of art song, contemporary classical music, and vocal chamber music repertoire. In contrast, the parallel vocal program at the Yale School of Music is focused on operatic performance. ♪

Longy School of Music of Bard College. The Longy School of Music in Cambridge, Massachusetts, offers graduate degree programs in Historical Performance for singers and instrumentalists. The program includes private lessons with Historical Performance voice faculty, master classes, courses in performance practice and special historical performance topics, and participation in chamber music ensembles and opera projects. Longy also has an undergraduate degree program in regular vocal performance that shares some of the same voice faculty. ♪

University of North Texas. The University of North Texas College of Music invites all members of the student body, including instrumentalists and singers, to participate in the many diverse activities of their Early Music Studies Area. It offers a variety of degree programs that feature early music components, including an MA, MM, DMA, and PhD. Voice teachers are listed as early music faculty, and while there is no special designation in the Bachelor of Music degree program, undergraduates may participate in early music performances and private lessons with early music faculty by audition. UNT boasts a large collection of early instruments, many different performing ensembles, and one of the largest and most active departments of its kind in North America. ♪

Boston University. The Boston University School of Music offers graduate degrees in Historical Performance for instrumentalists and singers. Singers in the MM and DMA programs focus on the music of the seventeenth and eighteenth centuries and study with a voice teacher who specializes in early music. Special guest performers give master classes and workshops. The program also includes continuo skills for non-keyboard players, courses in performance practice, and participation in chamber music ensembles. Singers in BU's other programs can also take advantage of baroque chamber music coached by historical performance faculty. The city of Boston has long been an international center for early music study and performance, and students are encouraged to take advantage of the many riches and opportunities the city has to offer. ♪

Eastman School of Music. The Eastman Early Music Program provides performance opportunities and instruction to undergraduate and graduate student instrumentalists and singers. The program has a number of chamber ensembles including both instrumental and vocal groups. Visiting artists give master classes and workshops in performance practice. Eastman also has a collection of period instruments available for student use. It offers a graduate degree program in plucked instruments and harpsichord, but it doesn't have resident early music faculty for other instrumental or vocal instruction. It looks like you can be in the regular conservatory vocal program and take advantage of the early music opportunities provided without getting a specialized degree. ♪

The Juilliard School. The Juilliard School in New York City offers a Historical Performance program for instrumentalists. With an instrumental faculty of world-renowned early music specialists, Juilliard students perform in chamber ensembles, solo recitals, and Juilliard415, the school's primary period instrument ensemble. The Historical Performance program also invites singers from the regular vocal program to collaborate in chamber music ensembles, oratorios, and fully staged baroque operas. Singers participating in these projects have the opportunity to work with leading conductors, directors, and instrumentalists in the early music field. ♪

University of Southern California. The Thornton School of Music at the University of Southern California offers graduate degrees in Early Music Performance that seem to be geared toward instrumentalists. It is not entirely clear if singers are included, though they do have a singer in their list of early music faculty. USC also has a regular vocal and opera program, and there may be easy overlap between the two departments. ♪

Case Western Reserve University. Case Western Reserve University in Cleveland offers a graduate degree program in historical performance practice within its MA program in musicology, and this program partners with faculty at the Cleveland Institute of Music. It seems to be geared for instrumentalists with a more academic focus. If you are in the vocal program at the Cleveland Institute, you may be able to take advantage of the early music offerings at Case Western. ♪

Other Academic Programs. Many other universities and conservatories, including Oberlin College, New England Conservatory, San Francisco Conservatory, Cornell University, Duke University, University of Toronto, Florida State University, and SUNY Stony Brook, have early music degree programs for instrumentalists. Many more schools have early music ensembles of some sort that may include a small or large choral group, viol consort, or recorder or other instrumental ensembles. Depending on what kind of music you want to sing, you may find opportunities at a particular school, or you may be able to create new ones.

Summer Workshops

A great way to learn about singing early music and get a chance to put it into practice is by attending a summer workshop. Programs are often only a week to a few weeks long and may include choral or small ensemble singing in addition to solo work in opera or chamber music. You may also get a chance to learn baroque dance or some basic instrumental skills.

Amherst Early Music. Amherst Early Music is one of the most respected presenters of early music workshops and performances in North America. In connection with the Amherst Early Music Festival, which takes place in July at Connecticut College, it offers weeklong workshops on a wide variety of topics for instrumentalists and singers. It also has weekend workshops throughout the rest of the year at various locations. Summer programs for pre-professional singers include the Baroque Academy for solo singers, an Ensemble Singing Intensive for those interested in consort singing, and a medieval program for voices and instruments. Some, but not all, of the programs require an audition.

Singers in the Baroque Academy may be performing in either opera or staged scenes. Students are coached by renowned specialists and participate in cantatas, opera productions, and small ensembles. ♪

Madison Early Music Festival. The University of Wisconsin–Madison Arts Institute hosts a highly respected two-week summer festival that includes concerts, lectures, and workshops for singers and instrumentalists of all levels. Participants can take classes in everything from Renaissance notation, court dance, and beginning recorder or viola da gamba to sixteenth-century vocal ensembles or seventeenth-century repertoire for voice and continuo. Concerts include student performances of works coached during the workshops and appearances by guest professional ensembles. ♪

Oberlin Baroque Performance Institute. Oberlin's Baroque Performance Institute (BPI) is an intensive two-week summer program for singers and instrumentalists of all levels. Focusing on baroque repertoire, students are coached in master classes and small ensembles by internationally known specialists. The institute culminates in faculty concerts as well as student performances of the pieces studied during the workshop. ♪

Queens College Baroque Opera Workshop. The Institute for Seventeenth-Century Music at Queens College offers a one-week summer intensive training program for singers and instrumentalists culminating in a production of a baroque opera. Singers receive coaching in style and ornamentation as well as instruction in baroque gesture and stagecraft. In master classes and rehearsals, participants work with well-known specialists in baroque singing style and early opera direction. Singers can apply through YAP Tracker, the online audition and vocal competition website. ♪

Tafelmusik Baroque Summer Institute. Tafelmusik, Canada's award-winning period instrument orchestra and chamber choir, offers a two-week intensive summer training institute in Toronto for advanced students as well as emerging and established professional singers and instrumentalists. The program consists of master classes and coachings in solo and chamber music repertoire, opera scene study, baroque dance instruction, small and large choir rehearsals, private lessons, and a wide range of lectures and workshops. The institute culminates in student and faculty performances. Tafelmusik also sponsors winter workshops and collaborates with the University of Toronto in graduate degree programs in historical performance. ♪

International Baroque Institute at Longy.   The Longy School of Music has been holding summer workshops in early music instruction for over twenty-five years. The ten-day program for singers and instrumentalists includes master classes, chamber music, choral and orchestral rehearsals, baroque dance instruction, and lectures. Each year the repertoire is chosen with a particular theme in mind and performances reflect the music that is studied in the workshop. ♪

Dartington International Summer School and Festival.   The Dartington Foundation and Estate, located in South East Devon in the United Kingdom, has been hosting a summer music school for seventy years. Originally a magnet for young performers, composers, and conductors interested in new music, the monthlong festival and school has become well-known for its early music programs that include instrumental, choral, and opera performances. Each week of the festival focuses on a different area of repertoire. Students may apply for specific courses related to individual weeks or stay for the entire month. Advanced courses requiring auditions are available for students and professionals, while other programs are open to students and amateurs of all levels. Vocal courses include large and small choral ensembles, as well as master classes in opera scenes and solo singing. ♪

San Francisco Early Music Society Summer Workshops.   The San Francisco Early Music Society sponsors a series of weeklong summer workshops on a wide variety of topics. Programs for instrumentalists and singers cover music from the medieval, Renaissance, baroque, and classical periods, for students, pre-professionals, and amateurs. The baroque workshop includes master classes, chamber music coaching, and solo song workshops, as well as classes in ornamentation, baroque dance, and continuo for non-keyboard players. ♪

Haymarket Opera Company Summer Opera Course.   Founded in 2011, the Haymarket Opera Company in Chicago started holding a summer opera workshop in 2016. During the one-week program, advanced students work with leading artists in the early opera field and receive private vocal coaching, Italian diction classes, and training in movement and acting. The course culminates in a performance of a baroque opera accompanied by the Haymarket Opera's period instrument orchestra. ♪

FOR AMATEURS

Choral Opportunities

One of the easiest and most common ways you can sing repertoire from before 1750 is in a chorus. Amateurs, students, and professionals may find opportunities to sing with choruses of all shapes and sizes, including everything from a large symphonic chorus to a small church choir to an a cappella consort. Some may hold auditions while others invite all comers. Some may perform repertoire from all periods while others specialize in early music exclusively.

Large Choruses. Most cities have at least one large choral organization. Smaller towns and communities usually support some kind of chorus as well. Large choruses may perform with the local symphonic orchestra or have their own concert series or both. Depending on the music director's interest and taste, a chorus may perform repertoire from all periods, both with and without instrumental accompaniment. Some of the most popular large choral works are the Bach *Passions* or Handel's *Messiah*. If you sing with a large chorus, chances are you will be part of a production of one of these beloved baroque works. Will you be performing at modern pitch with modern instruments or with period instruments at baroque pitch? Will the conductor ask for a historically informed approach to style or a more modern one? As we discussed in chapter 5, you will need to bring slightly different vocal skills and stylistic choices to the project depending on the answers to these questions.

If you sing in a large chorus, you should follow the instructions of the conductor and let them guide the overall vocal and musical style of the performance. The chorus may hire its own orchestra and be conducted by its regular music director. A large chorus may also be hired by an orchestra, in which case they might be prepared by their regular conductor but led in the performance by the orchestra's music director, or even a guest conductor. At Christmas and Easter, many of the major orchestras in the country, including the New York Philharmonic, Boston Symphony, Philadelphia Orchestra, and others put on their own productions of *Messiah* and the *Passions*. Depending on what kind of large chorus you sing with, you must be ready to adapt your vocal technique and style to fit the needs of the situation.

Specialty Baroque Choruses.   Some choruses define themselves as specializing in early music with a historically informed approach to style. These kinds of choruses can be large or small and include professional singers or amateurs or both. Most require an audition. Many of these choruses have their own period instrument orchestras or are associated with an established ensemble that performs at baroque pitch. The mission statement of the organization will usually explain what kind of repertoire and style the group promotes, but don't be surprised if these choruses present performances of *Messiah* and the *Passions*. If you want to participate in one of these groups, you should definitely bring your historically informed vocal technique and style with you. Some of the more well-known North American early music choruses include the Boston Handel and Haydn Society, Tafelmusik in Toronto, Philharmonia Baroque Orchestra and Chorale in the San Francisco Bay Area, Amor Artis in New York City, Music of the Baroque in Chicago, the Dallas Bach Society, and the Bethlehem Bach Choir. There are many more in the United States and even more in the United Kingdom and Europe. Some specific events, such as the Oregon Bach Festival and Carmel Bach Festival, hold special auditions for their festival choruses. ♪

Church Choirs.   There are as many different kinds of church choirs to sing with as choruses, and the interested amateur singer can easily find a situation that suits their needs. Check a church's website for information on its music program or talk to other singers in the area to learn more about the reputation and atmosphere of a specific church and choir. Church choirs can be small or large, casual or formal, made up of professional or amateur singers or a combination of both. Some choirs may want you to be a member of the church, and you may want to choose a church choir based on the denomination of the service. Repertoire can include everything from Gregorian chant to newly composed works and, depending on the taste of the music director and/or minister, can include a healthy dose of great sacred choral works of the Renaissance and baroque periods. Some church choirs invite anyone who wants to sing to join, while others require an audition and are highly selective. Some church choirs sing only for Sunday services, while others have their own concert series in addition to their liturgical duties. Extra concerts may require added rehearsals besides the regular weekly rehearsals for Sunday services.

Emmanuel Music in Boston presents a Bach Cantata every Sunday from September to May as part of the weekly Episcopal church service at Emmanuel Church. It also has an extensive calendar of other concerts and programs for singers and instrumentalists. Members of this world-class choir include both amateurs and professionals. Similarly, the choir at Trinity Church on Wall Street in New York City provides concert-quality music during Sunday church services as well as a busy schedule of other performances and events.

Small Consorts. Here is where the realms of early music and a cappella overlap and blur. There are so many different kinds of small vocal ensembles in the United States and elsewhere that it is almost impossible to categorize them. Some present early music exclusively while others extend their repertoire choices into contemporary, jazz, and Broadway selections. Some limit their focus to medieval chant, while others include music of the Renaissance and baroque. Some stick to music for voices only, while others invite instruments to join them. Some are true consorts of four to six voices, while others are small chamber choirs of fifteen or twenty. Some have a conductor or music director, while others are group led. Some feature male voices only, even on the treble parts, while others include female voices. Some are completely amateur, while others are completely professional.

A page with choral listings from the Early Music Chicago website shows fourteen different groups, half of them on the small side. If you search in your local area for early music vocal ensembles, I expect you will find a similarly varied selection of small choirs or consorts to investigate. If you don't find what you are looking for, start your own group! A page from Primarily A Cappella (singers.com), which lists early music ensembles, shows everything from the most highly regarded international profes-sional organizations such as the mixed male and female Tallis Scholars, to an all-male group from the Washington, DC, area called the Suspicious Cheese Lords. Singing in a small vocal ensemble is a great way to im-merse yourself in early music repertoire without having to be a soloist. ♪

Summer Workshops

As we saw in the previous section on summer workshops for students, many of the early music workshops offered in the summer are open to amateurs of all abilities. Amherst, Madison, Oberlin, San Francisco, Dartington, and Tafelmusik welcome singers of all ages and skills to their summer workshops. Western Wind, the internationally acclaimed vocal sextet, offers summer workshops focusing on small ensemble singing for singers of all levels. Styles covered include everything from medieval, Renaissance, and baroque repertoire to folk songs, jazz and pop improvisation, and more. The Early Music Shop in London website has a page of summer workshops in the United Kingdom that lists a variety of courses for singers and instrumentalists of all levels. ♪

FOR PROFESSIONALS

If you want to have a career as a professional singer, there are many paths you can take. You may want to focus primarily on early music, or include it as part of a varied diet of repertoire and styles. You may have a voice particularly suited to certain kinds of music or just see what opportunities open up for you. Within the realm of early music repertoire, you can investigate both choral and soloist opportunities, in both sacred and secular venues, including chamber music and opera.

Choral Positions

Most young professional singers have some sort of choral job, even if they aspire to be soloists. In the previous sections on choral opportunities for amateurs, we saw that many choruses, both large and small, secular and sacred, have paid positions for professional singers. Church choirs may have a core group of paid professionals or a solo quartet. Emmanuel Music in Boston and Trinity Church on Wall Street in New York City, just two examples, have numerous positions for professional singers who both sing in the chorus and perform the needed solo parts. These are great opportunities, especially when the music of the week is a Bach cantata or *Passion*. Some of the most highly regarded specialty baroque choruses are made up entirely of professional singers who also pursue solo performing careers. Boston's Handel and Haydn Society employs a professional solo quartet in the chorus, as does New York's Amor Artis. Chicago's Music of the Baroque chorus is made up entirely of professionals, as is the choir of the Bach Society of Houston, the Monteverdi Choir in London, the choir of Les Arts Florissants in Paris, and many others. ♪

When it comes to smaller choirs and consorts, many of the well-known groups are entirely professional and have busy year-round schedules of performances, touring, and recording. They may hold public auditions for open spots on their roster, or have auditions by invitation only, or even hire replacement singers from recommendations of musicians in their network. Gaining a position in a group such as Chanticleer, or the United Kingdom's Tallis Scholars, Tenebrae, or Gallicantus can make for a highly rewarding career singing early music. After nearly thirty years of touring and recording, the four female singers of Anonymous 4 have decided to move on to other pursuits, leaving the field open for up-and-coming female consorts. In Appendix A, my colleague Gabriel Crouch, who was a member of The King's Singers for many years, goes into more detail about what is needed to have a career as a consort singer. ♪

Young Artist Programs

Some of the larger and more prestigious professional choirs also have young artist training programs. The Monteverdi Choir in London has an apprentice program, Les Arts Florissant in Paris includes a program for young artists called Le Jardin des Voix, and Tenebrae in the United Kingdom has a year-long program for Associate Artists. The American Bach Soloists Festival in San Francisco has an academy for advanced students who participate in master classes, coaching and performances of chamber music, opera, and oratorio, both as soloists and chorus members. Both the Carmel Bach Festival and the Oregon Bach Festival hold programs for vocal fellows in the chorus who participate in special master classes and have opportunities to perform solos. The Boston Early Music Festival's Young Artists Training Program provides passes to all the festival concerts and events in exchange for singing in the ensemble of the main stage opera production. BEMF Young Artists also participate in master classes, opera scenes, and smaller chamber music concerts in the multitude of fringe events going on concurrent to the main festival. Opera Lafayette, Washington,

DC's baroque opera company, has a Young Artists Program that affords advanced students and young professional singers an opportunity to cover leading roles and perform smaller parts in the main stage productions, as well as being mentored by leading artists and presenting educational school programs and performances. ♪

Competitions

There are a few early music competitions in the United States and many more in Europe. The Handel Aria Competition takes place in conjunction with the Madison Early Music Festival and awards emerging artists cash prizes and performance opportunities. For over forty years, the Oratorio Society of New York Solo Competition has provided emerging solo singers with the opportunity to advance their careers. While the repertoire requirements for this competition include oratorio solos from all periods, singers can certainly present arias from works of Bach and Handel. Handel opera arias are also allowed in the Metropolitan Opera National Council Auditions. I have had two former students who, as countertenors, won the Met Auditions singing Handel. If you sing baroque arias in vocal competitions, however, make sure to find out if you will be singing with piano or modern orchestra at modern pitch or with period instruments in a more historically informed style. ♪

In Europe, there are many more opportunities to participate in early music competitions. The National Center for Early Music has an international competition for small ensembles, either instrumental, vocal, or combined, as part of the York Early Music Festival. Italy, France, Austria, Germany, and Poland all have solo vocal competitions for early music repertoire. Links for these events are listed on the travel page of the *Early Music Today* magazine. Emerging artists may apply for travel grants from Early Music America to attend these kinds of competitions. ♪

Opera Companies

More and more major opera companies are including works by Handel, Monteverdi, Rameau, and other baroque composers in their regular seasons. As we discussed in chapter 5 and previously in this chapter, you must find out if a production of a baroque opera will be

performed with period instruments at baroque pitch, with modern instruments at modern pitch, or some other combination. You must also
find out if you are responsible for your own ornaments or if the conductor will dictate the style and ornamentation for the production. There
are a few specialty baroque opera companies that always perform with
period instruments, including Opera Lafayette in Washington, DC,
American Baroque Opera Company in Dallas, and Haymarket Opera
Company in Chicago. There are many more in the United Kingdom
and Europe, including the Early Opera Company. Many of the early
music festivals I will mention shortly present a fully staged opera as part
of their schedule of performances, and many early music concert series
present concert versions of operas as well. If you establish a reputation
as a singer who knows how to perform early music, you may have many
opportunities to be considered for roles in baroque operas. ♪

Oratorio

Some singers spend their entire careers as oratorio soloists. Tenors
who specialize in the Evangelist roles in the Bach *Passions* can have
busy performing schedules for most of the year. Productions of *Messiah*
provide work for many soloists as well as choral singers. As an oratorio
soloist, you can include music from all periods in your repertoire and
participate in both modern and historically informed productions of
baroque works. As we have said before, make sure you know what kind
of instruments you will be performing with and at what pitch. Also, find
out the approach toward ornamentation and be prepared to defer to the
conductor in matters of style.

Chamber Music

As we said in chapter 6, a great deal of baroque vocal repertoire is
meant for a chamber ensemble. If you do an online search for early
music in your area, chances are that you will find many small chamber
music concerts. These can take place in small venues such as churches
or recital halls, and they can be sponsored by colleges, universities, art
museums, or other larger presenting organizations. Chamber music
concerts can feature established, internationally known groups and

soloists, or local ensembles. Some baroque chamber ensembles include one or more resident singers while other groups invite singers as special guests. You may be invited to perform a concert of baroque chamber music as a special guest of an established group, as part of a larger festival, or you may secure a position as a regular member of a baroque ensemble, in which case you may get to perform in a local concert series or find yourself with a busy schedule of touring and recording. Being a regular member of a baroque chamber ensemble is a wonderful opportunity for performing early music. If you can't find an existing group to perform with, start your own!

EARLY MUSIC FESTIVALS

A great place to learn about and hear a lot of early music is at one of the many specialty early music festivals that take place throughout North America and abroad. Each festival has its own character and approach to repertoire, historical performance practice, and scholarship, and each showcases its own distinct combination of local and international performers. If you plan your summer calendar carefully, you could spend May to September attending a different early music festival every other week. I have mentioned some of these festivals already, including Madison, Oberlin, and Amherst, in relation to summer workshops, young artist programs, and competitions. I will give more information on other major festivals here.

Boston

The Boston Early Music Festival (BEMF) has been recognized as a leader in the early music world since its founding in 1980. Presenting an annual winter concert series in Boston and New York and a biannual summer festival and exhibition in Boston, BEMF showcases international early music stars, produces lavishly staged operas, and supports the wide community of players and singers who engage in music of the medieval, Renaissance, and baroque periods with a variety of educational programs. Established artists, young professionals, students, and lovers of early music can all find many delights in their varied offerings. Whether it is performing in or attending a world-class concert or opera production, participating in a master class, searching for sheet music at the exhibition, networking with colleagues, or hearing an exciting fringe performance, anyone interested in early music should make a trip to BEMF. ♪

Berkeley

The San Francisco Early Music Society presents the Berkeley Festival and Exhibition (BFX) every other year alternating with the Boston Early Music Festival. Founded in 1990, BFX presents nationally known ensembles in main stage performances of larger works, chamber music and opera, as well as a young artist series, lectures, master classes, and fringe events. As in Boston, the exhibition features instrument makers, music publishers, educational organizations, performing ensembles, and much more. ♪

Vancouver

Early Music Vancouver (EMV) produces a wide variety of programs all through the year, including a summer festival in early August. Featuring internationally known groups such as The King's Singers, Canadian ensembles like Tafelmusik, as well as local West Coast musicians, EMV presents concerts of larger works, chamber music, and solo artists in music from the medieval, Renaissance, and baroque periods. ♪

London

The London Festival of Baroque Music has been featuring concerts of seventeenth- and eighteenth-century music since 1984. The week-long festival in May presents distinguished international artists as well as homegrown favorites from the United Kingdom. Concerts take place in churches around central London, including Westminster Abbey. ♪

York

The York Early Music Festival in the United Kingdom has been presenting historically informed performances of music from the medieval to the baroque since 1977. For ten days in early July, the York Early Music Festival features internationally recognized artists performing in beautiful medieval churches in York as well as at the magnificent York Minster. The festival also sponsors an Emerging European Ensembles project and an International Young Artists Competition every other year. ♪

Bruges

The MAfestival Brugge boasts a week of internationally renowned artists presenting early music concerts in the historical city of Bruges, Belgium. Known for its daring dash of innovation, Musica Antiqua Bruges includes a major concert series, fringe concerts for young and promising ensembles, an exhibition, an international competition for instrumental baroque soloists, and a musical bike ride, Vélo Baroque. ♪

Utrecht

Since 1982, the Utrecht Early Music Festival has hosted concerts by internationally renowned artists in the city of Utrecht in the Netherlands. For ten days in late August, the festival includes main stage themed concerts, an exhibition, fringe events for young artists, and a competition for early music ensembles. ♪

Regensburg

Another early music festival takes place in May in Regensburg, Germany. The long weekend of events features concerts by small and large ensembles from all over Europe and the United Kingdom, as well as from the United States. ♪

Bach Festivals

Festivals devoted specifically to the music of Johann Sebastian Bach make up their own distinct category. I have mentioned above several of the larger ones in North America, including Bethlehem, Carmel, and Oregon. Early Music Vancouver hosts a summer Bach Festival as well. Many cities, such as Dallas, Houston, and Washington, DC, have their own special Bach choirs, and there are doubtless many more Bach Festivals presented by colleges, universities, church choirs, and other local organizations throughout the United States. Leipzig, Germany, where Bach lived and wrote most of his major sacred choral works for the choir of the Thomaskirche (St. Thomas Church), hosts a special Bach Festival in June, as well as other Bach events throughout the year. The Bach Fest Leipzig features concerts by the Leipzig Gewandhaus Orchestra and the choirs of the Thomaskirche and Leipzig Opera, as well as internationally recognized artists and ensembles, such as the Monteverdi Choir and English Baroque Soloists. There are also lectures by noted scholars and an international competition for young artists that rotates specific solo instruments or voice from year to year. It is especially important with Bach festivals to find out what kind of instruments will be used and at what pitch. The Leipzig Gewandhaus Orchestra is a modern ensemble playing at 440, while the English Baroque soloists use period instruments. As we have said earlier, many possibilities exist, especially for Bach performances. ♪

OTHER RESOURCES

In addition to Early Music America, there are similar clearinghouses of information in the United Kingdom and Europe. In the United Kingdom, the National Center for Early Music in York sponsors the York Early Music Festival, and it also offers many other educational and networking programs. The National Early Music Association UK is a membership organization that holds conferences for performers and scholars to share knowledge about early music and performance practice. It also provides a database of events and useful networking contacts. *Early Music Today* is a magazine for early music enthusiasts in the United Kingdom with valuable listings of festivals, competitions, and performances, as well as articles about early music performers making headlines. The European Early Music Network, or REMA—Réseau Européen de Musique Ancienne—is a membership organization dedicated to providing an exchange of knowledge, information, and cooperation in the European early music field. It sponsors conferences and workshops, posts listings of events, festivals, and competitions, provides a biannual showcase for young artists, and much more. EarlyMusicNews.org was created in 2005 as a place to post news items and event listings relating to the international early music scene. Based in Canada, but covering events worldwide, the community networking site includes calendars of concerts, festivals, workshops, competitions, auditions, and web links to ensembles and academic programs. Links to all of these organizations can be found on the companion website for this book. ♪

Don't forget to search for early music events and listings in your local area. You will be surprised to discover how much is going on in any large city or even a small town. Whether you are an amateur, student, or professional interested in singing opera, chamber music, or choral repertoire, if you want to sing early music, a wealth of opportunities awaits you.

APPENDIX A

So You Want to Be a Consort Singer?
Gabriel Crouch

I can remember the first time I sang with a truly world-class vocal consort as if it were yesterday. It was my first audition with The King's Singers, a few days before my twenty-second birthday in September of 1995. I felt profoundly awkward during the obligatory small talk (despite the group's laudable efforts to put me at ease), but as soon as we all opened our mouths to sing, everything was different. In the ensuing minutes, all the precious secrets of vocal consort singing were revealed to me by these amiable masters of the craft. The first thing I noticed was the *breath*: We were breathing *for each other*, not just for ourselves, and the process of breathing had a pronounced and conscious physicality that I did my best to imitate. Second, I sensed the *listening* that was going on around me, and I realized that I was being "listened to" in a way I had never experienced before. My five colleagues leaned in toward each other, making tiny adjustments in vowels and tone color in the search for perfect ensemble, and they willed me to do the same. Finally, there was the *sound*. It wasn't what you would call "loud," but it *felt* loud within the group because it was crackling with energy. Everything was projected forward, toward the middle of the group, and I could see that my colleagues were physically exerting themselves to create the sound they wanted. It hardly matters what we were singing, but of course, I remember it—a beautiful villancico by Juan Vásquez called "Gentil señora mia." I was so overwhelmed by the experience that I exclaimed to the group as soon as the piece was finished that it was the most satisfying four minutes of music-making I had ever experienced in my life.

So let's look at these qualities in a little more detail and think about how we can harness them in the service of great consort singing.

LEARN TO COMMUNICATE WITH BREATH

Most vocal consorts have a musical director, but they less often have a real conductor. Conductors have a way of interfering in consort settings. If they stand out in front, they block most of the musical action, and if they stand to one side and sing, the ensemble feels lopsided—with the singers projecting their sound not toward the audience but to one side of the group. The best consorts are able to maintain their ensemble without a conductor, and they do this partly through eye contact and partly through breath. Eye contact is perhaps the more obvious option, but it is the least preferable since it can seriously detract from the effect of a performance if singers are more focused on each other's faces than on the audience they are addressing. However, on the other hand, breath (for a consort singer) bears the secret to life itself. A considered breath—free, healthy, and without gasping or heaving—may contain within it all the information one would need to create a perfect ensemble sound: tempo, dynamic, character, and tone color. These qualities can all be expressed within the singer's breath if one can master the art. For an established consort, the best way to do this is to practice with one's eyes closed. Get used to listening for perfect silence and recognizing those moments when the room is "ready" for music. Focus on recognizing that moment together and responding to it. Listen . . . breathe . . . *sing!*

REALLY, REALLY LISTEN

Listening is not just a part of consort music-making—it is *everything* in consort music-making! Without developing your ears to filter and isolate all the sounds around you, and without learning to respond instantaneously to what you hear, you will never be successful. And make no mistake about it—it's a hard skill to learn. We spend so much time as singers learning to listen to *ourselves* that we find it difficult to prioritize a different sound, fearful of the ugly tone or faulty intonation that might ensue if we are distracted. However, the point is not to *ignore* our own sound; rather, it is to hear it in the context of everything else: a balanced, melodic constituent in a contrapuntal texture, or a functioning, harmonic component of a chordal one. By truly listening, we can learn to appreciate the difference between solid intonation and *beautiful* intonation. We can recognize those moments when perfect balance and intonation excites the harmonic series and creates that effect that every consort singer strives for—of the room being "alive" with sound. Finally, we can respond instantaneously to the musical promptings of our colleagues, creating performances that are fresh and spontaneous and that respond to the peculiarities of the room, the atmosphere of that particular day, and the varying whims of the performers.

Develop a Truly Flexible Sound

Now that you're learning to listen properly, it's time to train your voice to respond to what you hear. This is where your vocal technique—and your approach to vocal technique—becomes so important. As solo singers, we tend to bring our vocal technique to the music we are performing so that the sound is recognizably ours. We practice until we understand how every note, every transition, and every phrase works in this carefully constructed voice of ours—and we commit this practiced approach to memory through repetition, so that it becomes our personal interpretation.

None of this works for a vocal consort. If you assemble a group of singers who are rigid in their beliefs and inflexible in their technique, then no matter how glorious their individual voices or how brilliant their level of musicianship, they will never sound consistently good together. World-class consort singers are able to adjust their vowels to match placement minutely. They have learned to add "grain" to the sound, as well as "richness," "warmth," "blade," "ping," and a wealth of other qualities that are more or less exclusive to this art form. Consort singers

tend to have flexible vibratos, which can vary in rate and extent according to the expressive needs of the music and the prevailing quality of
the group sound. Moreover, they can do all this without losing control
of their vocal technique or risking fatigue or other vocal health issues.
Acquiring this ability is, for me, more a matter of mindset than anything
else. A singer must be willing to experiment with where the sound is
placed and what its characteristic constituents are; and because there is
often a fine line between ugly and exquisite consort singing, they must
be unfazed by the possibility of sounding ugly. I sometimes practice by
sustaining any note on an "ah" vowel while moving an index finger from
the point of my nose, across my sinuses, and up to the top of my head,
then looping down to the back of my throat, forward to the roof of my
mouth, into the teeth, and finally dropping down to my chest cavity. I
make a conscious effort to "move" my sound so that I can feel it resonat-
ing where my finger is, and I try to learn the qualities of each different
sound. The really difficult part of this exercise is the seamless transition
from one kind of sound to another, so this is the aspect that needs most
careful practice.

NOW THAT YOU'RE BUILDING YOUR SKILLS, WHAT'S NEXT?

Before we go too deep into "consort philosophy," we should address
the question of how to make all this work in a practical sense: how to
do what you love most in the world and have it put food on your table.
It's not easy. There are a small number of full-time, salaried consorts
(The King's Singers, Chanticleer, and Voces8 among them), and entry
to these groups is, of course, extremely competitive. Most who earn a
successful living from consort singing are more loosely bound to several
different groups and combine these loose affiliations with either membership of professional choirs, a solo singing career, an institutional
teaching position, or any combination of the above. It is absolutely crucial—and I can't stress this enough—for a consort singer to be a stable
and flexible musician *and* colleague because life in this business can be
unpredictable. A broad palate of communication skills and a facility for

scholarly research will also serve you well, in addition to the technical and musical qualities we have already discussed.

Let's not kid ourselves—this is a rarified form of music-making, and there is not a limitless capacity in the professional music world for new vocal consorts. I have seen many excellent consorts start up over the years and almost as many that have ground to a halt. So what gives a new vocal consort the best chance of success? Of course, it is important that the members get along with each other and have compatible diaries, voices, and musical philosophies; but for me, the most important factor is the group's unshakeable understanding of why it exists at all. At your group's inception, you should ask yourselves: What music do we want to address, and what special things do we want to say with this music that hasn't been said before? Without knowing how you will make your unique contribution to music (that has been recorded many times before)—and I apologize for sounding rather blunt here—*how can you expect audiences to listen??*

The good news is that, whatever anyone may tell you, there is no one way to perform early vocal consort music. There is no truly *correct* sound or style. Your duty is to consider the received wisdom, to listen to the conventional approaches to sound, tone, vowels, vibrato, diction, and everything else, and then discard it all in favor of your own preferences. We don't need another King's Singers or another Tallis Scholars or any other revered early music consort sound. We need *your* sound, and you need to move us forward. I wish you the best of luck on that quest.

APPENDIX B

Singing with Players
Mary Benton, Patricia Hlafter, Judith Klotz, and Amy Warren
Members of the Viola da Gamba Consort La Spirita

La Spirita is a viola da gamba quartet that has been playing together for over twenty years. Our members have played and/or sung with various other groups and on various other instruments. After one concert, we were reminiscing about previous concerts and recitals in which we had participated that combined singers and players. We remembered the many kinds of problems and challenges that can arise. This appendix comes out of that discussion, along with quite a lot of brainstorming. While our focus tends to be early music, this guide applies to all periods of music, and we hope that our insights will be of help to singers who have little or no experience singing with instruments. This discussion does not address musical interpretation, but it does address ways to put together a successful concert when one combines singers with players.

As we all know, stunning concerts do not materialize on their own. They take preparation, coordination, communication, and rehearsal. What follows is a guide designed to help you through the process from the initial planning to the final bow. Most importantly, the overarching theme is to help you to develop a good ensemble. Ensemble playing begins with only two people making music together, but it is inescapable when there are three or more.

SPECIFIC CONCERNS FOR INSTRUMENTALISTS

Space

Space requirements vary with the kind of instrument, of course. A cellist needs more space than a recorder player, but both need space for a music stand. Some players will need chairs (such as the cellist) while others may prefer to stand. Keep in mind that the amount of room a string player needs depends on the arc of their full bowing range. It can be rather comical—as well as disconcerting (pun intended)—to be bowing into each other's ribs.

Chairs and Stands

Chairs without flat seats, like those curvy plastic jobs, can be miserable to sit and play on for long periods of time, and chairs with arms are downright impossible for members. Chamber music players usually bring their own music stand with them to rehearsals and performances. We have noticed that instrumentalists who are used to playing in orchestras or larger ensembles will not automatically bring a stand. Early music players probably will. Just be specific about what you need your musicians to bring with them to rehearsals and the final concert.

Lighting

This seems to be an obvious concern, but many performing spaces (churches, for example) may not have optimum lighting. A singer may be prepared to sing from memory, but instrumentalists must be able to see their music. The lighting may determine where and how you arrange the ensemble in the space.

Temperature

Of course, we all want to be comfortable, but unstable temperatures can wreak havoc with tuning—especially for early instruments with gut strings. Try to create or place your players in a temperate environment. We keenly remember an incident in which the treble viol player was in such a draft that all of her pegs slipped and her strings became grossly out of tune.

Placement of Players and Singers

The Importance of Seeing. Let's face it, you can't create "ensemble" if you and the players can't see each other. Churches often offer difficult challenges because they are designed for worship, not as performing spaces. It doesn't work for musicians to sit or stand in a straight row. We remember playing with a small group of singers in an auditorium designed for lectures. The stage was less than six feet deep so you could only see or hear the person directly next to you.

The Importance of Hearing. Good ensemble playing requires not only being able to see each other but also being able to hear everyone as well. The audience needs to be able to hear too! A space that is too live can be just as difficult to hear and perform in as one that is too dead. Carpets, arches, and alcoves can help or seriously hurt the sound. To counteract a space that is too live, instrumentalists will need to use a more detached style of playing or the music will sound like mush. On occasion, we have actually brought a rug with us to counteract this problem. If the space is dead and the ensemble cannot move elsewhere, plan to herd the audience to the best place in the hall. We usually check out the acoustics of an unfamiliar performing space ahead of time with one or two instruments to see what works for the audience and what does not. It is helpful to have someone listen from the back of the space. Also, remember that the audience itself will change the acoustics to some extent.

Create a Checklist

- Choose your performance space as early as possible so that you have the most options.
- Check both rehearsal and performance spaces to be sure both have sufficient room.
- Make sure that all chairs are suitable and that you have one for each player who needs to sit down.

- Check with your instrumentalists about their need for music stands.
- In your performance space, choose the area that has the best lighting for everyone.
- If you have no choice and the lighting is bad, ask the instrumentalists if they have stand lights they can use.
- Check the heating and cooling options, and choose the most temperate space available for your concert.
- Choose where the musicians will sit and stand with view lines in mind.
- Perform a sound check in advance of your rehearsal so that precious rehearsal time is not lost shifting your players around.

MUSIC AND MUSICIANS

Music Editions

Here are some things to think about when choosing which edition you will work from:

- Does the range of the music fit the range of the instruments? Make sure you know the ranges of the instruments you plan to use.
- What clefs does each instrument typically read?
- Is the music in score or parts? If it is in open score format, are there any page turn problems? If there are no page turn problems, a score will help to keep everybody together. It is especially helpful, but not essential, for instrumentalists to have the vocal line, as it not only helps players stay with the singer, but it also gives them cues about articulation and phrasing.
- Are there any cues in the music when instruments have multiple measures out?
- Are there measure numbers or rehearsal letters? If not, you may want to supply them. Otherwise, plan on spending a lot of time counting x number of measures from y during precious rehearsal time.
- Everybody should be using the same edition.

Choosing Players

- What instruments are needed? You may ask, "Doesn't it say so on the music?" Not necessarily if the music is from the eighteenth century or earlier. You may also need to substitute a different instrument for one you do not have available. Here again, you need to familiarize yourself with the ranges of the instruments and the music. Don't hesitate to ask for advice from someone who knows. Do you want to substitute recorders for flutes in a Bach cantata? Recorders sound an octave higher so a tenor recorder, not a soprano recorder, will be in the same range as a flute (or a soprano voice). Also, recorders do not have as great a range as flutes.

- What instruments work well together? Consider the timbre and volume of the sound of each instrument and the character of the music. Do you want a homogeneous sound? Choose instruments that will blend. Does the music call for each line to have its own character? Choose contrasting timbres.

- Will you use "original" instruments or "modern" instruments? You will probably have to make some compromises, but if you decide to mix early instruments with modern, watch out for the balance. A piano and a cello may drown out a recorder. If you mix "original" and "modern" instruments, remember that baroque instruments are usually, but not always, tuned to A415 rather than A440. The tuning of the keyboard may be the deciding factor. Viols can tune to A415 or A440, but wind instruments and baroque strings cannot. Do *not* try to "pull out" recorders, as they will not be in tune with themselves!

- Have you considered balance if you plan to have instruments doubling singers? What may work well with a chorus may not work with a soloist.

- Are all instrumentalists created equal? Of course not. Consider the difficulty of the music (Bach is extremely difficult). It is a good idea to get reliable recommendations before you ask a player to join the ensemble.

- Don't expect to get the best players at the last minute. Instrumentalists prefer as much lead time as possible to organize their schedules and to prepare the music.

Handing Out Music

Instrumentalists wish they had a third hand for turning pages. String players have a particularly hard time because they have an instrument in one hand and a bow in the other. If there are no parts, and if there are page turns in the middle of a song or movement, you may have to create parts by "cutting-and-pasting." Because the number of pages should be as minimal as possible, it goes without saying that instrumentalists cannot play from a piano-vocal score. Pale photocopies (you shouldn't be copying anyway), tiny study scores, or too many pages to fit on the stand will not only irritate your players but may also cause some missed notes.

Checklist

- Make sure the music you have chosen can be played by the instruments you have available.
- Make sure your players can play from the edition you give them. Check for: clefs, page turns, cues, and measure numbers.
- Consider instrumentation—what instruments will go together.
- Be sure the instrumentalists you have available can handle the music you have chosen.
- Be sure everyone knows whether you will be tuned to A415 or A440, otherwise DISASTER!

PREPARING FOR THE PERFORMANCE

Rehearsals and Time

One never seems to have enough time to put together the perfect performance. How often have we yearned for "just one more rehearsal"? Fortunately, there are things you can do to nudge time onto your side.

First and foremost, you will want to think about how many rehearsals you will need leading up to the concert. Of course, this will depend on how difficult the music is, individual schedules, and your budget, if you plan to pay your performers for rehearsals. Set rehearsal times as early as possible. Also, give consideration to how much time will pass between rehearsals. One day is usually not enough; conversely, a month or more gives everyone plenty of time to completely forget everything they practiced. Somewhere in the middle is often the correct solution.

Time-Efficient Rehearsals

- Provide the music and pertinent notes well in advance of the first rehearsal to give the musicians ample time to learn their parts. The pertinent notes could include basic tempi, tempo changes, repeats/ numbers of verses, ficta, and basic dynamics.
- Have the rehearsal space set up when the players arrive.
- Plan enough time for the number of pieces you need to work on.
- Allocate enough time for each piece, especially if you have only one rehearsal.
- Rehearse all of the music—don't get bogged down with one thing.

La Spirita finds it very rewarding to make musical decisions by consensus, but that's a luxury your rehearsal schedule may not permit.

Logistical Details

Even when you think you've made all the basic decisions, playing and singing together doesn't just happen. As you already know from singing with others, while the sheet music gives you basic instructions, much sensitive interaction needs to happen between musicians for the music to be together and come alive. For each piece, it must be decided:

- Who gives the starting tempo, and who leads the ending? If you are a vocal soloist, you might assume it's you, but the instrumentalists may start first or finish last.
- What's the pulse (in 3 or 6 . . . in 2 or 4)?
- How will you start and finish together? Clear body gestures and breathing should be all you need. Remember, you don't have a conductor.
- Can everyone see each other's gestures? Seating and standing arrangements really matter for this.

- Is everyone ready to start, and are they looking?
- As you already know, cadences within the piece (and at the very end) are particularly important places for everyone to make eye contact. There will be other passages, however, where eye contact between two individual players/singers is very important for a good ensemble. For La Spirita, finding and reveling in those are some of the joys of chamber music.
- The relative dynamic balance will often best be worked out during rehearsal so that the most important line at any moment comes out clearly. Don't be surprised that some instruments, such as recorders, have a narrow dynamic range.
- Will there be ornamentation? Where, when, and what type? Be consistent!

Other Important Details

When you are preparing for a recital or other special event, there will likely be enough excitement and stress at the performance without finding that some other key component has gone wrong. So why not treat your ensemble planning the way you might any other key part of a big event? Checklists and a calendar should help to keep you on track.

Attire. Most musicians will default to black, but if you have something different in mind, let everyone know early on.

Directions and Parking. Your ensemble members may be coming from several directions; make sure they are all clear on how to get to the performance space you have selected. Check ahead of time for potential parking issues. Do the spaces require a pass or payment? Are they far away from the entrance to the facility? Give special consideration to players with large instruments and lots of gear!

Amenities. A greenroom is nice to have but certainly not necessary. The ensemble will need to know, however, where they can put their "stuff" (preferably somewhere secure or within sight) and other practical matters, such as where the restrooms are located.

Concert Formalities

Take a moment to think about the choreography of the concert.

- Will everyone be on stage at the outset?
- Will the performers come in from a particular stage entrance? If not all of the musicians will be performing in all of the pieces, where will they escape to between numbers?
- When will the musicians tune? Ensembles tune before the concert, but when singing with early instruments that have gut strings, there needs to be a point during the concert for retuning. This can be at a planned intermission. Be prepared to deal with a tuning disaster. Remember the note about the viol player in a draft! Should that disaster happen, and it is rare, your having thought about how you will proceed will keep you in control.
- Tell your musicians how or if you plan to acknowledge them to the audience after the concert and how the group will handle bows.

Remuneration

Finally, are the ensemble players there only for the love of music, or also for a paycheck? Everyone will feel better about the experience if the arrangement is specified in advance. Of course, musicians are rarely paid what they're really worth, but for whatever you've promised—even an "honorarium"—it's courteous to have the check at the performance (or before) so that the musicians aren't placed in the awkward dilemma of whether to gently remind you later. Though we don't think anyone would ever engage a collection agency, forgetting your promise would take something away from the joy of making music together.

FINAL THOUGHTS

You've thought of it all. You have planned well, prepared and rehearsed with your musicians, dressed to knock'em dead, and the day of the concert has arrived. Take a deep breath, and enjoy your performance!

APPENDIX C

Approximating the Past
Jamie Reuland

Writing in an age before musical notation, the seventh-century encyclopedist Isidore of Seville asserted that "unless sounds are re-membered by man, they perish, for they cannot be written down."[1] Even after the development of a technology that would prove Isidore wrong—the ability to fix acoustic phenomena through pen and parch-ment—memory and oral tradition persisted as the major conduits of musical knowledge and practice well into the Renaissance. The distant and irrecoverable sound world posed by the earliest of early music proves a deterrent to some singers, a spur to the imagination for oth-ers, and a historical challenge to yet others. While this repertory is certainly old, it is far from old-fashioned, and there is much that is fresh and new to be discovered in it.

The term "early music" is really too broad to mean much of anything specific. In its most general sense, it designates works predating the period of common practice. That's a span of time only a few centuries shy of a millennium! Early music is, fundamentally, an invention of mo-dernity; the concept grew out of various antiquarian strains in the nine-teenth century, and as attitudes toward history and tastes in style have changed so too have modern expressions of "early" sound. Much of the music of the Middle Ages and Renaissance was written in a period when notions of authorship were not yet fixed, and part of the pleasure this affords for performers is the relative freedom from authorial control. Even so, it is helpful to have in mind some of the historical specificities of these diverse repertories.

Painting in somewhat broad strokes, we might say that the history of early music tracks roughly with the increasing professionalization of singers. It was for and by the church that the earliest repertories were written down in Western Europe, to be sung by members of monastic and cathedral choirs. The range in skill and ability among institutions must have been considerable, though it is likely that the institutions that produced the (very expensive) musical and liturgical manuscripts would have also been better endowed in singers. By the eighth century, the papacy had established the *Schola Cantorum* (literally "singing school" or "singing group") to provide training in style, repertory, and vocal technique to the choristers of the papal chapel. These choristers would have been the most talented men and boys in Rome. Non-monastic choirs such as these, in fact, would have consisted solely of men and boys. Women in convents, on the other hand, would have furnished their own liturgical music, making the abbey one of the few places in which women had some amount of musical agency.

Virtually no notated sources predate the ninth century, and those copied before the eleventh century are difficult to interpret with exactitude. Even so, scholar-performers willing to look beyond the score for musical evidence allow us to imagine what might lie behind the veil of oral tradition. Among the most compelling projects in this vein are Benjamin Bagby's recreations of medieval epic songs, including *Beowulf* and the Icelandic *Edda* poems. To create a plausible sound world for epic storytelling, Bagby employs traditional philological and musicological methods alongside other kinds of approaches, establishing, for instance, an epic's modal horizon through the evidence offered up by the tunings of harps found in ancient Germanic burial sites.

The advent of music writing in the ninth century doesn't solve everything for the modern performer, either. Scholars and singers frequently lament the lack of intervallic and rhythmic specificity conveyed by *neumes* (the notational signs used to transmit plainchant). However, that is a pessimistic view. Neume notation offers up a wealth of qualitative information that an adventurous singer or ensemble, with the time and inclination, can mine. These nuances are often suggested in the names of the neumes themselves, and they can also be found in the smattering of letter abbreviations added above or beside the neumes. The letter *c*, for instance, stands for *celeriter*, Latin for "fast." *T* is *tenere*, or "hold"; *tb tenere bene*, "hold well"; *st statim*, or "immediately"; and so on.

The music of the Early and High Middle Ages (up to around 1250) was once considered prohibitively distant to performers and audiences. Thanks to several generations of collaboration between musicologists and performers, there are now many well-informed and persuasive recordings that lay the foundations on which new generations can build. Moreover, the pedagogical approaches toward this repertory are increasingly user-friendly, opening the sound of the period up to broader audiences. An exceptionally easy-to-use manual is the medieval musical primer included by chant scholar Margot Fassler in her *Music in the Medieval West*.

What makes the music of the later Middle Ages and Renaissance slightly more accessible than that which came before? During the thirteenth century, Western Europe witnessed dramatic changes in social organization. These changes included urbanization, the vernacularization of culture, and, to a certain extent, secularization (though the church would continue to be the main bearer of culture for many centuries). In other words, the shifts that took place in this period presage those of modernity, making its forms of expression more recognizable to us today.

A musical anecdote told by the thirteenth-century Parmese chronicler Salimbene of Adam gives a flavor of the kinds of musical cross-fertilization this newly urban, vernacular, and somewhat secularizing society fostered. He remembers how his friend, Brother Henry, "wrote many songs and sequences (a form of liturgical composition)" and "once . . . wrote the words and music to the hymn, *Christe Deus, Christe meus, Christe rex et Domine!* through the inspiration of a little servant girl who was walking through the cathedral in Pisa singing, 'E s'tu no cure de me, e' no curarò de te (If you do not pay attention to me, I will not pay attention to you).'"[2] This clash of cultures and classes is characteristic of much of this repertory. We know from chronicle sources such as Salimbene's that singers and composers moved freely between clerical and secular realms, working and performing in both contexts.

The use of secular tunes in liturgical music (the process Salimbene describes, called *contrafactum*) is just one indication of this social fluidity. Another is the transfer of vocal style and performance practice from one context into another. Detractors of these stylistic promiscuities give us some valuable insight into what the overall feel of this musical atmosphere might have been at certain moments. Take, for instance, the moment of 1324 in Avignon when Pope John XXII issued a papal bull (so-called for the leaden seal attached to the pope's official documents), the highest form of ecclesiastical mandate, targeted at singers practiced in this "new style" of singing. This document, known as the *Docta Sanctorum*, brought the singing practices of the fourteenth century briefly into the realm of church politics and gives us a rather humorous glimpse of what it would have been like to witness the most new-fangled style of liturgical music being performed in its sacred setting. The pope complains of "certain disciples of the new school" who "hinder the melody [of plainchant] with hockets, deprave them with descants, and sometimes pad them out with upper parts made out of secular songs." He adds that their "voices move incessantly to and fro, intoxicating rather than soothing the ear, while the singers themselves try to convey the emotion of the music by their gestures."[3]

What valuable insight a passage such as this has to offer! Though speaking of liturgical polyphony, he describes a performance practice that is not staid or even particularly religious in feeling but one that is highly playful and sensual—erotic even. Spending time with textual sources is a valuable way to imagine the "historical ear" (as impossible as that concept ultimately is). Another musical portrait in Salimbene's chronicle describes a Brother Vita as "the best singer of his time anywhere in both styles, plainsong and harmony." We learn that he was "a lean and slender man, taller than Brother Henry, and his voice was better suited to a small room than to the sanctuary."[4] Mundane as these details might seem, they help tune our attention, along with our ears, to salient sonic differences registered by a thirteenth-century listener: differences between the acoustics of a monumental space such as a sanctuary and a small chamber such as the ones in which these singer-composers, and perhaps a few discerning listeners, might have gathered on an informal basis. At least part of the fascination lies in the fact that the bodies of these medieval people are long gone, and so too, for the most part, the rooms and buildings in which they sang. Through these descriptions, the medieval past becomes somewhat less remote, for we remember that this music resonated through real, historical bodies and through spaces either intimate or monumental.

Another rewarding way to draw nearer to this repertory is to work from original sources. Singing from facsimile (literally meaning "make-like," these are high-end reproductions of prints or manuscripts) was once a recherché pastime restricted to those with access to the major research libraries that own these expensive materials. With so many libraries digitizing their holdings, you can now browse deluxe musical manuscripts from your couch.

Take an example found on the eleventh folio of the manuscript Harley 978, housed physically in the British Library, but digitally right here ♪. The famous thirteenth-century *rota* (Latin for "wheel," or "round") *Sumer is icumen in* is an easy demonstration of the kind of fun and insight to be had working with original sources. The Middle-English text, given in black ink, describes a summer scene, the protagonist of which is the cuckoo. Beneath this text is a Latin text in red ink that expounds a bit of Christological theology. Either text will fit the musical setting, and the agricultural language in both generates a great deal of intertextual play between them. This is a perfect example of the porousness Salimbene describes between secular and sacred realms, writing, as he did, as a near-contemporary of this source.

The entire song falls across the space of a single page. However, how many voices are on this page, and where does each start? Take a look at the black-ink block of text on the right side of the page, about three-quarters of the way down. This is the canon, from the Greek word *kanón,* or "rule." Our modern use of the musical term canon is a metonym for this original, medieval sense. This "rule," often given verbally, as here, instructs the singers on how to realize the additional parts. In this case, the canon tells us that four friends should sing the round, in addition to the two additional voices on the *pes* (the lower two voices occupying half the length of the page each). One friend begins, and when he or she arrives at the red cross above *Lhu*-de, the next should enter, and so on and so forth.

However, what about the notes and their respective values? Two shapes predominate: a quadrangle with a downward stem on the

right, and a lozenge. Sing the quadrangle twice as long as the lozenge, except for when the quadrangle appears in groups of three (as
in "sing cuccu"), or before a long hash mark, in which case, give the
quadrangle three times the length of the lozenge. What is the hash
mark? A rest. These should be held for the value of three lozenges.
Once you get used to this pattern of longs and shorts, it becomes quite
intuitive. But be careful! The pattern changes midway through the
final phrase, over *"cuccu ne swik."* Here there are two quadrangles
followed by a lozenge, and you will need a 3–2–1–3 pattern. How
did this rearrangement of note shapes force this local change in the
rhythm? Such technicalities are beyond the scope of this short essay,
but the thirteenth-century music theorist Franco of Cologne provides
a thorough and lucid rationale behind these rhythms in his *Ars cantus
mensurabilis,* a treatise that plays an indispensable role in our knowledge of thirteenth-century rhythmic notation.[5]

The painstaking process of editing and transcribing sources lags far
behind the rapid speed at which digital imaging is taking place, and
many more original sources are available in digital format than are
modern transcriptions of them. Lagging even farther behind, of course,
is the recording and programming of these works. This makes it an exciting time for the amateur performer, who has the opportunity make fresh
discoveries in the repertory and to perform works that have not been
heard, in some cases, for nearly a millennium. Willi Apel's *The Notation
of Polyphonic Music* has long been a standby reference for students
willing to tackle early notation. More recent is chant scholar Thomas
Forrest Kelly's *Capturing Music: The Story of Notation,* an entertaining
and useful introduction for the general audience. An online tutorial on
fourteenth-century French notation, designed by musicologist Elizabeth Eva Leach, is part of the many resources available through the
Digital Image Archive of Medieval Music (DIAMM). Today, the number of early music ensembles singing from manuscript or print facsimile
is steadily growing, as is amateur interest in the kinds of interpretive
insights these materials can provide. ♪

NOTES

1. *The Etymologies of Isidore of Seville,* translated by Stephen A. Barney, W. J. Lewis, J. A. Beach, Oliver Berghof (Cambridge: Cambridge UP, 2006), 95.

2. *The Chronicle of Salimbene de Adam,* translated by Joseph L. Baird (Binghamton, NY: Medieval & Renaissance Texts & Studies, 1986), 172–3.

3. Henry Raynor, *A Social History of Music from the Middle Ages to Beethoven* (New York: Schocken Books, 1972), 36–37.

4. *The Chronicle of Salimbene de Adam,* 174–5.

5. Franco's *Ars cantus mensurabilis* is available in English translation in *Strunk's Source Readings in Music History II: The Early Christian Period and the Latin Middle Ages,* edited by James McKinnon (New York: Norton, 1998), 226–44.

GLOSSARY

BEMF: Acronym for Boston Early Music Festival.

Boston Early Music Festival: Early music festival with an annual winter concert series in Boston and New York and a bi-annual summer festival and exhibition in Boston.

BFX: Acronym for Berkeley Festival and Exhibition.

Berkeley Festival and Exhibition: Early music festival with a bi-annual summer festival and exhibition in Berkeley, California.

CPDL: Acronym for Choral Public Domain Library. Also known as ChoralWiki.

Choral Public Domain Library: A free database of choral and vocal music in the public domain, including repertoire from the medieval period to the present.

ChoralWiki: See Choral Public Domain Library.

EMA: Acronym for Early Music America.

Early Music America: A non-profit organization providing information and services to its members aiming to increase awareness about the music of the medieval, Renaissance, baroque and classical periods. It produces a magazine, e-newsletter, and online databases of scores, concerts, workshops, festivals and educational opportunities.

EMV: Acronym for Early Music Vancouver.

Early Music Vancouver: A concert producing organization with a wide variety of programs throughout the year and a summer early music festival.

IMSLP: Acronym for International Music Score Library Project.

International Music Score Library Project: A virtual library of musical scores in the public domain. It includes over 370,000 scores from over 14,000 composers including both new works as well as old and new editions of old works. It is supported through subscriptions.

REMA: Acronym for Réseau Européen de Musique Ancienne, or the European Early Music Network.

Réseau Européen de Musique Ancienne: A membership organization dedicated to providing an exchange of knowledge, information and cooperation in the European early music field.

European Early Music Network: See Réseau Européen de Musique Ancienne.

SSCM: Acronym for Society for Seventeenth-Century Music.

Society for Seventeenth-Century Music: A membership organization that produces a scholarly journal, hosts scholarly conferences, and provides a wealth of other services to its members and the general public.

Accenti: Italian term for grace notes, or graces. Small ornamental gestures, including appoggiaturas and trills, that do not significantly alter the contour of the melody.

Adagio Style: A compositional style for baroque arias in which the music moves slowly, sometimes also called the pathetic style. Arias with a slower, more-introspective feeling require a certain approach to ornamentation that complements the musical style.

Affect: The attitude or emotional quality of a movement or piece of music.

Agréments: French term for graces, small ornaments that don't significantly alter the contours of the melody.

Air de cour: A French term ("court air") describing a secular solo song form popular in sixteenth- and seventeenth-century France, especially at the court of Louis XIII.

Allegro Style: A compositional style for baroque arias in which the music moves in a fast and active tempo. Arias with a more energetic and outgoing character demand a showy and bravura type of ornamentation.

Anthem: A short, sacred choral composition, used in the Anglican Church service.

Appoggiatura: One of the most important Italian ornaments, made by leaning on an auxiliary note, either above or below the principal note. It often creates dissonance and adds more contrast and interest to the musical phrase. It is sometimes notated but often not.

Ariette: French term meaning "small aria."

Ars Nova: Latin term ("new art") that refers to the new style of music composition developed in the fourteenth century. New systems of musical notation allowed for wider possibilities in rhythm and meter, a better indication of word underlay, and more complex polyphony.

Baroque Pitch: A=415 Hz, approximately a half step lower than A=440 Hz. In the late twentieth century, musicians decided on a modern standard of baroque pitch for period instrument performances as a convenient solution to the complex problem of different pitch standards in seventeenth-century Europe. We do know from fixed pitch instruments that, in general, the pitch was a good deal lower in the baroque era than today.

Basso Continuo: See Figured Bass.

Cadence: A musical term with numerous associations. It can refer to the closing of a musical phrase, a specific inflection of the voice, a particular kind of French ornament, or vocal vibrato.

Cadenza: An extensive ornamental flourish at the final cadence of an aria, often improvised, usually completed in one breath on the penultimate syllable of text. It should show off a singer's virtuosity while staying within the character of the specific aria.

Cantabile Style: A smooth and connected type of articulation which emulates the legato of singers, also sometimes called the adagio or pathetic style. This approach is appropriate for slower, more introspective music.

Cantata: A setting of dramatic poetry for solo voice and instruments. It typically includes several arias alternating with sections of recitative. The topic of the text can be sacred or secular.

Cantus firmus: Latin term ("fixed song") for medieval plainchant. An existing chant melody was used as the basis for a new polyphonic composition.

Castrato: A male singer castrated before puberty to preserve the boy soprano or alto voice. Adult male sopranos and altos were highly sought after in the baroque period to sing in churches and opera houses throughout Europe.

Chanson: A secular vocal composition, using a French text. Medieval chansons were single line melodies with texts concerning heroes and lovers. Later chansons were polyphonic works for two, three, or four voices.

Choirbook Format: A style of music notation used before the sixteenth century in which each line of counterpoint is written out separately instead of in full score format.

Clef: A musical symbol used to indicate the pitches of written notes on a staff.

Coloratura: Florid passages in vocal music. The term came from the practice of dividing a longer note value into smaller, faster notes, or coloring in a white note with black notes.

Concerto: A musical composition for solo instrument accompanied by an orchestra.

Consort: In a musical context, a group of instruments or singers.

Continuo: Also known as basso continuo, the bass line and chordal accompaniment that became popular in the early baroque. It also refers to the combination of instruments used to play the accompanying chords and bass line. This can include a harpsichord, organ, or plucked instrument, such as a lute, to play chords combined with a bowed string instrument, or other low instrument to play the bass line.

Counterpoint: The relationship between different independent lines of music. Rules of counterpoint attempt to organize interacting melody lines so that the resulting harmony is pleasing.

Countertenor: Also known as counter tenor, counter-tenor, or contra tenor, a male singing voice with the range of a female alto or mezzo-soprano.

Cornetto: A Renaissance wind instrument.

Critical Editions: A scholarly edition of a text or musical composition that includes commentary and annotation about the sources used to make editorial decisions. Critical editions strive to present a work as close to its original intent as possible; sometimes known as an Urtext edition or scholarly edition.

Da Capo Aria: A form of solo vocal composition popular throughout the baroque era, featuring a solo singer accompanied by either a chamber group or small orchestra. It is organized in three sections; an opening A section followed by a contrasting B section and ending with a return of the A section, in which the singer is expected to add ornaments and variations.

Declamatory Solo Song: The new style of vocal composition that became popular at the beginning of the seventeenth century. It made use of the recitative style and was promoted by the members of the Florentine Camerata.

Diminutions: Florid ornaments in vocal music in which a larger note value is divided into smaller, faster notes. See also *passages*, divisions, coloratura.

***Dispositione*:** Italian term describing the agility and flexibility ("disposition") of the voice necessary to execute florid ornaments with speed and clarity.

Divine Office: The daily cycle of Christian liturgies performed throughout the course of a day, usually in monasteries.

Divisions: Florid ornaments in vocal music in which a longer note value is divided into smaller, faster notes.

***Esclamazione*:** A seventeenth-century Italian ornament in which the voice enters softly followed by a crescendo.

Facsimile: A reproduction of an old book, manuscript, map, musical score, or other item of historical value that attempts to maintain the original source as accurately as possible.

Falsetto: A high vocal range above the normal chest register. It can be considered the same as head voice, or something distinctly different depending on the writer and the context. It can refer to male and female voices, again depending on the writer and context.

Feigned Voice: A term used in early vocal treatises to indicate falsetto or head voice.

Figured Bass: Also known as thoroughbass or basso continuo, a shorthand system for indicating chords and harmony to be played with a bass line. Numbers and symbols, or figures, instruct a keyboard or lute player as to which additional notes to play to fill out the accompaniment.

Flaté: A French term used to describe a specific trembling type of ornament. It can also refer to vocal vibrato.

Formes Fixes: Latin term ("fixed forms") used to describe the standard musical and poetic structures that became popular for setting song texts in the fourteenth and fifteenth centuries. The forms included patterns of repetition with verses and refrains. The three standard fixed forms are the ballade, virelai, and rondeau.

Full Score: A form of music notation in which all the different instrumental and vocal lines of music are arranged in a vertical order so that musicians can see everything that is going on in the musical texture all at once.

Gavotte: A graceful French dance form that starts on an upbeat and has two strong beats per measure.

Graces: Small ornamental gestures in vocal music that don't significantly alter the contour of the melody, including appoggiaturas and trills.

Gregorian Chant: A standardization during the ninth century of the earlier Roman Catholic plainchant. The name refers to either Pope Gregory I (r. 590–604) or Pope Gregory II (r. 715–731), but scholars believe that the unaccompanied sacred chants developed later.

Gorgia: Italian term for improvised florid ornamentation in sixteenth-century vocal music. The term also refers to the flexibility and agility of the throat required to execute the florid passages with speed and clarity.

Gruppo: Early seventeenth-century Italian ornament in which two pitches alternate, either a half or a whole step; later known as the trill.

Haut-contre: A very high tenor range featured in French baroque repertoire.

Head Voice: The high part of the vocal range, above the chest voice. It can indicate the same sound as falsetto, or something different depending on the writer and the context.

Historical Performance Practice: The study of how music was performed in the composer's day. Musical performances based on information gained from historical sources that aim to recreate the sound and style of the period are also known as Historically Informed Performances.

Homophony (Homophonic): A form of musical composition in which the main melody, usually the top part, is supported by several other parts providing harmony.

***Inégalité*:** French term ("inequality") to describe the practice of performing evenly written notes with a slightly unequal rhythm.

Liturgy: The customs and traditions of worship of a specific religion, including texts, music, and ritual. It is undertaken by those participating in the divine actions of the religious service.

Lute: A general term for plucked stringed instruments with a neck, frets, and a pear-shaped body, popular in the sixteenth and seventeenth centuries. The instrument came in different sizes, known as the archlute, chitaronne, and theorbo. They were used for solo music and song accompaniment.

Madrigal: A secular form of vocal polyphony popular in the Renaissance and early baroque periods.

Magnificat: One of the oldest parts of the Christian liturgy, taken from the Gospel of Luke, also known as the Canticle of Mary. It was part of the divine office, or daily prayers, performed in early church services. This particular text inspired musical settings by many composers.

Manuscript: Any document, or musical score written by hand, often representing the author's or composer's original version. An illuminated manuscript includes elaborate decoration.

Medieval: Period in European history, also known as the Middle Ages, which lasted from the fifth to the fifteenth centuries. The beginning is marked by the fall of the Roman Empire and the end transitions into the Renaissance.

Melisma: A phrase of music in which one syllable is sung over a series of pitches in a row. This kind of music is called melismatic as opposed to syllabic in which each syllable gets its own pitch.

***Messa di voce*:** Italian vocal ornament with a crescendo and decrescendo on one note.

Minnesingers: Professional singer-/songwriters of the twelfth and thirteenth centuries in German regions. See Troubadours.

Minuet: A dance form characterized by three beats per measure. This traditional court dance could be elegant and noble in a slow tempo, or gracefully lilting in a slightly faster tempo.

Modern Pitch: A=440, established in 1939 at an international conference in London.

Monody: Songs or music with one melodic line. Sacred chants or secular songs are called monophonic if they have only one line of melody.

Monophony (Monophonic): Music with a single part or melody, usually without accompaniment.

Motet: An early form of medieval and Renaissance polyphony in which a new text and additional lines of melodic counterpoint were added to an existing chant melody. The new text could be sacred or secular, in Latin or a vernacular language.

Musica Ficta: Literally "false" or "feigned" music, a term that refers to accidentals that were added to the music of the medieval and Renaissance periods to make the cadences come out in accordance with the rules of music theory. Performers would often add accidentals that were not notated in order to make the intervals and the counterpoint sound pleasing and correct.

Neumes: An early form of musical notation prior to the invention of five-line staff notation.

Obbligato: A distinctive and often elaborate musical line that accompanies a principal melody and is essential (obligatory) to the overall musical texture.

Oboe d'amore: Italian for "oboe of love." The mezzo-soprano member of the oboe family, pitched a third lower than the oboe.

Oratorio: A large-scale composition for vocal soloists, choir, and orchestra, usually on a text of religious theme, intended for concert performance as opposed to theatrical presentation.

Organum: An early form of sacred polyphony in which a new melody line is added either above or below an existing chant. Usually, the two lines move in parallel motion, but one line can move more slowly while the other line has more notes that move more quickly.

Passages: French term for diminution or division.

Passion: Part of the Christian liturgy describing the arrest, trial, and crucifixion of Jesus. Musical settings of these Gospel texts were often used in services during Holy Week.

Pathetic Style: See Adagio Style.

Period Instruments: A term used to describe a variety of instruments used for historically informed performances of early music. They can be restored original instruments or new reproductions of early instruments made with special materials and construction to replicate those of earlier centuries.

Piano Reduction: See Piano-Vocal Score.

Piano-Vocal Score: A reduction of many lines of music into two staves, intended to be played at the piano. Multiple instrumental parts are transcribed into a two-handed piano version meant to accompany a vocal part. Also called piano reduction.

Plainchant: Unaccompanied, unison melodies for singing Latin texts in early Christian church services of the fifth and sixth centuries.

Polyphony: Two or more distinct, independent melodic lines sounding simultaneously. When the individual melody lines move in different directions and with different rhythms, it results in counterpoint. This is in contrast to a single, dominant melodic line with accompaniment that generally moves in the same rhythm, which is called homophony.

***Portamento*:** An Italian term ("carrying") used to describe a gentle slide from one pitch to another.

***Port de voix*:** A French term ("carrying the voice") used to describe a specific appoggiatura-type ornament.

Realized Accompaniment: A fleshed-out version of a figured bass line. A continuo player, or an editor, creates a complete accompaniment from a bass line and its numerical indications of harmony. Modern editions often include a piano accompaniment as a realization of the figured bass seen in an original manuscript or early edition.

Recitative: A style of sung music in which the singer delivers the text in a manner close to ordinary speech. It is used in opera, oratorio, and cantatas, and it is also called the declamatory style.

Renaissance: Period in European history spanning the fourteenth to the seventeenth centuries. Begun in Italy, it is characterized by a flowering of literature, art, architecture, and music and an emphasis on humanistic values and the pleasures of the senses.

Rhetoric: The art of persuasive speech. Rules of rhetorical speech, practiced by ancient Greek and Roman orators, found their way into the music and poetry of the seventeenth and eighteenth centuries and influenced the composition and performance of baroque repertoire.

Rhythmic Alteration: The practice of performing rhythms differently from how they are notated. Scholars group together various situations under this umbrella term, including the execution of dotted figures and triplets as well as decisions about making contrasting rhythms agree.

***Ritornello*:** An Italian term ("return") that refers to a recurring instrumental section in a vocal work or concerto.

Sackbut: A medieval and Renaissance brass instrument that uses a slide mechanism to change pitch; forerunner of the trombone.

Schleifer: Type of German ornament known as the slide in which the main note is preceded by at least two decorative notes.

Seconda prattica: Italian term ("second practice") referring to the new style of vocal composition popular at the beginning of the seventeenth century. The new music featured a solo vocal line with text set in a declamatory fashion and a simple accompaniment of bass line and chords.

Shawm: A medieval and Renaissance double reed wind instrument, the forerunner of the oboe.

Solfège: A method of music education developed by the eleventh-century Italian monk Guido of Arezzo to help singers learn to sight-read music, also known as solmization. Syllables are assigned to the notes of a scale to aid in mentally hearing and remembering the melody.

Sprezzatura: Italian term for rubato, used by Caccini in his *Le nuove musiche*.

Stile antico: Italian term ("ancient style") used to describe the polyphonic music of the sixteenth century and earlier.

Tablature: A system of music notation for fretted instruments, such as lute or guitar, which indicates fingerings rather than pitches.

Terraced Dynamics: Using dynamics to shift volume levels suddenly to build contrasting phrases or sections of music, as opposed to gradual crescendos or decrescendos.

Theorbo: A large bass lute with a long neck; a relative of the archlute that is able to play in a low range. It was popular as a continuo instrument.

Thoroughbass: Also known as basso continuo; see Figured Bass.

Treatise: A formal, systematic written discourse on a particular subject.

Treble: The higher range of voices or music. It can refer to the highest vocal part or range, or a clef for writing music in a higher range.

Tremblement: French term meaning trembling, but with many other associations. In early writings about singing, the term can refer to a specific ornament, or to the quality of vocal vibrato.

Tremolo: An Italian term with numerous meanings relating to variations in pitch. It can refer to a specific trill ornament, or to a quality of vocal vibrato.

Trill: One of the most important Italian ornaments, used in English, French, and German music as well. It is made by alternating two neighboring pitches, either a half step or a whole step, sometimes notated, but often not. The trill is expected on the penultimate note at major cadences, usually started on the upper note, and it can include various prefixes and/or suffixes.

Trillo: Early seventeenth-century Italian ornament in which one pitch is rearticulated; sometimes called tremolo.

Troubadours: Professional singer-/songwriters of the twelfth and thirteenth centuries; also called trouvères in French regions and Minnesingers in German regions. Their songs, most often strophic, told stories of courtly love and adventure.

Urtext: German term for "original text." An Urtext edition is also known as a critical edition, authoritative edition, or scholarly edition.

Viol: Also known as viola da gamba, or gamba ("legs" in Italian), a stringed instrument popular in the Renaissance and baroque periods. It comes in a variety of sizes and ranges, typically has six strings and frets, and is played with an underhand bow grip. No matter the size, it is held vertically between the legs, hence the name "viol of the legs."

Voce di petto: Italian term meaning "chest voice."

Voce di testa: Italian term meaning "head voice."

Vorschlag: German term for appoggiatura.

INDEX

ABOUT THE AUTHOR AND CONTRIBUTORS

Martha Elliott has enjoyed a rich career performing, teaching, and writing. Her book, *Singing in Style: A Guide to Vocal Performance Practices*, was published by Yale University Press in 2006 and was the first book of its kind to present information on four centuries of historical performance practice for singers. The book earned praise from soprano Dawn Upshaw, countertenor and opera director Drew Minter, and has been widely used throughout the United States, United Kingdom, and Australia. Her new book, *So You Want to Sing Early Music*, expands upon the information first presented in *Singing in Style* and presents it in an inviting and accessible format for a more general audience.

As a singer, Elliott has performed a wide range of repertoire, including baroque music with period instruments, opera, chamber music, and avant-garde contemporary music. She has appeared throughout the United States and in Europe, Asia, and South America with groups such as Concert Royal, Continuum, Marlboro Music, the New England Bach Festival, Oberlin Baroque Performance Institute, Philadelphia Chamber Music Society, Brentano String Quartet, New Millennium Ensemble, New Jersey Symphony, Philadelphia Orchestra, Atlanta Symphony, and the Odessa Philharmonic in Ukraine.

Educated at Princeton University and the Juilliard School, Elliott has been a member of the performance faculty of Princeton University since 1985. She has taught private lessons, courses in baroque chamber music, and has coached many baroque opera productions in addition to frequently performing with the Richardson Chamber Players and Princeton University Orchestra. Her former students have gone on to perform with such opera companies as the Metropolitan Opera, Houston Grand Opera, and English National Opera.

Elliott has presented talks, workshops, and master classes at several national and international conferences, including the National Association of Teachers of Singing (NATS), International Congress of Voice Teachers (ICVT), and the National Early Music Association (NEMA) in the United Kingdom, as well as at colleges and universities throughout the United States. Additional research interests include menopause and mindfulness, and she has written articles on these topics for the *Journal of Singing*. She is also an avid cyclist and coleader of Princeton Insight Meditation. Elliott lives in Skillman, New Jersey, with her husband, Michael Pratt, conductor of the Princeton University Orchestra.

Gabriel Crouch is director of choral activities and senior lecturer in music at Princeton University. He began his musical career as an eight-year-old in the choir of Westminster Abbey, where he performed a solo at the wedding of HRH Prince Andrew and Miss Sarah Ferguson. After completing a choral scholarship at Trinity College, Cambridge, he was offered a place in the renowned a cappella group The King's Singers in 1996. Over the next eight years, he made a dozen recordings (one of which received a Grammy nomination) and gave more than 900 performances in almost every major concert venue in the world. In 2008, he was appointed music director of the British early music ensemble Gallicantus, with whom he has released numerous recordings that have received rave reviews and a Grammy nomination. When the academic calendar allows, Crouch maintains parallel careers in singing and record production, crossing the Atlantic frequently to appear with such ensembles as Tenebrae and the Gabrieli Choir.

Mary Benton, **Patricia Hlafter**, **Judith Klotz**, and **Amy Warren** are all members of the viola da gamba consort La Spirita. This ensemble performs Renaissance and baroque music for voice and treble, tenor and bass viols, often with guest singers and other gambists. They specialize in the polyphony of the seventeenth century, including the music of William Byrd, Orlando Gibbons, John Jenkins, Henry Purcell, and Giovanni Gabrieli. The name La Spirita derives from a famous *canzona* by Gabrieli that was played on the group's first concert. Since 1995, La Spirita has been regularly performing in New Jersey and Pennsylvania. In 2004, the members of La Spirita founded the Guild for Early Music, a consortium of early music ensembles and musicians from central New Jersey and eastern Pennsylvania.

Jamie Reuland is an assistant professor of music at Princeton University. Her research focuses on the intellectual, aesthetic, and political history of medieval music and on the intersections between musical texts, oral culture, and political life in the late-medieval Mediterranean. Her courses include the history of musical notation, liturgical chant, and medieval song. She is also director of the Princeton Facsimile Singers and associated faculty at the Seeger Center for Hellenic Studies. She has received fellowships from the Andrew W. Mellon Foundation, Fulbright Foundation in Greece, and the Medieval Academy of America. Educated at Dickinson College and Princeton University, Reuland taught at Stanford University before returning to Princeton to join the faculty.

Wendy LeBorgne is a voice pathologist, speaker, author, and master class clinician. She actively presents nationally and internationally on the professional voice and is the clinical director of two successful private practice voice centers: the ProVoice Center in Cincinnati and BBIVAR in Dayton. Dr. LeBorgne holds an adjunct professorship at University of Cincinnati College-Conservatory of Music as a voice consultant, where she also teaches voice pedagogy and wellness courses. She completed a BFA in musical theater from Shenandoah Conservatory and her graduate and doctoral degrees from the University of Cincinnati. Original peer-reviewed research has been published in multiple journals, and she is a contributing author to several voice textbooks. Most recently, she coauthored *The Vocal Athlete* textbook and workbook with Marci Rosenberg. Her patients and private students currently can be found on radio, television, film, cruise ships, Broadway, Off-Broadway, national tours, commercial music tours, and opera stages around the world.

Scott McCoy is a noted author, singer, conductor, and pianist with extensive performance experience in concert and opera. He is professor of voice and pedagogy, director of the Swank Voice Laboratory, and director of the interdisciplinary program in singing health at Ohio State University. His voice science and pedagogy textbook, *Your Voice: An Inside View*, is used extensively by colleges and universities throughout the United States and abroad. McCoy is the associate editor of the *Journal of Singing* for voice pedagogy and is a past president of the National Association of Teachers of Singing (NATS). He also served NATS as vice president for workshops, program chair for the 2006 and 2008 national conferences, chair of the voice science advisory committee, and a master teacher for the intern program. Deeply committed to teacher education, McCoy is a founding faculty member in the NYSTA Professional Development Program (PDP), teaching classes in voice anatomy, physiology, acoustics, and voice analysis. He is a member of the distinguished American Academy of Teachers of Singing (AATS).